After the Science Wars

The science wars have recently taken center stage as a popular debate not only across the academic disciplines but also in the popular media. The "war" is between scientists who believe that science and its methods are objective, and an increasing number of social scientists, historians, philosophers, and others gathered under the umbrella of Science Studies. The latter group have disputed that science is impartial and in some cases whether it comes close to the truth at all.

After the Science Wars is an exciting new collection that seeks to move the debate from its stalemate to a more fruitful dialogue. The "war" was intensified by the Sokal affair—which at first appeared to raise the status of science in relation to its critics, and now that the dust has settled has also managed to damage it. The book contains a contribution from Sokal, explaining his motivation for writing "Transgressing the boundaries: toward a transformative hermeneutics of quantum gravity," which was later revealed as a hoax, and his conclusions from the affair. Then follow original essays by leading philosophers and scientists from a broad spectrum of views, including feminist, postcolonial, and anthropological, and two pieces of science fiction. The essays all attempt to bridge the wide interdisciplinary gulfs in this discussion and move it forward.

After the Science Wars is essential reading for all those interested in the debates surrounding the status of science and its relation to society and culture.

Contributors: Philip S. Baringer, Alan D. Sokal, Adrian L. Melott, Gabriel Stolzenberg, Barry Shank, Shari Speer, Alan Thompson, Sarah Wayland, Ann E. Cudd, Keith M. Ashman, Ziauddin Sardar, Robert L. Park, David Norman Smith, Steve Fuller, James Gunn.

Editors: Keith M. Ashman is Assistant Professor of Physics at Baker University. Philip S. Baringer is Professor of Physics at the University of Kansas.

After the Science Wars

Edited by Keith M. Ashman
and Philip S. Baringer

London and New York

First published 2001
by Routledge
11 New Fetter Lane, London EC4P 4EE

Simultaneously published in the USA and Canada
by Routledge
29 West 35th Street, New York, NY 10001

Routledge is an imprint of the Taylor & Francis Group

Typeset in Times by
The Running Head Limited, Cambridge
Printed and bound in Great Britain by
TJ International, Padstow, Cornwall

British Library Cataloguing in Publication Data
A catalogue record for this book is available from the British Library

Library of Congress Cataloging in Publication Data
After the science wars / edited by Keith Ashman and Philip Baringer
       p. cm.
   Includes bibliographical references and index.
   1. Science–Social aspects. 2. Science and state. I. Ashman, Keith M., 1963– II.
Baringer, Philip S. (Philip Shively), 1956–
Q175.55.A38   2000
501—dc21   00-058263

ISBN 0–415–21208–1 (hbk)
ISBN 0–415–21209–X (pbk)

Contents

Contributors

Keith M. Ashman, Department of Physics, Baker University, also Department of Physics and Astronomy, University of Kansas

Philip S. Baringer, Department of Physics and Astronomy, University of Kansas

Ann E. Cudd, Department of Philosophy, University of Kansas

Steve Fuller, Department of Sociology, University of Warwick

James Gunn, Department of English, University of Kansas

Adrian L. Melott, Department of Physics and Astronomy, University of Kansas

Robert L. Park, Department of Physics and Astronomy, University of Maryland

Ziauddin Sardar, City University, London

Barry Shank, Division of Comparative Studies, Ohio State University

David Norman Smith, Department of Sociology, University of Kansas

Alan D. Sokal, Department of Physics, New York University

Shari Speer, Department of Linguistics, Ohio State University

Gabriel Stolzenberg, Department of Mathematics, Northeastern University

Alan Thompson, National Institute of Standards and Technology

Sarah Wayland, Entropic Research Laboratories

1 Introduction: the "science wars"

Philip S. Baringer

Somewhere in this book you will find something to disagree with. Perhaps strongly. Perhaps so strongly that you will feel like throwing the book across the room, but please resist the urge. While our publisher takes the utmost care to produce a high-quality volume, books are not really engineered to be missiles. And besides, after you cool off a bit I am sure you will want to pick the book back up and resume reading.

How can I be so sure of your reaction? The subject of this collection of essays is the so-called "science wars," a topic that provokes strong opinions. My reactions to writings on this topic can vary greatly, even within the span of a single essay. In one paragraph I may admire the writer's clarity of thought and clever means of expression, and then in the next, I will be scribbling angry notes in the margins and wondering how anyone would dare to inflict such drivel upon the world. My opinion of what is brilliant (or drivel) is most likely very different from yours. In exploring the "science wars" we must explore some of the deepest philosophical issues around—what is the ultimate nature of "reality"? Is there any single objective reality? How can mere humans best try to comprehend different aspects of our world(s)? What is science and is its role at all special? Everyone has opinions on these issues, and they are often strongly held.

Unlike most other collections on the science wars, we have tried to represent a broad spectrum of opinion in this book, which is another reason I can be sure you will find something objectionable somewhere in these pages. It is hard to imagine a person who can embrace all these diverse opinions simultaneously. Each essay covers a somewhat different aspect of science or science criticism, so I recommend you read every one, even (perhaps especially) those with which you think you may disagree. It is useful to have your philosophical assumptions challenged. The authors may not make you change your mind about anything, but they will almost certainly help you refine and deepen your thinking on these issues.

Our contributors come from a variety of academic disciplines, ranging from English to sociology to astrophysics. One of the few ground rules imposed on the writers was to make their piece accessible to readers coming from a broad variety of backgrounds. This meant a limited use of jargon, explaining what jargon they did choose to employ, and an assumption that they were not preaching to the converted.

This book grew out of an interdisciplinary conference called "Science and Its Critics" that had similar ground rules and took place at the University of Kansas in 1997 from February 28 through March 2. "Science and Its Critics" was the first conference in the United States to bring together scientists and the social scientists who study them (very shortly followed by many others). In December 1994 Steve Fuller organized a conference in Great Britain that was the first of this kind anywhere; he provided the Kansas organizers with a great deal of helpful advice. The meeting, like this book, mainly focused on issues involving the history and philosophy of science, especially postmodern criticisms of scientific practices. Unlike this book, the conference also covered a variety of other topics ranging from creationism to science journalism.

This book is not a conference proceedings—only a small subset of the conference speakers are represented here (and we also have contributors who did not attend the conference)—but the book did draw its inspiration from the conference. We thus owe a debt to the people who made the conference possible and this is as good a place as any to acknowledge them. "Science and Its Critics" was conceived by the University of Kansas History and Philosophy of Science Committee in the wake of the "Sokal Hoax" (about which more below). Our two keynote speakers at the conference, Alan Sokal and Steve Fuller, are represented in this volume as are several members of the organizing committee: myself, Adrian Melott, Ann Cudd, and James Gunn. The other members of the organizing committee were Allan Hanson, Rudolf Jander, and Donald Marquis. John Pattinson of the University of Kansas Division of Continuing Education played a critical role in the success of the conference—he dealt with the many practical details while people like myself were busy philosophizing. I would also like to thank the many excellent speakers at the conference who are not represented here because of our desire to more narrowly focus the book.

In early 1997, the issues discussed at "Science and Its Critics" and many other similar conferences gained widespread attention not just in numerous academic departments but in the popular media as well. The "science wars" were discussed in publications ranging from *Physics Today* and *Scientific American* to the *New York Times*. "Science and Its Critics" drew the attention of the international media, with *Nature* reporter Colin McIlwain in attendance. (McIlwain's piece on the science wars appeared in the May 22, 1997 issue.) Sharon Begley of *Newsweek* interviewed several conference presenters for her piece on the science wars in the April 21, 1997 issue.

While the media attention has died down in the ensuing years, the core issues behind the science wars continue to simmer. Some may feel we are being overly optimistic to entitle this volume "After the Science Wars." Maybe these essays would be better viewed as part of ongoing "science peace talks." I think it is fair to say that the rhetoric on both sides has toned down a little and, as exemplified by the essays in this volume, there are genuine attempts at communication between the "sides."

To begin to understand the issues in this conflict, let us briefly examine some recent history, starting with C. P. Snow's famous essay "The two cultures and the scientific revolution." Snow was both a scientist and a writer, and so had experience with the literary and the scientific set in Britain. He described the vast gulf between the two cultures and the difficulty of communication between them. As science evolved as a discipline, specialization became the norm and it was rare for individuals to contribute to both science and literature. Snow describes the disconnection he observed between the scientific and literary cultures in the late 1950s:

> The non-scientists have a rooted impression that the scientists are shallowly optimistic, unaware of man's condition. On the other hand, the scientists believe that the literary intellectuals are totally lacking in foresight, peculiarly unconcerned with their brother men, in a deep sense anti-intellectual, anxious to restrict both art and thought to the existential moment. And so on. Anyone with a mild talent for invective could produce plenty of this kind of subterranean back-chat. On each side there is some of it which is not entirely baseless. It is all destructive. Much of it rests on misinterpretations which are dangerous.
>
> (Snow 1959: 5–6)

This disconnection had not yet translated into open hostility, but the situation would soon get worse.

Next let us consider the publication and reception of Thomas Kuhn's work of science philosophy, *The Structure of Scientific Revolutions* (Kuhn 1970/ 1962). This is the book that brought the phrase "paradigm shift" into common usage. Kuhn described the history of science as periods of normal science, when scientists work within a commonly accepted conceptual framework (the "paradigm"), occasionally broken by revolutions, the result of which is the acceptance of a new paradigm. Revolutions are brought on by the accumulation (and recognition of the importance) of anomalous results that don't fit the old paradigm. An example of a paradigm shift was when Einstein's relativity supplanted Newton's framework for mechanics.

It was not so much Kuhn's notion of the paradigm that caused later controversy, but rather Kuhn's observation that sociological forces play a hand in whether and how a new paradigm becomes accepted. This was a departure from the "pure" picture of science wherein scientists reach their conclusions based solely on the evidence they gather from nature. Kuhn suggested that the human interactions among scientists help to determine at least the speed with which new ideas come to be accepted. Other writers picked up on Kuhn's work and expanded on the notion that scientific theories, like other forms of knowledge, are "social constructs"—conventions brought about by some process of building consensus among a group of people. In the "strong" form of constructivism, there is a denial that objective reality plays any role in this consensus building. This radical point of view is related to philosophical relativism, the notion that no grounds can be found for preferring any one set of beliefs over another. Kuhn later objected to these extrapolations from his work. His stated goal was to make scientists aware of such social influences so they could better shield themselves from them and not to imply that the social influences were an inextricable part of the process.

This leads us to the development of "postmodernism" and its influence on the emerging field of the sociology of science. How exactly to define postmodernism is rather difficult to pin down. In some ways it is easier to discuss what postmodernism is not. As the name suggests, it is not "modernism," an attitude that evolved from the late seventeenth-century European period known as the Enlightenment. In this period the scientific method was ascendant and the restraints on thought imposed by a theological orthodoxy were being loosened. Because of its successes in the physical sciences (due to Galileo, Newton, and company), reason and logic were celebrated and there was an optimistic feeling that everything of importance could be understood by the systematic application of rational thought. In his recent bestseller *Consilience*, Edward O. Wilson exemplifies this Enlightenment spirit and provides us with a point of view that can be regarded as the antithesis of postmodernism. Wilson states early in his book his complete faith in a rational agenda to bring together diverse areas of scholarship. He says, "The ongoing fragmentation of knowledge and resulting chaos in philosophy are not reflections of the real world but artifacts of scholarship. The propositions of the original Enlightenment are increasingly favored by objective evidence, especially from the natural sciences" (Wilson 1998: 8).

Wilson also offers a sort of definition of postmodernism: "Postmodernism is the ultimate polar antithesis of the Enlightenment . . . Enlightenment thinkers believe we can know everything, and radical postmodernists believe we can know nothing" (Wilson 1998: 44).

Compare this rather unsympathetic statement to a more sympathetic one from Steve Fuller:

> "Postmodernism" emerged in the late 1970s to capture the changed character of the sciences in the 20th century, which called into question the idea that the organized pursuit of knowledge has a unique and natural course of development that, in turn, can provide the basis for the general improvement of humanity, typically in the form of rational statecraft . . . The term "Enlightenment" is increasingly used for the tendency in the history of Western thought that postmodernism is said to have undermined.
>
> (Fuller 2000)

I would claim that Wilson and Fuller, coming from very different viewpoints, are in substantial agreement about the main distinction between postmodernism and modernism.

If we need to label the "sides" in the science wars, one possibility would be the postmodernists and the modernists. Although it requires more of a knowledge of jargon, this might be more accurate than talking of, say, the scientists and the critics, for indeed some scientists, especially social scientists, have postmodern leanings, and some critics are more modern in outlook. The labels I slightly prefer are the rationalists and the romantics. Historically, the Romantic movement was a reaction to the Enlightment that rejected the scientific worldview with all its logic and empirical evidence and preferred a more personal, emotional, and intuitive approach to Truth. (See David Norman Smith's contribution to this volume for more on the Romantic movement.) The postmodernists, with their added spice of philosophical relativism, are the current inheritors of this tradition.

Of course, in all of this labeling it must be remembered that it is simplistic to speak of there being two "sides" to this argument. There is really a spectrum of views. Even under the banner of postmodernism there is no single philosophy or attitude, but a variety. It is our purpose to survey a large part of the spectrum of opinion on the "science wars" with the essays in this book. I should admit out front, though, that the more radical positions of the strong constructivists are not represented here. As Keith Ashman argues in his essay, it is hard to imagine how scientists and strong constructivists could engage in a meaningful dialogue.

In case anyone thinks I slighted postmodernism by declaring it difficult to define, let me digress a little here in order to point out that "science" is equally difficult to define. We all think we know what science is, but when we sit down to define it, one person's definition may differ from another's in significant ways. Here, for example, is one reasonable definition offered by Michael Shermer, publisher of *Skeptic* magazine: "[Science is] a set of methods designed to describe and interpret observed or inferred phenomena, past or present, and aimed at building a testable body of knowledge open to rejection or confirmation" (Shermer 1997: 18). This is fine as far as it goes, but leaves open the question of the "set of methods." He goes on to say that defining this set of methods, the "scientific method, is not so simple."

The usual prescription, the cartoon version of the scientific method, is that of making hypotheses, gathering evidence, and then revising your hypotheses as needed. In reality, science is more complicated and harder to pin down, but we can discuss the knowledge that one derives from science and see if we can contrast it with other types of knowledge. Scientific knowledge can take the form of a theory—"a well-supported and well-tested hypothesis or set of hypotheses" (Shermer 1997: 19)—or a fact—"A conclusion confirmed to such an extent that it would be reasonable to offer provisional agreement" (Shermer 1997: 19; in this and subsequent quotations, original emphasis is retained). Further, "A theory may be contrasted with a *construct*: a nontestable statement to account for a set of observations" (Shermer 1997: 20).

To take a simple example, suppose we observe the transformation of water into two gases, hydrogen and oxygen, via an electric current. One explanation for the observation is that "God made this happen," a second explanation is that "water is made of molecules built from hydrogen and oxygen atoms and the current split apart the molecules." The first explanation is a construct, the second a scientific theory. Note that the statements are not mutually exclusive, both (or neither) may be true, but only the second is a testable scientific statement.

Shermer goes on to say, "Through the scientific method, we aim for *objectivity*: basing conclusions on external validation. And we avoid *mysticism*: basing conclusions on personal insights that elude external validation" (Shermer 1997: 20). Further, "Science leads us toward *rationalism*: basing conclusions on logic and evidence . . . And science helps us avoid *dogmatism*: basing conclusions on authority rather than logic or evidence" (Shermer 1997: 20). This is not to say that personal insight has no role to play in science: "Many great scientists have attributed their important ideas to insight, intuition, and other mental leaps hard to pin down . . . But intuitive ideas and mystical insights do not become objective until they are externally validated" (Shermer 1997: 20). Also: "Dogmatic conclusions are not necessarily invalid, but they do beg other questions: How did the authorities come by their conclusions? Were they guided by science or some other means?" (Shermer 1997: 21).

Having presented part of the scientist's view of what science is, let us return to our brief history of the science wars. Kuhn opened the door to a new field—the sociology of science. Because science, like any other human endeavor, is influenced by social forces, it provides fertile ground for the historian or sociologist to ask a number of very interesting questions. About this there is little controversy. The arguments arise over the extent to which the ideas of relativism and social construction are used in science studies. Here is how Collins and Yearly make the case for methodological relativism:

> The importance of the philosophical arguments about relativism in the 1970s was, in retrospect, not that they showed that relativism was true but that it was tenable and therefore could be used as a methodology for the study of science.
>
> (Collins and Yearly 1992: 303)

Further, they explain how relativism is used by the scholar:

> A clear prescription that emerged from relativism was . . . [that] sociologists of scientific knowledge should treat correct science and false science equally; they should analyze what are taken by most scientists to be true claims about the natural world and what are treated by most as mistaken claims in the same way. The idea was that the construction of the boundary between the true and the false would become the topic rather than the starting point as in existing sociologies of science.
>
> (Collins and Yearly 1992: 302)

This is quite similar to the approach anthropologists would take in addressing a new culture that was very different from their own. The new culture may have a system of beliefs that appears very strange, even wrong in some sense, from the perspective of the culture the anthropologist comes from. In order for anthropologists to gain insight into the new culture they must take a relativist stance; they can make no judgment (when acting as anthropologists) on the relative merits of the culture's beliefs because to do so would bias their study. If one starts out assuming some belief is just delusional, it will be impossible to uncover why the belief is held in that cultural context. Note that anthropologists can be methodological relativists, they can suspend their disbelief for the purposes of the study but still privately hold their own belief system to be superior; they need not necessarily be philosophical relativists.[1]

I think it is fair to say that most scientists took little notice of these developments in the philosophy and sociology of science until the publication of *Higher Superstition: The Academic Left and Its Quarrels with Science* by Paul Gross and Norman Levitt. The book examines much postmodern literature, finds it to be profoundly anti-science in attitude, and quotes some leading practitioners, holding up their statements as examples of either excess or outright nonsense. Here follow some samples from the book. First a comment on viewing science through the lens of relativism:

> Once it has been affirmed that one discursive community is as good as another, that the narrative of science holds no privileges over the narratives of superstition, the newly minted cultural critic can actually revel in his ignorance of deep scientific ideas. That this is a canny political act is accepted as an article of faith, no matter how much it seems to elevate wishful thinking over hard social fact.
>
> (Gross and Levitt 1994: 85)

Gross and Levitt make plain their disdain for relativism, claim that the philosophy has been adopted in some quarters for political reasons, and assert that it has led to sloppy scholarship, such as writers not bothering to learn much about the science they are criticizing. Further, they say this sloppy scholarship has been given a "free ride" because of a misguided sense of political correctness:

> To these sympathizers, the very act of putting on the table questions about the competence and objectivity of science, about its complicity with the injustices of capitalism, racism, and patriarchy, is praiseworthy in and of itself; nagging doubts about the competence and fairness with which this is done are easily deferred.
>
> (Gross and Levitt 1994: 238)

Gross and Levitt also fault postmodern writers for inconsistencies such as rejecting science (as a tool of capitalism, a barrier to social progress, and so on) yet using the results of science (for example, research into global warming) when it suits their purpose: "The relativism of cultural constructivist doctrine is the perfect tool for discounting science as biased or corrupt if and when it inconveniences one's political program" (Gross and Levitt 1994: 162).

It is easy to see how the publication of *Higher Superstition* escalated the conflict between the academic cultures. On the one hand, scientists see how postmodern philosophers and sociologists of science have been disparaging their work. Science is portrayed not merely as influenced by social forces and not merely as a means of political repression, but as fundamentally without meaning. On the other hand, philosophers and sociologists see Gross and Levitt calling them muddleheaded, accusing them of poor scholarship, and attacking the theoretical underpinnings of their work. Small wonder irate words started flowing from both camps.

Gross and Levitt's frontal assault on the postmodernist culture was followed two years later by a sort of Trojan Horse attack. Alan Sokal published in *Social Text* the article "Transgressing the boundaries: toward a transformative hermeneutics of quantum gravity" (Sokal 1996). After its appearance in print, Sokal revealed the piece to be a hoax, a parody of postmodern thought that the editors mistook for the genuine article. Here is a small sample of the parody:

> the postmodern sciences deconstruct and transcend the Cartesian metaphysical distinctions between humankind and Nature, observer and observed, Subject and Object. Already quantum mechanics, earlier in this century, shattered the ingenuous Newtonian faith in an objective, prelinguistic world of material objects "out there" . . . Just as quantum mechanics informs us that the position and momentum of a particle are brought into being only by the act of observation, so quantum gravity informs us that space and time are contextual, their meaning defined only relative to the mode of observation.
>
> (Sokal 1996: 227–228)

To rationalists like Sokal, statements like the above should provoke laughter, but the editors of *Social Text*, presumed romantics, found the article plausible. Sokal's hoax was instrumental in bringing the debate over science studies to an even broader audience and brought the science wars to their peak intensity. "Science and Its Critics," various other conferences, and numerous books shortly followed. And now in this volume we examine the aftermath of the science wars and where things stand on some of these issues.

The eleven pieces in this volume provide a variety of perspectives on science and science criticism. We lead off with Alan Sokal himself, who discusses his motivation for the parody and in the process gives his take on many of the issues that drove the "science wars." Sokal opens the debate in an essay taken from his keynote talk at the conference, "What the *Social Text* affair does and does not prove: a critical look at 'science studies'."

Other authors in this volume offer their reactions to the issues Sokal brings up, as well as other related issues. First, Adrian Melott, a cosmologist and a former Unitarian minister, brings us "Randomized thoughts of a cultural turncoat," in which he presents a variety of short subjects. Gabriel Stolzenberg next explores these issues much as he did in a three-week course he offered for faculty at Rutgers entitled "The Science Wars: Tragedy or Farce?" In his essay "Reading and relativism: an introduction to the science wars," he explores the rigor and fairness of statements made by Sokal and others. In "science wars" discussions, the rationalists claim that the arguments of neo-romantic writers such as Jacques Derrida, Bruno Latour, and Luce Irigaray don't stand up under scrutiny. But do these arguments in turn stand up under scrutiny? Stolzenberg presents case studies in which he finds holes in some of these arguments, then tackles some of the tough philosophical questions that lie at the core of the conflict.

One of the main bones of contention in the science wars is the notion that scientific theories are purely social constructions with no more claim to the label "truth" than other socially constructed ideas. To some this notion is a given, a starting point for further investigation. To others it is utterly nonsensical. If we are to communicate across disciplines and move away from the polarization of the science wars, we must somehow tackle the issue of objectivity. Four colleagues from very different fields got together to discuss these issues. Barry Shank (American studies), Shari Speer (speech, language, and hearing), Alan Thompson (physics), and Sarah Wayland (neurology) present the results of their collaboration in this volume. Not only is the paper interesting in its own right, but the origins of the paper also give us one model for communication across disciplines. In "Pure objects and useful knowledges" they offer us a possible compromise on the truth claims in different disciplines.

Another significant criticism of science is that historically it has been dominated by white male scientists. Suppose we accept for the sake of argument that science is measuring something real, some aspect of reality that exists independent of human observers. If that is the case, then does it matter who the scientists are or what their background, culture, or worldview might be? How does the white male worldview affect the questions that are asked or the answers that are found by science? Ann Cudd addresses gender and race issues in her contribution to this volume, "Objectivity and ethno-feminist critiques of science."

There are other barriers to objectivity in science in addition to race and gender issues. One is the simple human capacity to want to hold on to preconceived notions. To what extent do scientists find the answers that they wanted to find through the power of wishful thinking? How does the scientific method try to enforce objectivity? How well does it succeed? Keith Ashman presents us with an interesting case from recent events in astrophysics in "Measuring the Hubble constant: objectivity under the telescope."

Next, Ziauddin Sardar reminds us that there are other worldviews besides the Western ones and that Western science owes a great and often unacknowledged debt to non-Western cultures. Science and math were alive and well in the civilizations of China, India, and Islam long before the Enlightenment hit Western Europe. We have spoken of the "two cultures" of literature and science, but these are both Western cultures. How is the philosophy and practice of science viewed in non-Western cultures? There is an even broader multiplicity of views to be examined and in his essay, "Above, beyond, and at the center of the science wars: a postcolonial reading," Sardar argues that the emergence of the field of postcolonial science studies may ultimately have more impact than the current "science wars." In the postcolonial view, Western science is trying to "colonize" non-Western science. The resistance of non-Western science and the reconsideration of some basic tenets of Western science make postcolonial science studies a field to watch.

Science and technology are two different but closely interrelated fields. Technology makes more sophisticated science possible and science makes more sophisticated technology possible. One of the great contributions of modern science and technology is the extension of the human life-span through the development of science-based medicine. This is not to say that science or technology are universally regarded as unmixed blessings. In fact, many examples of anti-science backlash can be found in our society. Paradoxically, there are a number of people who feel compelled to explain their fundamentally non-scientific beliefs in the language of pseudo-science. Robert Park is one scientist who takes on the duty of separating science from pseudo-science. He discusses this in his essay "Voodoo medicine in a scientific world."[2]

This leads us to the question of rationality. Science relies not only upon the notion that there actually is an objective reality, but also on the application of rational argument for discovering knowledge of that reality. One charge that is made against pseudo-science and postmodernism alike is that it is irrational. Sociologist David Norman Smith would remind us that irrationalism is an observable part of human society that has a long history. In other words, irrationalism has an objective reality. For example, antisemitism exists—it is a social construct of a certain group of people, and it unfortunately has very real consequences. David Norman Smith, in his paper "The stigma of reason: irrationalism as a problem for social theory," discusses some recent history of irrationalism and shows us some of the uses of the concept of social construction.

Next, Steve Fuller not only takes on some of the deepest issues in the philosophy of science in his essay "The reenchantment of science: a fit end to the science wars?," but he also engages the really big questions of Truth and Justice. He explores the "enchanted" and "disenchanted" worldviews (a distinction somewhat like the one drawn here between romantic and rational) and whether "science" can be generalized in such a way as to bridge the current divides between the natural sciences, social sciences, and humanities. We have put Sokal and Fuller at opposite ends of this book for good reason, but each is seeking middle ground in their own way.

The final piece in the volume is a selection of two science fiction writings from author James Gunn. Science fiction can be viewed as a true synthesis between the "two cultures" of science and literature, so I find it a fitting conclusion to the volume. Scientific and literary ideas meet and produce unique results. Some science fiction is in the form of a thought experiment. We can examine the human consequences of science and technology through literature. Perhaps more importantly for this book, Gunn here examines several issues highly relevant to our themes. What might be the consequences of anti-science attitudes, or anti-intellectualism in general? And what about the criticism that science is not politically progressive, in the sense that it does not admit human values and aspirations into its methods for establishing truths. Gunn looks at one alternative: what if science gave way to, say, magic?

Having completed our survey of the essays in this volume, and knowing that it is a rare reader that perseveres this far into an introduction, this is a safe place for me to offer some of my own observations. First, I would like to point out that literature and science put language to very different purposes. This is a point that became increasingly apparent to me in the fascinating process of editing this collection. The scientist strives to avoid ambiguity as much as possible because a central component of the scientific method is that results must be reproducible. Another theorist should be able to reconstruct my calculation and another experimentalist should be able to obtain my result with their apparatus, so I must communicate as clearly and unambiguously as possible my findings. Scientific writing is full of specialized jargon where ordinary words, like "momentum," are given technical meanings (in this case mass multiplied by velocity). When a scientist writes that they had "one kilogram of mass," another scientist on the other side of the world knows how to get exactly that amount of material to within the limits of their measuring technology. In literary writing, on the other hand, ambiguity and imprecision may be highly desired in order to provide richness, texture, and depth of meaning. The goals are quite different: the passive voice, technical use of language, and emotional neutrality of the scientific journal article would generally doom a literary piece to failure. I am thus highly skeptical when postmodernists use techniques borrowed from literary criticism to examine science. It seems self-evident that carefully weighing and measuring the physical properties of the book does little to understand the contents of Shakespeare's plays written within. It seems to me equally self-evident, although obviously this view is not as widely shared, that doing a close literary analysis of an article in *Physical Review* will cast little light on the science being put forth.

Next, a word about "progress." One of the livelier discussions at the "Science and Its Critics" conference ensued from Steve Fuller's remarks on "the myth of progress." Can any social endeavor—and let's freely admit that the practice of science is a social endeavor—be said to make "progress"? Critics of science can cite numerous case studies that demonstrate how the workings of scientific society can lead to erroneous or misleading results. Scientists respond that in the long run the scientific method, with its rigorous techniques of external verification, overcomes our human foibles. As time goes on, say the scientists, we develop a more and more accurate picture of the way nature works. In a word, the scientists say they are making "progress." Critics of science claim that this notion of progress is a "myth." Much of the discussion at the conference involved what exactly was meant by "progress." Certainly, if you focus on the social, ethical, and political connotations of "progress," as Fuller does at least in part, it is much harder to make a case for progress than if you take a narrower view.

I would like to suggest here a very narrow view of progress that I believe scientists can defend. Let us assert that scientists make "progress" if their predictions become either more accurate, more numerically precise, or encompass a broader range of phenomena. This notion of progress has the advantage that it can to a large extent be objectively measured. Have weather forecasts become more accurate over the last century? Can we more precisely predict the orbit of a satellite? Can we anticipate the reaction of the human body to a wider variety of drugs? I focus on predictions because they most clearly distinguish science from other types of knowledge. Many fields offer explanations, and certainly explanations are also at the heart of science. But scientific explanations, if they have merit, allow one to predict the future behavior of the system under study.

One can certainly argue for a broader definition of scientific progress than this. The falsification of a theory, finding new data to support an existing theory, or recasting a theory in a more elegant mathematical form, can all be fairly said to be "progress" even though they do not immediately lead to improved predictions. I suggest, though, that when one broadens the definition, one makes claims of scientific progress less distinct from claims of social, ethical, or artistic progress and more open to relativist arguments.

One final thought. One final reason for reading the essays in this volume and for thinking about these deep knotty philosophical issues—it's fun. Now I am not supposed to say this, but I am safe because no one is still reading this. I am supposed to say it is significant or profound or highly relevant, but I think I have implied those things already. What I have not mentioned is the sheer fun of a good intellectual argument. After all, in terms of my professional development I should be spending my time doing physics experiments (which in fact is how I spend most of my time) and not editing books like this. I am doing this for the fun of it (and, OK, also for the learning experience). It was either edit this book or watch a rerun of *The Simpsons*. (More accurately, I could have watched hundreds of reruns of *The Simpsons* in the time spent on this.) Bringing a sense of fun to these arguments may be one of the best ways to defuse some of the tensions of the science wars. This presupposes that mutual respect has been reestablished between the disciplines. The atmosphere at the "Science and Its Critics" conference and the cooperative effort that went into this book give me great cause for optimism in that regard.

So I hope you will find these essays enlightening, thought provoking and . . . fun. And remember, please do not employ the book as a projectile no matter how much your thoughts get provoked.

Notes

1 I can't resist making an analogy with the natural sciences here. Physicists or biologists necessarily use a materialist point of view in their work. That is, they explain all observations in terms of matter and the interaction between material things. Scientists can privately believe in non-material forces, such as God, they need not be atheists, but they cannot directly take non-material forces into account in their research (while acting as a natural scientist) without undermining it.
2 I should note that the related talk Park gave at the "Science and Its Critics" conference generated a great deal of discussion. Some claimed Park's remarks on Deepak Chopra's writings (similar remarks lead off his essay) and his use of the word "voodoo" displayed a bias against non-Western cultures. Park's defenders asserted that ideas from non-Western cultures, like any ideas, should be expected to withstand empirical testing if they are to be considered scientifically valid. Park's defenders also noted that most of his criticisms were directed towards homeopathic medicine, a field that came out of Western Europe based on some rather mystical views of chemistry. (His essay in this book takes on the field of magnet therapy that developed in Europe and the US.)

Bibliography

Collins, H. M. and Yearly, Steven (1992) "Epistemological chicken," in Pickering, A. (ed.) *Science as Practice and Culture*, Chicago and London: University of Chicago Press.

Fuller, Steve (2000) "Postmodernism," to appear in McInnis, Ray (ed.) *Discourse Synthesis: A Conceptual Dictionary*, Westport CT: Greenwood Press.

Gross, Paul and Levitt, Norman (1994) *Higher Superstition: The Academic Left and Its Quarrels with Science*, Baltimore: Johns Hopkins University Press.

Kuhn, Thomas (1962) *The Structure of Scientific Revolutions*, 2nd edn, Chicago: University of Chicago Press.

Shermer, Michael (1997) *Why People Believe Weird Things: Pseudoscience, Superstition, and Other Confusions of Our Time*, New York: W. H. Freeman and Company.

Snow, C. P. (1959) *The Two Cultures and the Scientific Revolution*, New York: Cambridge University Press.

Sokal, Alan D. (1996) "Transgressing the boundaries: toward a transformative hermeneutics of quantum gravity," *Social Text* 46–47 (Spring/Summer): 217–252.

Wilson, Edward O. (1998) *Consilience: The Unity of Knowledge*, New York: Knopf.

2 What the *Social Text* affair does and does not prove

A critical look at "science studies"[1]

Alan D. Sokal

I confess to some embarrassment at addressing a conference devoted to questions of the philosophy, history, and sociology of science. After all, I'm neither a philosopher nor a historian nor a sociologist. I'm merely a theoretical physicist with an amateur interest in the philosophy of science and perhaps some modest skill at thinking clearly. *Social Text* co-founder Stanley Aronowitz was absolutely right when he called me "ill-read and half-educated" (Scott 1996).

So, what am I doing here? I guess you all know at least the bare bones of the story. I wrote a parody of postmodern science criticism, entitled "Transgressing the boundaries: toward a transformative hermeneutics of quantum gravity," and submitted it to the cultural studies journal *Social Text* (of course without telling the editors that it was a parody). They published it as a serious scholarly article (Sokal 1996a) in their spring/summer 1996 special issue devoted to the "science wars" (a term that I dislike, by the way, because I certainly don't see this debate as a "war"). Three weeks later I revealed the hoax in an article in *Lingua Franca* (Sokal 1996b), and all hell broke loose.[2]

This affair has brought up an incredible number of issues, and I can't dream of addressing them all in forty-five minutes. So let me start by circumscribing my talk, listing some issues that I won't address now, but which we might want to discuss later. First of all, I won't belabor *Social Text*'s failings either before or after the publication of my parody: *Social Text* is not my enemy, nor is it my main intellectual target. I won't go into the ethical issues related to the propriety of hoaxing (although in the question period I'd be glad to defend my ethics). I won't address the obscurantist prose and the uncritical celebrity-worship that have infected certain trendy sectors of the American academic humanities. I won't try to analyze the media fallout from this affair and what it may indicate both about academia and about the larger society.[3] I won't say much about the political implications of this "affair"—although in fact it was my concern for the future of leftist politics that was my principal motivation for writing the parody, and I'd be glad to discuss this further if people are interested.[4] I won't attempt to address the social and political role of science and technology, nor the problem of reconciling technical expertise with democratic control: these are very important issues but they would take us too far afield. Nor will I go too deeply into the subtler issues of the philosophy of science.[5] What I would like to do in this talk is to take a critical look at the discipline sometimes referred to as the "new" sociology of science, but often simply called science studies. In particular, I want to take issue with the philosophical and methodological presuppositions that underlie some (and I emphasize the word "some") of this work.[6]

But first, so that you don't get the idea that I'm an arrogant physicist who rejects all sociological intrusion on our "turf," I'd like to lay out some positive things that I think social studies of science can accomplish. The following propositions are, I hope, noncontroversial:

1   Science is a human endeavor, and like any other human endeavor it merits being subjected to rigorous social analysis. Which research problems count as important, how research funds are distributed, who gets prestige and power, what role scientific expertise plays in public policy debates, and in what form scientific knowledge becomes embodied in technology and for whose benefit—all these issues are strongly affected by political, economic, and, to some extent, ideological considerations, as well as by the internal logic of scientific inquiry. They are thus fruitful subjects for empirical study by historians, sociologists, political scientists, and economists.

2   At a more subtle level, even the content of scientific debate—what types of theories can be conceived and entertained, and what criteria are to be used for deciding between competing theories—is constrained in part by the prevailing attitudes of mind, which in turn arise in part from deepseated historical factors. It is the task of historians and sociologists of science to sort out, in each specific instance, the roles played by "external" and "internal" factors in determining the course of scientific development. Not surprisingly, scientists tend to stress the "internal" factors while sociologists tend to stress the "external," if only because each group tends to have a poor grasp of the other group's concepts. But these problems are perfectly amenable to rational debate.

3   There is nothing wrong with research informed by a political commitment, as long as that commitment does not blind the researcher to inconvenient facts. Thus there is a long and honorable tradition of socio-political critique of science and technology, often quite scathing: the leftist critique of military and industrial technologies, the ecological critique of the same, the antiracist critique of anthropological pseudo-science and eugenics (for example, Gould 1996), and feminist critiques of psychology and parts of medicine and biology (for example, Fausto-Sterling 1992, Tavris 1992). These critiques typically follow a standard pattern: first one shows, using conventional scientific arguments, why the research in question is flawed according to the ordinary canons of good science, then, and only then, one attempts to explain how the researchers' social prejudices

(which may well have been unconscious) led them to violate these canons. Of course, each such critique has to stand or fall on its own merits; having good political intentions does not guarantee that your analysis will constitute good science, good sociology, or good history. But this general two-step approach is sound, and empirical studies of this kind, if conducted with due intellectual rigor, could, I think, shed useful light on the social conditions under which good science (defined normatively as the search for truths or at least approximate truths about the world) is fostered or hindered.[7]

I don't want to claim that these three points exhaust the field of fruitful inquiry for historians and sociologists of science, but they certainly do lay out a big and important area. Yet some sociologists and literary intellectuals over the past two decades have gotten greedier: roughly speaking, they want to attack the normative conception of scientific inquiry as a search for truths or approximate truths about the world; they want to see science as just another social practice, which produces "narrations" and "myths" that are no more valid than those produced by other social practices; and some of them want to argue further that these social practices encode a bourgeois, Eurocentric, or masculinist worldview. Of course, like all brief summaries this one is an oversimplification; and in any case there is no canonical doctrine in the "new" sociology of science, just a bewildering variety of individuals and schools. More importantly, the task of summarization is made more difficult here by the fact that this literature is often ambiguous in crucial ways about its most fundamental claims (as I'll illustrate later using the cases of Latour and Barnes–Bloor). Still, I think most scientists and philosophers of science would be astonished to learn that "the natural world has a small or nonexistent role in the construction of scientific knowledge," as prominent sociologist of science Harry Collins claims (Collins 1981: 3),[8] or that "reality is the consequence rather than the cause" of the so-called "social construction of facts," as Bruno Latour and Steve Woolgar assert (Latour and Woolgar 1979: 237).

But let me back up for a second to consider the "*Social Text* affair," and ask what (if anything) it proves—and also what it does not prove, because some of my over-enthusiastic supporters have claimed too much. In this analysis, it's crucial to distinguish between what can be deduced from the fact of publication and what can be deduced from the content of the article.

From the mere fact of the publication of my parody I think that not much can be deduced. It certainly does not prove that the whole field of cultural studies, or cultural studies of science, or sociology of science, is nonsense. Nor does it prove that intellectual standards in these fields are generally lax. (This might be the case, but it would have to be established on other grounds.) It proves only that the editors of one rather marginal (but trendy) journal were derelict in their intellectual duty, by publishing an article on quantum physics that they admit they could not understand, without bothering to get an opinion from anyone knowledgeable in quantum physics, solely because it came from a "conveniently credentialed ally" (as *Social Text* coeditor Bruce Robbins later candidly admitted: see Robbins 1996), flattered the editors' ideological preconceptions, and attacked their "enemies."[9]

To which one might say "so what?"[10]

The answer comes from examining the content of the parody. In this regard, one important point has gotten lost in much of the discussion of my article: Yes, the article is screamingly funny—I'm not modest, I'm proud of my work—but the most hilarious parts of my article were not written by me. Rather, they're direct quotes from the postmodern Masters, whom I shower with mock praise. In fact, the article is structured around the silliest quotations I could find about mathematics and physics (and the philosophy of mathematics and physics) from some of the most prominent French and American intellectuals; my only contribution was to invent a nonsensical argument linking these quotations together and praising them. This involved, of course, advocating an incoherent mishmash of trendy ideas—deconstructive literary theory, New Age ecology, so-called "feminist epistemology,"[11] extreme social-constructivist philosophy of science, even Lacanian psychoanalysis—but that just made the parody all the more fun. Indeed, in some cases I took the liberty of parodying extreme or ambiguously stated versions of views that I myself hold in a more moderate and precisely stated form.

I said that I structured the article around the silliest quotes I could find, but what precisely do I mean by "silliness"? Here's a very rough categorization: first of all, one has meaningless or absurd statements, name-dropping, and the display of false erudition. Second, one has sloppy thinking and bad philosophy, which come together notably (although not always) in the form of glib relativism.

The first of these categories would not be so important, perhaps, if we were dealing with a few assistant professors of literature making fools of themselves pontificating on quantum mechanics or Gödel's theorem.[12] It becomes more relevant because we're dealing with important intellectuals, at least as measured by shelf space in the cultural-studies section of university bookstores. Here, for instance, are Gilles Deleuze and Félix Guattari pontificating on chaos theory:

> To slow down is to set a limit in chaos to which all speeds are subject, so that they form a variable determined as abscissa, at the same time as the limit forms a universal constant that cannot be gone beyond (for example, a maximum degree of contraction). The first functives are therefore the limit and the variable, and reference is a relationship between values of the variable or, more profoundly, the relationship of the variable, as abscissa of speeds, with the limit.
>
> (Deleuze and Guattari 1994: 119)

(By the way, if you worry that I'm quoting out of context, just follow my footnotes, look up the originals, and decide for yourself. You'll find that these passages are even worse in context than out of context.)

And there's much more—Jacques Lacan and Luce Irigaray on differential topology, Jean-François Lyotard on cosmology, Paul Virilio on relativity, Michel Serres (member of the Académie française) on nonlinear time—but let me not spoil the fun. (For an extensive compilation of postmodern French philosophers' abuses of mathematics and physics, along with commentary for non-experts, see Sokal and Bricmont 1998.)

Nor is all the nonsense of French origin. Connoisseurs of fashionable American work in the cultural studies of science will find ample food for thought.

The science studies contingent in the audience might now object: maybe some of our friends in the English department take Lacan or Deleuze seriously, but no one in our community does. True enough; but then take a look at Bruno Latour's semiotic analysis of the theory of relativity, published in *Social Studies of Science*, in which "Einstein's text is read as a contribution to the sociology of delegation" (Latour 1988: 3). Why's that? Because Latour finds Einstein's popular book on relativity full of situations in which the author delegates one observer to stand on the platform and make certain measurements and another observer to stand on the train and make certain measurements; and of course the results won't obey the Lorentz transformations unless the two observers do what they're told! You think I exaggerate? Latour emphasizes Einstein's

> obsession with transporting *in*formation through *trans*formations without *de*formation; his passion for the precise superimposition of readings; his panic at the idea that observers sent away might betray, might retain privileges, and send reports that could not be used to expand our knowledge; his desire to discipline the delegated observers and to turn them into dependent pieces of apparatus that do nothing but watch the coincidence of hands and notches.
>
> (Latour 1988: 22; original italics)

Furthermore, because Latour does not understand what the term "frame of reference" means in physics—he confuses it with "actor" in semiotics—he claims that relativity cannot deal with the transformation laws between two frames of reference, but needs at least three:

> How can one decide whether an observation made in a train about the behaviour of a falling stone can be made to coincide with the observation made of the same falling stone from the embankment? If there are only one, or even *two*, frames of reference, no solution can be found since the man in the train claims he observes a straight line and the man on the embankment a parabola. Thus nothing tells us if it is the same stone

acting according to the same law of physics . . . Einstein's solution is to consider *three* actors: one in the train, one on the embankment and a third one, the author [enunciator] or one of its representants, who tries to superimpose the coded observations sent back by the two others.

(Latour 1988: 10–11; original italics)

Finally, Latour somehow got the idea that relativity concerns the problems raised by the relative location (rather than the relative motion) of different observers. (Of course, even the word "observer" here is potentially misleading: it belongs to the pedagogy of relativity, not to the theory itself.) Here is Latour's summary of the meaning of relativity:

provided the two relativities [special and general] are accepted, more frames of reference with less privilege can be accessed, reduced, accumulated and combined, observers can be delegated to a few more places in the infinitely large (the cosmos) and the infinitely small (electrons), and the readings they send will be understandable. His [Einstein's] book could well be titled: "New Instructions for Bringing Back Long-Distance Scientific Travellers."

(Latour 1988: 22–23)

Latour has thus produced forty pages of comical misunderstandings of a theory that is nowadays routinely taught to intelligent college freshmen; and *Social Studies of Science* found it a worthy scholarly contribution.[13]

So much for examples of nonsense (although many more are available). More interesting intellectually, I think, are the sloppy thinking and glib relativism that have become prevalent in many parts of science studies (albeit not, by and large, among serious philosophers of science). When one analyzes these writings, one often finds radical-sounding assertions whose meaning is ambiguous, and which can be given two alternative readings: one as interesting, radical, and grossly false; the other as boring and trivially true.

Let me start again with Latour, this time taken from his book *Science in Action*. His so-called Third Rule of Method reads as follows:[14] "Since the settlement of a controversy is the *cause* of Nature's representation, not the consequence, we can never use the outcome—Nature—to explain how and why a controversy has been settled" (Latour 1987: 99, 258; original italics). Note how Latour slips, without comment or argument, from "Nature's representation" in the first half of this sentence to "Nature" *tout court* in the second half. If we were to read "Nature's representation" in both halves, then we'd have the truism that scientists' representations of nature (that is, their theories) are arrived at by a social process, and that the course and outcome of that social process can't be explained simply by its outcome. If, on the other hand, we take "Nature" seriously in the second half, linked as it is to the word "outcome," then we would have the claim that the external world is created by scientists' negotiations: a claim that is bizarre to say the least, given that the external world has been around for about ten billion years longer than the human race.[15] Finally, if we take "Nature" seriously in the second half but expunge the word "outcome" preceding it, then we would have either (a) the weak (and trivially true) claim that the course and outcome of a scientific controversy cannot be explained solely by the nature of the external world (obviously some social factors play a role, if only in determining which experiments are technologically feasible at a given time, not to mention other, more subtle social influences); or (b) the strong (and manifestly false) claim that the nature of the external world plays no role in constraining the course and outcome of a scientific controversy.[16]

On the other hand, if we apply the First Rule of Interpretation of Postmodern Academic Writing—"no sentence means what it says"—we can perhaps make sense of Latour's dictum. Let's read it not as a philosophical principle, but rather as a methodological principle for a sociologist of science—more precisely, for a sociologist of science who does not have the scientific competence to make an independent assessment of whether the experimental or observational data do in fact warrant the conclusions the scientific community has drawn from them. (The principle applies with particular force when such a sociologist is studying contemporary science, because in this case there is no other scientific community besides the one under study who could provide such an independent assessment. By contrast, for studies of the distant past, one can always look at what subsequent scientists learned, including the results from experiments going beyond those originally performed.) In such a situation, the sociologist will be understandably reluctant to say that "the scientific community under study came to conclusion X because X is the way the world really is"—even if it is in fact the case that X is the way the world is and that is the reason the scientists came to believe it— because the sociologist has no independent grounds to believe that X is the way the world really is other than the fact that the scientific community under study came to believe it.

Of course, the sensible conclusion to draw from this cul de sac is that sociologists of science ought not to study scientific controversies on which they lack the competence to make an independent assessment of the facts, if there is no other (for example, historically later) scientific community on which they could justifiably rely for such an independent assessment. But it goes without saying that Latour and at least some of his colleagues would not enjoy this conclusion, because their goal, as Steve Fuller put it, is to "employ methods that enable them to fathom both the 'inner workings' and the 'outer character' of science without having to be expert in the fields they study" (Fuller 1993: xii).[17]

It seems to me that much sloppy thinking in science studies, like that in Latour's Third Rule of Method, involves conflating concepts that need to be distinguished. Most frequently this conflation is accomplished by terminological fiat: the author intentionally uses an old word or phrase in a radically new sense, thereby undermining any attempt to distinguish between the two meanings. The clear goal here is to achieve by definition what one could not achieve by logic. For example, one often finds phrases like "the social construction of facts" (Latour and Woolgar 1979) that intentionally elide the distinction between facts and our knowledge of them. Or, to take another example, philosophers usually understand the word "knowledge" to mean "justified true belief" or some similar concept; but Barry Barnes and David Bloor redefine "knowledge" to mean "any collectively accepted system of belief" (Barnes and Bloor 1981: 22 n.). Now perhaps Barnes and Bloor are uninterested in inquiring whether a given belief is true or rationally justified; but if they think these properties of beliefs are irrelevant for their purposes, then they should say so and explain why, without confusing the issue by redefining words.[18]

More generally, it seems to me that much sloppy thinking in science studies involves conflating two or more of the following levels of analysis:

1   *Ontology*. What objects exist in the world? What statements about these objects are true?
2   *Epistemology*. How can human beings obtain knowledge of truths about the world? How can they assess the reliability of that knowledge?
3   *Sociology of knowledge*. To what extent are the truths known (or knowable) by humans in any given society influenced (or determined) by social, economic, political, cultural, and ideological factors? The same question applies to the false statements erroneously believed to be true.
4   *Individual ethics*. What types of research ought a scientist (or technologist) to undertake (or refuse to undertake)?
5   *Social ethics*. What types of research ought society to encourage, subsidize, or publicly fund (or, alternatively, discourage, tax or forbid)?

These questions are obviously related—for example, if there are no objective truths about the world, then there is not much point in asking how one can know those (nonexistent) truths—but they are conceptually distinct.

For example, Sandra Harding (1991: Chapter 4)—citing the work of Forman (1987)—points out that American research in the 1940s and 1950s on quantum electronics was motivated in large part by potential military applications. True enough. Now, quantum mechanics made possible solid-state physics, which in turn made possible quantum electronics (for example, the transistor), which made possible nearly all of modern technology (for example, the computer). And the computer has had applications that are beneficial to society (for example, in allowing the postmodern cultural critic to produce her articles more efficiently) as well as applications that are harmful (for example, in allowing the US military to kill human beings more efficiently). This raises a host of social and individual ethical questions: Ought society to forbid (or discourage) certain applications of computers? Forbid (or discourage) research on computers *per se*? Forbid (or discourage) research on quantum electronics? Or solid-state physics? Or quantum mechanics? And likewise for individual scientists and technologists. (Clearly, an affirmative answer to these questions becomes harder to justify as one goes down the list, but I do not want to declare any of these questions *a priori* illegitimate.) Similarly, sociological questions arise, such as: To what extent is our (true) knowledge of computer science, quantum electronics, solid-state physics and quantum mechanics—and our lack of knowledge about other scientific subjects, for example, the global climate—a result of public policy choices favoring militarism? To what extent have the erroneous theories (if any) in computer science, quantum electronics, solid-state physics and quantum mechanics been the result (in whole or in part) of social, economic, political, cultural, and ideological factors, in particular the culture of militarism?[19] These are all serious questions, which deserve careful investigation adhering to the highest standards of scientific and historical evidence. But they have no effect whatsoever on the underlying scientific questions: whether atoms (and silicon crystals, transistors, and computers) really do behave according to the laws of quantum mechanics (and solid-state physics, quantum electronics, and computer science). The militaristic orientation of American science has quite simply no bearing whatsoever on the ontological question, and only under a wildly implausible scenario could it have any bearing on the epistemological question. (For example, if the worldwide community of solid-state physicists, following what they believe to be the conventional standards of scientific evidence, were to hastily accept an erroneous theory of semiconductor behavior because of their enthusiasm for the breakthrough in military technology that this theory would make possible.)

The extreme versions of social constructivism and relativism—such as the Edinburgh "Strong Programme"—are, I think, largely based on the same failure to distinguish clearly between ontology, epistemology, and the sociology of knowledge. Here is how Barnes and Bloor describe the form of relativism that they defend:

> Our equivalence postulate is that all beliefs are on a par with one another with respect to the causes of their credibility. It is not that all beliefs are equally true or equally false, but that regardless of truth and falsity the fact of their credibility is to be seen as equally problematic. The position we shall defend is that the incidence of all beliefs without exception calls for empirical investigation and must be accounted for by finding the specific, local causes of this credibility. This means that regardless of whether the sociologist evaluates a belief as true or rational, or as false and irrational, he must search for the causes of its credibility . . . All these questions can, and should, be answered without regard to the status of the belief as it is judged and evaluated by the sociologist's own standards.
>
> (Barnes and Bloor 1981: 23)

It seems clear from this passage, as well as from the paragraph that precedes it, that Barnes and Bloor are not advocating an ontological relativism: they recognize that "to say that all beliefs are equally true encounters the problem of how to handle beliefs which contradict one another," and that "to say that all beliefs are equally false poses the problem of the status of the relativist's own claims" (Barnes and Bloor 1981: 22). They might be advocating an epistemological relativism—that all beliefs are equally credible, or equally rational—and indeed, their attack on the universal validity of even the simplest rules of deductive inference (such as *modus ponens*) lends some support to this interpretation (Barnes and Bloor 1981: 35–47). But more likely what they are advocating is some form of methodological relativism for sociologists of knowledge. The problem is, what form?

If the claim were merely that we should use the same principles of sociology and psychology to explain the causation of all beliefs irrespective of whether we evaluate them as true or false, rational or irrational, then I would have no particular objection (although one might have qualms about the hyper-scientistic attitude that human beliefs can always be explained causally, and about the assumption that we have at present adequate and well-verified principles of sociology and psychology that can be used for this purpose). But if the claim is that only social causes can enter into such an explanation—that the way the world is cannot enter—then I cannot disagree more strenuously.

Let's take a concrete example: Why did the European scientific community become convinced of the truth of Newtonian mechanics somewhere between 1700 and 1750? Undoubtedly a variety of historical, sociological, ideological, and political factors must play a role in this explanation—one must explain, for example, why Newtonian mechanics was accepted quickly in England but more slowly in France[20]—but certainly some part of the explanation must be that the planets and comets really do move (to a very high degree of approximation, although not exactly) as predicted by Newtonian mechanics.[21] Or to take another example: Why did the majority view in the European and North American scientific communities shift from creationism to evolutionism over the course of the nineteenth century? Again, numerous historical, sociological, ideological, and political factors will play a role in this explanation; but can one plausibly explain this shift without any reference to the fossil record or to the Galápagos fauna?

In the unlikely event that the argument is not already clear, here's a more homely example. Suppose we encounter a man running out of a lecture hall screaming at the top of his lungs that there is a stampeding herd of elephants in there. What we are to make of this assertion, and in particular how we are to evaluate its "causes," should, I think, depend heavily on whether or not there is in fact a stampeding herd of elephants in the lecture hall—or, more precisely, since I admit that we have no direct, unmediated access to external reality, whether when I and other people peek (cautiously) into the room we see or hear a stampeding herd of elephants (or the destruction that such a herd might recently have caused before themselves exiting the room). If we do see such evidence of elephants, then the most plausible explanation of this set of observations is that there is (or was) in fact a stampeding herd of elephants in the lecture hall, that the man saw or heard it, and that his subsequent fright (which we might well share under the circumstances) led him to exit the room in a hurry and to scream the assertion that we overheard. And our reaction would be to call the police and the zookeepers. If, on the other hand, our own observations reveal no evidence of elephants in the lecture hall, then the most plausible explanation is that there was not in fact a stampeding herd in the room, that the man imagined the elephants as a result of some psychosis (whether internally or chemically induced), and that this led him to exit the room in a hurry and to scream the assertion that we overheard. And we'd call the police and the psychiatrists.[22] I daresay that Barnes and Bloor, whatever they might write in journal articles for sociologists and philosophers, would do the same in real life.

The bottom line, it seems to me, is that there is no fundamental "metaphysical" difference between the epistemology of science and the epistemology of everyday life. Historians, detectives, and plumbers—indeed, all human beings—use the same basic methods of induction, deduction, and assessment of evidence as do physicists or biochemists.[23] Modern science tries to carry out these operations in a more careful and systematic way—using controls and statistical tests, insisting on replication, and so forth—but nothing more.[24] Any philosophy of science that is so blatantly wrong when applied to the epistemology of everyday life must be severely flawed at its core.

In summary, it seems to me that the "Strong Programme," like Latour's Third Rule of Method, is ambiguous in its intent; and, depending on how one resolves the ambiguity, it becomes either a valid and mildly interesting corrective to the most naive psychological and sociological notions—reminding us that "true beliefs have causes too"—or else a gross and blatant error.

I'd like to conclude with some remarks on the so-called—and I think grossly misnamed—"science wars." The term was apparently first coined by *Social Text* coeditor Andrew Ross, who explained that

> the Science Wars [are] a second front opened up by conservatives cheered by the successes of their legions in the holy Culture Wars. Seeking explanations for their loss of standing in the public eye and the decline in funding from the public purse, conservatives in science have joined the backlash against the (new) usual suspects—pinkos, feminists, and multiculturalists.
> (Ross 1995: 346 and 1996: 6)

This theme was further elaborated in the now-famous special issue of *Social Text*.[25] But, just as in the dreary "culture wars," the truth is rather more complicated than this Manichean portrayal would allow. The alleged one-to-one correspondence between epistemological and political views is a gross misrepresentation.[26] So, too, is the idea that in this debate there are only two positions, or that this is a conflict between disciplines (scientists versus sociologists, with philosophers in the middle).[27]

This conception of debate as combat is, in fact, probably the main reason why the *Social Text* editors fell for my parody. Acting not as intellectuals seeking the truth, but as self-appointed generals in the "science wars," they apparently leapt at the chance to get a "real" scientist on their "side." Now, ruing their blunder, they must surely feel a kinship with the Trojans.

But the military metaphor is a mistake: the *Social Text* editors are not my enemies. Ross has legitimate concerns about new technologies and about the increasingly unequal distribution of scientific expertise. Aronowitz raises important questions about technological unemployment and the possibility of a "jobless future" (Aronowitz and DiFazio 1994). But, *pace* Ross, nothing is gained by denying the existence of objective scientific knowledge; it does exist, whether we like it or not. Political progressives should seek to have that knowledge distributed more democratically and to have it employed for socially useful ends. Indeed, the radical epistemological critique fatally undermines the needed political critique, by removing its factual basis. After all, the only reason why nuclear weapons are a danger to anyone is that the theories of nuclear physics on which their design is based are, at least to a very high degree of approximation, objectively true.[28]

Science studies' epistemological conceits are a diversion from the important matters that motivated science studies in the first place: the social, economic, and political roles of science and technology. To be sure, those conceits are not an accident; they have a history, which can itself be subjected to sociological study.[29] But science studies practitioners are not obliged to persist in a misguided epistemology; they can give it up and go on to the serious task of studying science. Perhaps, from the perspective of a few years from now, today's so-called "science wars" will turn out to have marked such a turning point.

Notes

1 This chapter is based on a talk given at the University of Kansas, February 28, 1997. A version of it first appeared in *A House Built on Sand: Exposing Postmodernist Myths about Science*, edited by Noretta Koertge, New York: Oxford University press (1998). Reprinted with permission.

2 The "official" reply from the editors of *Social Text* appears in Robbins *et al.* 1996, along with a brief rejoinder from myself and letters from readers. For a more detailed explanation of my motivations in undertaking the parody, see Sokal 1996c and 1997. For further commentary, see, for example, Frank 1996, Pollitt 1996, Weinberg 1996, Willis 1996, and Boghossian 1996.

3 For some interesting comments, see Willis 1996.

4 See Albert 1996, Sokal 1996c, 1997, Epstein 1997, and Sokal and Bricmont 1998: Chapter 12.

5 Some of these issues are discussed in Sokal and Bricmont 1998: Chapter 4.

6 For a more detailed discussion, see Sokal and Bricmont 1998: 85–105.

7 Of course, I don't mean to imply that the only (or even principal) purpose of the history of science is to help working scientists. History of science obviously has intrinsic value as a contribution to the history of human society and human thought. But it seems to me that history of science, when done well, can also help working scientists.

8 Two qualifications need to be made: first, this statement is offered as part of Collins's introduction to a set of studies (edited by him) employing the relativist approach, and constitutes his summary of that approach; he does not explicitly endorse this view, though an endorsement seems implied by the context. Second, while Collins appears to intend this assertion as an empirical claim about the history of science, it is possible that he intends it neither as an empirical claim nor as a normative principle of epistemology, but rather as a methodological injunction to sociologists of science: namely, to act as if "the natural world ha[d] a small or non-existent role in the construction of scientific knowledge," or in other words to ignore ("bracket") whatever role the natural world may in fact play in the construction of scientific knowledge. I shall argue below, in discussing Barnes–Bloor, that this approach is seriously deficient as a methodology for sociologists of science.

9 The "science wars" special issue of *Social Text* was conceived primarily to attack Gross and Levitt 1994. See Ross 1996; and see also Ross and Aronowitz 1995.

10 Indeed, a mainstream journal in the sociology of science would almost certainly not have fallen for my parody. (On the other hand, *Social Studies of Science* published a long article on the theory of relativity which, if it was not in fact a parody, might as well have been: see below.) I chose *Social Text* because my primary motivation was political: see Sokal 1996c, 1997.

11 I emphasize that this term is a misnomer, as these ideas are hotly debated among feminists, among whom I include myself. For incisive feminist critiques of "feminist epistemology," see Haack 1992, 1993a and Radcliffe-Richards 1996.

12 It is not unknown for physicists to make fools of themselves holding forth on Shakespeare.

13 For a more detailed analysis of this article, see Sokal and Bricmont 1998: Chapter 6, and Huth 1998.

14 This "rule" is the culmination of an argument (Latour 1987: 96–99) in which ontology, epistemology and the sociology of knowledge are gradually conflated. See Sokal and Bricmont 1998: 94–97 for a detailed analysis.

15 You might worry that here my argument is circular, in that it takes for granted the truth of the current scientific consensus in cosmology and paleontology. But this is not the case. First of all, my phrase "given that . . ." is a rhetorical flourish that plays no essential role in the argument; the idea that the external world is created by scientists' negotiations is bizarre irrespective of the details of cosmology and paleontology. Second, my phrase "the external world has been around . . ." should, if one wants to be super-precise, be amended to read: "there is a vast body of extremely convincing (and diverse) evidence in support of the belief that the external world has been around . . . ; and if this belief is correct, then the claim that the external world is created by scientists' negotiations is bizarre to say the least." Indeed, all of my assertions of fact—including "today in New York it's raining"— should be glossed in this way. Since I shall claim below that much contemporary work in science studies elides the distinction between ontology and epistemology, I don't want to leave myself open to the same accusation.

16 Re (b), the "homely example" in Gross and Levitt 1994: 57–58 makes the point clearly.

17 For a more detailed analysis of the Third Rule of Method, see Sokal and Bricmont 1998: 92–99. For further analysis of *Science in Action*, see Amsterdamska 1990.

18 Note also that Bloor fails to use systematically this new notion of "knowledge"; from time to time he falls back on the traditional sense of the word, without alerting the reader to the confusion (and perhaps without noticing it himself). Thus, he begins by offering the following radical redefinition:

> Instead of defining it as true belief—or perhaps, justified true belief— knowledge for the sociologist is whatever people take to be knowledge. It consists of those beliefs which people confidently hold to and live

by. . . . Of course knowledge must be distinguished from mere belief. This can be done by reserving the word "knowledge" for what is collectively endorsed, leaving the individual and idiosyncratic to count as mere belief.

(Bloor 1991: 5)

But only nine pages later, he reverts without comment to the standard definition of "knowledge," which he contrasts with "error": "it would be wrong to assume that the natural working of our animal resources always produces knowledge. They produce a mixture of knowledge and error with equal naturalness . . ." (Bloor 1991: 14).

19 I certainly don't exclude the possibility that present theories in any of these subjects might be erroneous. But critics wishing to make such a case would have to provide not only historical evidence of the claimed cultural influence, but also scientific evidence that the theory in question is in fact erroneous. (The same evidentiary standards of course apply to past erroneous theories; but in this case the scientists may have already performed the second task, relieving the cultural critic of the need to do so from scratch.)

20 The consensus of historians appears to be that the slow acceptance of Newtonian mechanics in France arose from scholastic attachment to Cartesian theories as well as from certain theological considerations: see, for example, Brunet 1931 and Dobbs and Jacob 1995.

21 Or more precisely: There is a vast body of extremely convincing astronomical evidence in support of the belief that the planets and comets do move (to a very high degree of approximation, although not exactly) as predicted by Newtonian mechanics; and if this belief is correct, then it is the fact of this motion (and not merely our belief in it) that forms part of the explanation of why the eighteenth-century European scientific community came to believe in the truth of Newtonian mechanics.

22 For what it's worth, these decisions can presumably be justified on Bayesian grounds, using our prior experience of the probability of finding elephants in lecture halls, of the incidence of psychosis, of the reliability of our own visual and auditory perceptions, and so forth.

23 The analogy with historians and detectives was used earlier by Haack 1993b: 137 and 1998: 96–97.

24 Please note: I am not claiming that inference from scientific observations to scientific theories is as simple or unproblematic as inference from seeing elephants in front of me to the conclusion that elephants are in front of me. (In truth, even this latter inference is not so simple or unproblematic: to fully ground it requires some knowledge about optics and about the mechanisms of human vision.) As all practicing scientists and historians of science well know, the reasoning from scientific observations to scientific theories is far more indirect, and typically involves a vast web of empirical evidence rather than a single observation. My point is simply that in all of these cases—Newtonian mechanics, Darwinian evolution, or elephants—it is absurd to try to explain the "causes" of people's beliefs without including the natural (non-social) world as one of those causes.

25 Five of the essay titles (Martin, Nelkin, Franklin, Kovel, Aronowitz) include the term "science wars," and three more titles (Rose, Winner, Levidow) contain assorted martial metaphors.

26 My own leftist political views are a matter of record, as are those of many of my supporters (for example, Michael Albert, Barbara Epstein, Meera Nanda, Ruth Rosen, and James Weinstein, among many others). Even Gross and Levitt, the original targets of Ross's wrath, make clear that their political views are basically left-liberal; they note that one of them (Levitt as it turns out) is a member of Democratic Socialists of America (Gross and Levitt 1994: 261, note 7).

27 For an eminently reasonable "middle ground" position, which coincides almost completely with my own views, see Kitcher 1998.
28 This point was made over a decade ago by Margarita Levin (1988).
29 For an interesting conjecture, see Nanda 1997: 79–80. For a different (but not incompatible) conjecture, see Gross and Levitt 1994: 74, 82–88, 217–233. Both these conjectures merit careful empirical investigation by intellectual historians.

Bibliography

Albert, Michael (1996) "Science, postmodernism and the left," *Z Magazine* 9(7/8) (July/August): 64–69.

Amsterdamska, Olga (1990) "Surely you are joking, Monsieur Latour!" *Science, Technology, and Human Values* 15: 495–504.

Aronowitz, Stanley and DiFazio, William (1994) *The Jobless Future: Sci-Tech and the Dogma of Work*, Minneapolis: University of Minnesota Press.

Barnes, Barry and Bloor, David (1981) "Relativism, rationalism and the sociology of knowledge," in Hollis, Martin and Lukes, Steven (eds) *Rationality and Relativism*, Oxford: Blackwell.

Bloor, David (1991) *Knowledge and Social Imagery*, 2nd edn, Chicago: University of Chicago Press.

Boghossian, Paul (1996) "What the Sokal hoax ought to teach us," *Times Literary Supplement* 13 December: 14–15.

Brunet, Pierre (1931) *L'Introduction des théories de Newton en France au XVIIIe siècle*, Paris: A. Blanchard (reprinted by Slatkine, Genève 1970).

Collins, Harry (1981) "Stages in the empirical programme of relativism," *Social Studies of Science* 11: 3–10.

Deleuze, Gilles and Guattari, Félix (1994) *What Is Philosophy?* Translated by Hugh Tomlinson and Graham Burchell, New York: Columbia University Press (French original: *Qu'est-ce que la philosophie?* Paris: Éditions de Minuit, 1991).

Dobbs, Betty Jo Teeter and Jacob, Margaret C. (1995) *Newton and the Culture of Newtonianism*, Atlantic Highlands, NJ: Humanities Press.

Epstein, Barbara (1997) "Postmodernism and the left," *New Politics* 6(2) (Winter): 130–144.

Fausto-Sterling, Anne (1992) *Myths of Gender: Biological Theories about Women and Men*, 2nd edn, New York: Basic Books.

Forman, Paul (1987) "Behind quantum electronics: national security as basis for physical research in the United States, 1940–1960," *Historical Studies in the Physical and Biological Sciences* 18: 149–229.

Frank, Tom (1996) "Textual reckoning," *In These Times* May 27: 22–24.

Fuller, Steve (1993) *Philosophy, Rhetoric, and the End of Knowledge*, Madison: University of Wisconsin Press.

Gould, Stephen Jay (1996) *The Mismeasure of Man*, 2nd edn., New York: Norton.

Gross, Paul R. and Levitt, Norman (1994) *Higher Superstition: The Academic Left and Its Quarrels with Science*, Baltimore: Johns Hopkins University Press.

Haack, Susan (1992) "Science 'from a feminist perspective'," *Philosophy* 67: 5–18.

Haack, Susan (1993a) "Epistemological reflections of an old feminist," *Reason Papers* 18 (Fall): 31–43.

Haack, Susan (1993b) *Evidence and Inquiry: Towards Reconstruction in Epistemology*, Oxford: Blackwell.

Haack, Susan (1998) *Manifesto of a Passionate Moderate: Unfashionable Essays*, Chicago: University of Chicago Press.

Harding, Sandra (1991) *Whose Science? Whose Knowledge? Thinking from Women's Lives*, Ithaca, NY: Cornell University Press.

Huth, John (1998) "Latour's relativity," in Koertge, Noretta (ed.) *A House Built on Sand: Exposing Postmodernist Myths About Science*, New York: Oxford University Press.

Kitcher, Philip (1998) "A plea for science studies," in Koertge, Noretta (ed.) *A House Built on Sand: Exposing Postmodernist Myths About Science*, New York: Oxford University Press.

Latour, Bruno (1987) *Science in Action: How to Follow Scientists and Engineers through Society*, Cambridge, MA: Harvard University Press.

Latour, Bruno (1988) "A relativistic account of Einstein's relativity," *Social Studies of Science* 18: 3–44.

Latour, Bruno and Woolgar, Steve (1979) *Laboratory Life: The Social Construction of Scientific Facts*, London: Sage.

Levin, Margarita (1988) "Caring new world: feminism and science," *American Scholar* 57: 100–106.

Nanda, Meera (1997) "The science wars in India," *Dissent* 44(1), (Winter): 78–83.

Pollitt, Katha (1996) "Pomolotov cocktail," *The Nation* June 10: 9.

Radcliffe-Richards, Janet (1996) "Why feminist epistemology is not," in Gross, Paul R., Levitt, Norman, and Lewis, Martin W. (eds) *The Flight from Science and Reason*, *Annals of the New York Academy of Sciences*: 775.

Robbins, Bruce (1996) "*Social Text* and reality," *In These Times* July 8: 28–29.

Robbins, Bruce, Ross, Andrew, Sokal, Alan, *et al.* (1996) "Mystery Science Theater," *Lingua Franca* 6(5) (July/August): 54–64.

Ross, Andrew (1995) "Science backlash on technoskeptics," *The Nation* 261(10) (2 October): 346–350.

Ross, Andrew (1996) "Introduction," *Social Text* 46–47 (Spring/Summer): 1–13.

Ross, Andrew and Aronowitz, Stanley (1995) unpublished letter to the author (and to other contributors to the "Science Wars" issue), March 8.

Scott, Janny (1996) "Postmodern gravity deconstructed, slyly," *New York Times* May 18: 1, 22.

Sokal, Alan (1996a) "Transgressing the boundaries: toward a transformative hermeneutics of quantum gravity," *Social Text* 46–47 (Spring/Summer): 217–252.

Sokal, Alan (1996b) "A physicist experiments with cultural studies," *Lingua Franca* 6(4) (May/June): 62–64.

Sokal, Alan (1996c) "Transgressing the boundaries: an afterword," *Dissent* 43(4) (Fall): 93–99 (a slightly abridged version of this article was also published in 1996 in *Philosophy and Literature* 20: 338–346).

Sokal, Alan (1997) "A plea for reason, evidence and logic," *New Politics* 6(2) (Winter): 126–129 (an extended version of this article appeared under the title "Truth, reason, objectivity, and the left" in *Mistaken Identities: The Second Wave of Controversy over "Political Correctness,"* edited by Cyril Levitt, Scott Davies, and Neil McLaughlin, New York: Peter Lang, 1999, 285–294).

Sokal, Alan and Bricmont, Jean (1998) *Fashionable Nonsense: Postmodern Intellectuals' Abuse of Science*, New York: Picador USA; published in the British Commonwealth under the title *Intellectual Impostures: Postmodern Philosophers' Abuse of Science*, London: Profile, 1998.

Tavris, Carol (1992) *The Mismeasure of Woman*, New York: Simon and Schuster.

Weinberg, Steven (1996) "Sokal's hoax," *New York Review of Books* 43(13) (August 8): 11–15.

Willis, Ellen (1996) "My Sokaled life," *Village Voice* [New York] (June 25): 20–21.

3 Randomized thoughts of a cultural turncoat

Adrian L. Melott

This is not an essay. Do not look for coherence or sequence, unless you are compulsive or like wasting time.

I enjoyed Alan Sokal's spoof. I knew it was coming and eagerly awaited the reaction. I fully support what he did, although I have deep disagreements with him. I do not think epistemology is the core issue, at least not as he has framed it ("objective reality"). What was (for me at least) wildly funny was the absolutely absurd uses to which the physics was put. It is bizarre, crazy, and can't escape attention—if you know any physics. Nevertheless, it fooled the editors of *Social Text*, at least two of whom have written about physics.

I no longer care to read or talk about the nature of "objective reality." A great deal of the time we are deluded into thinking questions are meaningful because they can be formulated in our native language. The existence of objective reality is an assertion (or maybe it is not even an assertion, but just sounds like one) that I know no way to test. Rather, my experience says that by assuming it I can make a series of increasingly useful approximations to something that works for me. But I have found it a useful procedure to assume it does exist, and so do the postmodernists who avoid stepping out into heavy traffic.

It is our fault, mostly. What used to be called the counterculture in fact picked up a lot of trash from nooks and crannies. In large measure, we replaced the trash we had been fed with different trash—which led to today's array of wonders, from the wildly popular Celestine Prophecy to the pseudo-highbrow stuff in *Social Text*. I confess to having nurtured some of the early trash and now I have penance to do.

Science is definitely a social phenomenon. It is done by people and not in isolation. It is therefore clearly affected by attitudes, by fashion, by funding priorities, and so on. A sociology of science is possible, yet in numerous examples it is flubbed. Assertions are made which are plainly silly, due to a lack of understanding of the sciences. Physicists, according to one Edinburgh

School publication, are accused of paying attention to one experiment while ignoring another (with opposing implications). In fact, one was cleverly direct and clear, while the other was complicated and subject to many contaminating influences which had to be taken into account. This was ignored, even though the difference is not subtle.

Once, in the days of the Garden, when we all lived in idyllic harmony with Nature, two people went out hunting, separately. One hunter, while walking the jungle, thought there was a tiger, but passed it off as a trick of light and shadow. The tiger had a nice meal. The other one was never near a tiger, but was sure he had seen one. That one was the parent of humanity. The moral: there can be a terrible evolutionary penalty for failing to notice something, but usually considerably less for imagining something. Self-delusion may waste some energy, but is seldom lethal. Given today's technology, this is no longer true. An imagined threat may precipitate a war.

   We are genetically hard-wired to be gullible. One experience with a copper bracelet and pain relief, and we are sold. We do not notice (or remember) the failures. One of the most wonderful things about science is the methodology it has developed to combat self-delusion. It is not perfect, but it is a big improvement over nothing—which is what most people use.

Journalists are a key problem area. Everyone of course likes to bash them, mostly about their "spin." I would like to focus on a simpler thing: accuracy. Lately I have taken to asking people (in the case of news stories in which they have personal knowledge of the contents) if they have ever seen a story without at least one substantial error. Let me stress that this is restricted to stories in which they either were personally involved in the events recounted or were expert in the area being described. So far I have had two positive responses out of forty-five inquiries. Part of the reason for this is "checkback." Checkback is a process of checking the factual accuracy of a story before submission. However, journalists are taught not to go back to a source with the story, as that could introduce censorship of a kind. In the case of reporting facts, this often leads to massive errors. Another serious problem is "even-handedness"— stories play better in a conflict mode, so marginal or even silly viewpoints get major billing. Based on science, there is very little doubt that humans are causing the most rapid species extinction rates in tens of millions of years and are modifying the Earth's climate with possibly catastrophic consequences. There is also little doubt that there is no evidence for serious danger from the electromagnetic radiation of common devices or from silicone breast implants. Yet the public is generally told these are controversial topics. The press magnifies a 1 percent viewpoint into a 50/50 proposition.

Postmodern writers adopt a kind of ostentatious awareness of the arbitrariness of form and value, of how contingent everything is upon the culture in which it is found. This is not new: the "pointing at" is at least there in

Jonathan Swift, the Vienna Circle, early Zen, and Charlie Chaplin. So why all the fuss?

The practice of science is distorted by many things, particularly the funding priorities of grant-giving foundations and agencies. Those are often skewed towards research with expected practical applications. However, any research whose outcome can be predicted and has an obvious payoff is almost certainly marginal, with no deep or lasting impact beyond a few years. Nearly all of what we call "technology" today is just applied quantum mechanics. Three quarters of a century later, the impact is still growing out of the abstract, fundamental theory that was needed to understand a few odd properties of atoms. If funding agencies had been able to direct research in the 1880s we would have very efficient steam engines, belt drive to transfer power, and a fast new method for tapping out Morse code (they would call it the information super-riverboat).

Science is a human activity. People active in research are well aware of this. Our progress is further distorted by the eloquence of certain people or by their academic pedigree, by accidents of place and time, by our unwillingness to accept the incredible, or by our attempt to make it happen. Still we do not like the tone of most "science studies." They would say it is a turf issue, but it seems to me they repeatedly just miss the point. The missing of the point is usually due to not knowing much about the science area they are studying. They think they do not need to; to me their assertions are often very funny.

Science study descriptions of working science seem mostly to ignore nature. While the interactions described are mostly between people, the raw stuff (rocks, fish, stars) would dominate much of our work experience. We feel nature guiding us—sometimes gentle hints or a whack on the head. This core experience, so central to everything, is usually absent or, when present, looks like a parody (as in Latour). I do not mean that science-study people should necessarily be scientists, but that their narrative of the process is terribly incomplete if the interaction with nature is left out or distorted. It cannot be experienced by observing science. This, above all, explains why I doubt if there will ever be a great deal of mutual respect between most working scientists and most practitioners of "science studies."

A flying saucer crashed in Roswell, New Mexico. About fifteen years later, Demi Moore was born in Roswell, New Mexico. Coincidence? You decide.

4 Reading and relativism

An introduction to the science wars[1]

Gabriel Stolzenberg[2]

> When Larry was a kid his mother . . . sometimes, out of curiosity, stopped the dial at a place where foreign languages came curling out of the radio's plastic grillwork: Italian or Portuguese or Polish . . . "Jibber, jabber," Larry's father called this talk, shaking his head, apparently convinced, despite all reason, that these "noises" meant nothing, that they were no more than a form of elaborate nonsense. Everything ran together; and there weren't any real words the way there were in English. These foreigners were just pretending to talk, trying to fool everyone.
>
> (Carol Shields, *Larry's Party*)

Late one afternoon in the spring of 1996, I heard part of a radio interview with a physicist named Alan Sokal. It was about something he had just done. He explained that he had been inspired to do it by reading *Higher Superstition*, a book by Paul Gross and Norman Levitt (1994) that also inspired Robert Bork (1996). Several years earlier, a colleague had tried to persuade me to read this book by shoving it under my nose open to a page on which an opaque remark by Jacques Derrida is alleged by the authors to reveal his "eagerness to claim familiarity with deep scientific matters." The remark begins, "The Einsteinian constant is not a constant, is not a center." My colleague expected me to find this ridiculous but I explained that I could not find it anything because I had no idea what it means. The authors talked as if they did but they gave me no reason to believe them.[3] Later, after some investigation, I concluded that not only did they not know what Derrida meant, they probably did not care. They were engaged in an attempt at humiliation, not scholarship.

Therefore, imagine my astonishment when Sokal's one example of inspiration provided by *Higher Superstition* turned out to be Derrida's alleged "eagerness to claim familiarity with deep scientific matters." Sokal offered no proof of the allegation—at least, nothing one would normally think of as a proof. He merely read the remark aloud, said that he had no idea what it meant and paused for the interviewer to burst out laughing.[4]

For all I know, Derrida really did not know what he was talking about thirty-three years ago, when he made this remark as part of an answer to a question following a lecture about structuralism. I think he did. I even have an interpretation that I find plausible. But I have no proof that he did, so I do not say so. However, no such epistemic niceties deterred either Gross and Levitt or Sokal from pronouncing Derrida's remark nonsense. Nor were these isolated cases. In the literature spawned by Sokal's hoax, I often found high-minded talk about the importance of "doing it right," keeping company with readings and arguments as shabby or non-existent as in the attacks on Derrida mentioned above. For example, in *A House Built on Sand*, the editor, Noretta Koertge, writes, "We intend to provide a place where reason and good sense can be brought to bear on a field that has lost its mechanism of scholarly self-control . . . Our only target is shoddy scholarship" (Koertge 1998: 5).

Yet in the opening chapter, Sokal's mechanism of scholarly self-control goes haywire[5]. Then, in the next chapter, the analytic philosopher Paul Boghossian touts his discipline's "subtle discussion of concepts in the philosophy of language and the theory of knowledge." Yet his scholarship is as shoddy as Sokal's.[6] Also, at least two other chapters are disfigured by hostile misreadings[7] that could easily have been eliminated during the vetting process.

Alas, my concerns were not widely shared. The attitude I usually encountered among scientists and old-fashioned humanists was "Why are you worrying about this? It's the other guys who are on trial." And, *sotto voce*, "In a war, the good guys do dirty things too." Welcome to the science wars! I confess that I found it exciting. Sokal's unerring sense of what he could get away with never ceased to amaze me. Forget about the Derrida caper on the radio or even his success at getting *Social Text* to publish his hoax. I was far more impressed by his self-serving polemic that immediately became the received wisdom about how to read the hoax (where to laugh), why he did it, and why the editors of *Social Text* published it—the last of which Sokal almost surely did not know when he wrote this piece. I was also very impressed by Steven Weinberg's influential essay "Sokal's hoax" (1996). On a non-skeptical reading, it is clear and convincing. Yet on a skeptical reading, as Weinberg would have seen had he made one, it is riddled with confusion.[8] That he did not bother to do so suggests that he intuited, correctly, that few readers would look closely at what he said and that those who did could be ignored.[9]

Initially, I saw the science wars as the Derrida case writ large—otherwise respectable academics accusing others of spouting nonsense about science or mathematics on the basis of perverse and often preposterous interpretations of their texts, and *other* otherwise respectable academics cheering them on.[10] Critical thinking seemed to have taken a holiday. In "Hatchet jobs," below, I consider representative examples of these attacks. All of them have the appearance of self-fulfilling prophecies. People hunt for nonsense in statements of authors suspected of being partial to it and, when they find what looks like it, they consider themselves done. Yet had they hunted instead, or in addition, for more generous interpretations, they almost surely would have found them, as I did.[11] So much depends upon the reader's trust! As a cautionary tale, before turning to the hatchet jobs, I consider an authoritative-looking remark about physics by the nonsense hunter, Thomas Nagel (1998: 36). On a literal reading, he is spouting nonsense about the special theory of relativity. But the physics alone does not enable me to judge how well this reading reflects his grasp of the theory and, at the end of the day, it seems to be solely the extent of my trust in that grasp that determines how I make the call.

Although my attention was first limited to examples of this kind, I learned soon enough that the allegations of nonsense-spouting were not limited to science and mathematics. Much of the ridicule was directed towards statements about our relationship to reality. I learned also that the alleged nonsense-spouting was attributed to the pernicious influence of relativism and social constructivism, philosophies whose alleged denial of objective truth and justification were said to license disdain for logic, evidence, truth and even intelligibility. The reasoning went something like this:

> If one does not admit the possibility of objective truth and justification, then anything goes. Reasoning is merely a form of rhetoric, science is just another belief system and there is no need to master a subject before holding forth on it because there is no such thing as "getting it right."

The existence of people who fit this description may be a logical possibility. I can just barely imagine a world in which people are indoctrinated to think and behave this way. But it requires no act of the imagination to reflect with awe upon the scholarship produced over the centuries by scholars skeptical about simplistic conceptions of objectivity hardly different from some of those paraded in the science wars. It is dismaying that so many people who should know better believe that skepticism of this kind licenses nihilism. Even worse, many believe that the sky has already fallen. Skepticism about objectivity, in the form of a "postmodern" relativism in which ideology trumps truth, is believed to have taken over entire sectors of the academy and with "the expected" consequences.[12]

Gradually, relativism and social constructivism and the evils attributed to them became the focus of my concerns. People were said to hold beliefs that imply that we can alter reality[13] at our whim, that before there were humans, there were no dinosaurs and that what we call scientific knowledge is the result of negotiation, not inquiry![14] What are relativism and social constructivism? Why are they thought to have such preposterous implications? And why do they generate such hostility, even fear? After "Hatchet jobs," I begin to offer answers. In "Relativism and social constructivism," I contest the conventional wisdom that these two isms deny context-independent truth and justification. In fact, they neither deny nor affirm them.[15] The exemplar of this agnosticism, which is radically different from denial, is the philosophy of Ludwig Wittgenstein after the *Tractatus*.[16] Although some philosophers worry that this agnosticism collapses into denial, what seems to bother people most is Wittgenstein's unwillingness to affirm that beliefs like the laws of physics are objectively true and ones like witchcraft and astrology are objectively false. That he affirms such things in the ordinary way does not alleviate their concern, which seems to have its root in Wittgenstein's view that reasons go just so far, beyond which there is at most trust.

In "Reality is hard to talk about," I use a version of the belief/knowledge distinction to show that seemingly innocuous realist statements about reality are, on realism's own terms, badly confused. This confusion is one source of realist misrepresentations of relativism and social constructivism. The same method is then used to expose a more serious confusion that I believe is the main source of realist objections to constructivist science studies. Here, a powerful intuition that the truth of a belief often figures significantly in explaining what makes us believe it makes it extremely difficult for scientists to cotton on to an equally powerful counter-intuition that the growth of scientific knowledge should be explained purely as a process of belief formation.

This completes my introduction to my introduction to the science wars. The rest is a series of case studies, divided into the three sections described above. Although little that I argue for is difficult to prove, almost all of it stands the conventional wisdom on its head. This, I suppose, is its significance for the science wars. However, for me personally, this chapter is primarily an attempt to persuade readers that trying to make sense of another human being is no less interesting a challenge and noble a pursuit than trying to make sense of the physical world. And that we are not yet very good at it.

Hatchet jobs

> Read it as you would a love letter.[17]

The philosopher Thomas Nagel is a great admirer of the part of *Fashionable Nonsense* that is devoted to mocking people for spouting nonsense about science and mathematics. Indeed, in his review of this book (Nagel 1998), he applauds the authors for their useful "hatchet job."[18] But how can we tell whether a statement about science or mathematics is nonsense? Nagel seems to believe that he knows it when he sees it.[19] But it is trickier than he supposes. To see why, consider the following statement that Nagel makes in his review:

> The world of Einstein's special theory of relativity, in which the interval between two widely separated events cannot be uniquely specified in terms of a spatial distance and a temporal distance, is not one that can be intuitively grasped, even roughly, by a layman.[20]

I will offer two readings of this. The first is ungenerous and unforgiving. But two physicists signed off on it, one of whom joked, "Let's put Nagel in a remedial relativity course with Latour."[21] The second reading is generous and forgiving. Another physicist persuaded me of it. I greatly prefer it because I would much rather have a good opinion of Professor Nagel than a bad one.

An unforgiving reading

Contrary to what Nagel says, the interval between any two events can be uniquely specified in terms of a spatial distance and a temporal one. Maybe he meant to say that the space–time interval between two different events does not uniquely specify associated spatial and temporal distances. But this is true even in a single reference frame and has nothing to do with the physics. The hypotenuse of a right triangle does not uniquely specify its opposite sides, yet nobody believes that the world of Euclid's theory of plane geometry "cannot be intuitively grasped, even roughly, by a layman."

This is not a malicious reading. It is not even a skeptical one. An unintelligible statement in the *New Republic* stands out. Moreover, everything I say is correct, although not necessarily as a reading of what Nagel meant. I take "interval" to mean "space–time interval." For the special theory of relativity, I do not know what other kind of interval "between two events" he could have meant. When I say that the interval between two events can be uniquely specified in terms of a spatial distance and a temporal one, I am relying upon the standard mathematical interpretation of "uniquely specified in terms of." I also rely on it in the second sentence, in which I, in effect, allow that Nagel may have meant to say instead "does not uniquely specify."

A forgiving reading

For a forgiving reading, I assume that Nagel has a reasonably good layman's grasp of special relativity but was muddled when he wrote this. I then try to guess what point he "really" meant to make. A natural guess is "in the special theory of relativity, neither the spatial nor temporal distance between two different events is the same in every reference frame." Thus we pretend that Nagel did not say "widely" and we assume that he was not talking about the space–time interval. Indeed, we assume that when Nagel used the word "interval," he was not talking about anything. He was just having trouble finding a phrase like "for any two different events" and settled instead on the unhappy choice of "the interval between two widely separated events." As in the unforgiving reading, we also assume that when he said "cannot be uniquely specified in terms of," he really meant to say "does not uniquely specify." This leaves us with something more awkward than the guess I made above but the content is essentially the same. There is one more point: the spatial distance between two events is relative even in classical physics.[22] Therefore, to capture what is special about special relativity, Nagel should have contented himself with something like, "The temporal distance between events is not the same in all frames." However, for most readers of the *New Republic*, the relativity of simultaneity would have been an even better choice.

To me, the unforgiving reading seems fair, the forgiving reading wildly generous. But which, if either, of these impressions is accurate depends on whether Nagel "really" knew what he was trying to say. If, as I prefer to believe, he did, then the wildly generous reading is far more accurate. If he did not, it is not. But this is not a question a physicist can settle for us. Indeed, physicists endorsed both readings. Also, even if the generous reading is more accurate, what ended up in the *New Republic* is best seen as gibberish.[23]

What's this, Polus?

> Socrates: What's this, Polus? You're laughing? Is this yet another kind of refutation which has you laughing at ideas rather than proving them wrong?
>
> (Plato's *Gorgias*, 473e, Waterfield translation)[24]

In the same review of *Fashionable Nonsense*, Nagel writes, "The chapters dealing in more detail with individual thinkers reveal that they are beyond parody. Sokal could not create anything as ridiculous as this, from Luce Irigaray:

> Is $E = Mc^2$ a sexed equation? Perhaps it is. Let us make the hypothesis that it is insofar as it privileges the speed of light over other speeds that are vitally necessary to us. What seems to me to indicate the possibly sexed nature of the equation is not directly its uses by nuclear weapons, rather it is having privileged what goes the fastest . . ."

This may send Nagel into convulsions but how does he know that it is her problem not his? How can he possibly know unless he knows what Irigaray means by "sexed" and "privileges" and that her reference to speeds is not an ironic metaphor? If he does not know these things, then he is kidding himself. But if he does know, why does he not tell us, so that we can join in the fun of mocking Irigaray? Instead of fulfilling his obligation as a philosopher to give us a reason to believe what he says, Nagel encourages us to trust that whatever Irigaray means is refuted by the authors' "comically patient" observation,

> Whatever one may think about the "other speeds that are vitally necessary to us," the fact remains that the relationship $E = Mc^2$ between energy (E) and mass (M) is experimentally verified to a high degree of precision, and it would obviously not be valid if the speed of light (c) were replaced by another speed.

This shows especially poor judgment. If Sokal and Bricmont think that something that is privileged can easily be replaced, there is little reason to suppose that they have any idea what Irigaray is talking about.[25] And by mocking her instead of giving us an argument, Nagel makes it appear that neither does he.

I am not a reference frame

> "Incompetent individuals were less able to recognize competence in others," the researchers concluded.
>
> (Erica Goode 2000)

In the opening chapter of *A House Built on Sand*, Sokal presents what he considers to be some of the silliest statements that he could find "about mathematics and physics . . . from some of the most prominent French or American intellectuals."

> Now, what precisely do I mean by "silliness"? Here's a very rough categorization: First of all, one has meaningless or absurd statements, name-dropping, and the display of false erudition. Second, one has sloppy thinking and poor philosophy, which come together notably (though not always) in the form of glib relativism.[26]

Almost any statement that Sokal offers as an example of silliness serves as a caution that merely being a scientist does not make one competent to assess the use of scientific-looking language in non-scientific texts. One also must know how to read. I think that Sokal has no idea how difficult this can be. Consider, for example, his claim that Bruno Latour "does not understand what the term *frame of reference* means in physics—he confuses it with *actor* in semiotics." His evidence is that Latour says (1988: 10–11)

> If there are only one, or even two, frames of reference, no solution can be found . . . .[27] Einstein's solution is to consider three actors: one in the train, one on the embankment and a third one, the author [enunciator] or one of its representants, who tries to superimpose the coded observations sent back by the two others.

To misread this as Latour confusing the concept of a frame of reference in physics with that of an actor in semiotics requires a high degree of silliness.[28] Sokal knows that Latour is discussing relativity theory as expounded in a popular book by Einstein and that the two frames of reference are ones that Einstein introduces. One is stationary with respect to a train, the other with respect to an embankment. Each also is stationary with respect to an actor: one on the train, the other on the embankment. Hence, when we specify one of the actors, we specify one of the frames and conversely. All this is Einstein and it is why Latour can shift from talk about the two frames of reference to talk about the first two actors without changing the subject. Latour's only contribution is the third actor, whose work requires not only a frame of reference but the Lorentz transformations between it and the first two frames.[29] However, bear in mind that although I am not a reference frame, all the ones with respect to which I do not move are uninterestingly different from the standpoint of special relativity. In this sense, actors do come close to specifying reference frames. The converse is obviously false.

Places in space

Consider next Sokal's claim that Latour "somehow got the idea that relativity concerns the problems raised by the relative *location* (rather than the relative *motion*) of different observers." It is impossible to read Latour's essay about relativity without noticing that it is dominated by a consideration of two reference frames in relative motion—the two discussed above. But perhaps Sokal forgot this when he came upon the following passage from Latour's essay, which is the evidence he offers for his accusation:

> Provided the two relativities [special and general] are accepted, more frames of reference with less privilege can be assessed, reduced, accumulated and combined, observers can be delegated to a few more places in the infinitely large (the cosmos) and the infinitely small (electrons), and the readings they send back will be understandable. His [Einstein's] book could well be titled: "New Instructions for Bringing Back Long-Distance Scientific Travellers."
>
> (Latour 1988: 22–23)

Is Sokal assuming that Latour is talking about places that are stationary with respect to us? Why would Latour do that? When we talk about a place outside the earth, we almost always have in a mind a material body, like Mars or Alpha Centauri, and almost every material body in the universe is in motion with respect to us. This already is telling. But the best evidence I have against Sokal's reading of the passage is Latour's reference to electrons. If an electron is a place to which an observer can be delegated, how likely is it that Latour has in mind only places that are stationary with respect to us?[30]

This argument notwithstanding, I don't pretend to know what Latour had in mind when he wrote this passage. But I don't need to know. Sokal does because he made the accusation. Finally, in criticizing Sokal's misreadings of Latour's essay, I do not mean to suggest that it does not merit criticism. On the contrary, the very passages that Sokal quotes make me wonder whether Latour mistook things that Einstein has his cartoon observers do in order to explain the theory of relativity for what real physicists do when they use that theory.

Masculine channels and feminine flows

In "Gender encoding in fluid mechanics: masculine channels and feminine flows," N. Katherine Hayles explores the thesis that fluid mechanics, or at least hydrology,[31] is "gender encoded masculine" (Hayles 1992: 16–44). In his contribution to *A House Built on Sand*, Phillip Sullivan finds fault with almost everything in the account of fluid mechanics that Hayles uses to explore the thesis. But after six pages of authoritative criticism that apparently suffice to make his case, instead of declaring victory and going home, Sullivan presses on with a page of accusations that are false and unfair.[32] Here I consider the least trivial of the allegations.

The excision of the observer

Sullivan accuses Hayles of misconstruing the history of the calculus by saying that when the calculus was made rigorous, "rigor [was] equated with the excision of the observer—a fundamental premise in the ideology of objectivity." Hayles supports the claim with a quote from the introduction to Carl Boyer's history of the calculus. Sullivan counters with a longer quote from the conclusion of Boyer's book, his distillation of which is that "rigor in mathematics is associated with excision of 'irrelevant elements'." He then asks sarcastically, "But what meaning can be attached to Hayles's assertion that rigor requires 'excision of the observer': that mathematical arguments cannot be observed?" Ignoring Sullivan's attempt at humor, we can begin to answer this by noting that Hayles does not say that rigor requires the excision of the observer. She says that, as a matter of historical fact, this is the view that informed the rigorization of the calculus (Sullivan 1998: 82–83). She is right, although Boyer's history of the calculus does not provide an adequate account of this. The importance attached to the idea of mathematics as "a reality independent of us" caused Gottlob Frege and others to insist that all traces of a subject/constructor/observer be removed.[33] So, for example, because a rule presupposes a subject/constructor/observer that executes it, in the rigorized mathematics a function is no longer a rule but a set.[34] Sullivan is not a philosopher of mathematics, so his ignorance of these foundational matters is understandable. But it does not excuse the sarcasm that he directs at Hayles for failing to share it.

When a mathematical point moves

Sullivan also accuses Hayles of misunderstanding the concept of a particle of matter, or mass point, in Newtonian mechanics (Sullivan 1998: 82–83). Here is her offending remark as quoted by Sullivan.

> Euler . . . wanted to develop a theory of hydraulics that would be based on the trajectories of particles as they moved through the flow.[35] The simplest way to deal with the particles was to treat them as mathematical points. But, by definition, a point has no extension and consequently no mass. When a point moves, nothing in the material world changes.

Sullivan has no patience for this. He writes,

> Every undergraduate physics student knows that Hayles's statement is
> nonsense. Newton's three laws of motion show that the motion of a body
> under the action of external forces can be calculated exactly by concen-
> trating all the body's mass at a single point in its interior known as the
> *center of mass.*[36]

Given the context, this is outrageous. The statement Sullivan trashes is part
of Hayles's description of how Euler thought about fluid flow. Sullivan does
not contest its accuracy. But if it is accurate, then, according to him, Euler
too needed to learn freshman physics. This is a serious blunder. Sullivan
should either have checked the accuracy of Hayles's account or taken a pass.
Yes, for computation, it often helps to pretend that there are point masses,[37]
ignoring the consideration that each would have to be infinitely dense. But
for a continuum model of fluid flow like Euler's, it is the opposite of helpful.
If any point in a body of fluid has positive mass, and mass varies continu-
ously with position, then the body of fluid has infinite mass. This is not a
useful idealization. According to Hayles, Euler worked instead with point
densities, which in this context is a very useful idealization.

The oracle of deconstruction

Derrida's remark about "the Einsteinian constant" occurred during an exchange with his colleague, Jean Hyppolite, following a lecture by Derrida on
structuralism, much of which was devoted to the history of the idea of a
center for a structure (Derrida 1970: 247–272). Although the lecture had
nothing overtly to do with physics, Hyppolite asked a question about the
theory of relativity in an attempt to clarify the notion of a center. In "Sokal's
hoax," after mocking Derrida as "the oracle of deconstruction" and calling
the "Einsteinian constant" remark babble,[38] Steven Weinberg says, "I have
no idea what it is intended to mean" (Weinberg 1996a: 11). So far, this is no
different from Sokal on the radio. But Weinberg goes on to say that although
there are fields like physics that require a technical language that cannot be
understood without a special training, "Derrida and other postmoderns do
not seem to be saying anything that requires a special technical language"
(Weinberg 1996a: 11). This is silly. If Weinberg has no idea what the remark
is intended to mean, how can he tell whether it requires a special technical
language? Later, in a reply to George Levine's (1996: 54) objection to the
emptiness of this reasoning, Weinberg tries harder.[39] He now argues that "the
Einsteinian constant" and "center" are bluff, fancy looking jibber-jabber
designed to create an impression of profundity (Weinberg 1996b: 56).

The Einsteinian constant

Weinberg remarks that "the Einsteinian constant" is not an expression used by physicists (Weinberg 1996b: 55–56). Indeed, a glance at the text (1970: 267) shows that Derrida introduced it merely as a way of referring, in the context of the exchange, to whatever is the constant that Hyppolite connects to Einstein. However, it is just this use of the expression to refer to whatever it is that Hyppolite is talking about, without having to say or ask what it is, that makes Weinberg think that Derrida is bluffing. He thinks Derrida "just started talking about the Einsteinian constant without letting on that (as seems evident) he had no idea of what Hyppolite was talking about" (Weinberg 1996b: 55–56). But "as seems evident" is hardly an argument. His accusation is only a suspicion.

Also, remember that Hyppolite started this by not bothering to tell Derrida explicitly what constant he had in mind. Why would he do that? One possibility is simple carelessness. But another is that this was not the first time that he and Derrida had talked about this subject. Furthermore, the back and forth that follows Derrida's reply strongly suggests that Hyppolite, if not Weinberg, believed that Derrida knew what Hyppolite was talking about.[40] Was Derrida that good a bluffer? Note also that although Derrida does not say what the Einsteinian constant is, he is willing to say things about it. If he is bluffing, this is a risky thing to do. For example, if Hyppolite's constant is either the speed of light or the space–time interval, then calling it "the very concept of variability" does not seem like a good idea. So, contra Weinberg's bluff hypothesis, we have support for the idea that both Derrida and Hyppolite thought that Derrida knew what Hyppolite was talking about and even for the possibility that he actually did. For Weinberg to show that he is not just peddling his prejudices here, he has to give an argument that is not vulnerable to such objections. This he has not done and that he pretends that he has is itself a bit of a bluff.

A center for a structure

For "center," Weinberg offers two pieces of evidence. The first consists in quoting one of the twenty-nine sentences in Derrida's lecture about the idea of a center and reporting, "This is not of much help" (Weinberg 1996b: 56). Indeed it is not. Perhaps neither are the other twenty-eight sentences, but how do we know? Weinberg's other piece of evidence is that Hyppolite's exchange with Derrida shows that, even after hearing both the lecture and Derrida's response to his question, Hyppolite still does not know what a center is (Weinberg 1996b: 56). So it seems. However, the question that Hyppolite asks shows that he knows at least this much: that a center for a structure is supposed to be constant with respect to any variation that the structure can sustain without loss of identity. By contrast, Weinberg, who feels confident to say what Hyppolite does and does not know, gives us no reason to think that he knows even this. Like Weinberg, I doubt that Derrida is attempting to introduce a precise concept in his discussion of "a center for a structure." But I draw a different conclusion from this because I take seriously Derrida's "reiterated warning that his texts are not a store of ready-made 'concepts' but an activity resistant to any such reductive ploy." I am quoting Christopher Norris (1996: 24), author of *Against Relativism* (1997), a book Weinberg would do well to read before beginning his next exegesis of the Derrida quote. In it, he will find the "physics babbler" enlisted as an important ally in a defense of the privileged status of science. Life is complicated.

Weinberg concludes his surmising with a flourish. "It seems to me that Derrida in context is even worse than Derrida out of context" (Weinberg 1996b: 56). I am sure it does. But why is Weinberg so sure that he read Derrida in the relevant context? I see no evidence of it. For example, Derrida talks about the idea of a center in a historical context that extends backwards to antiquity.[41] Does Weinberg think this is irrelevant? Michael Harris's wickedly perceptive observation about a related conceit of Sokal and Bricmont applies to Weinberg's without significant change:

> In some cases, we have quoted rather long passages, at the risk of boring the reader, in order to show that we have not misrepresented the meaning of the text by pulling sentences out of context (Sokal and Bricmont 1998: 17)

> This may satisfy those who imagine that the context of page 50 is pages 48–52, say, but if the context is an ongoing literary debate or an entire culture's orientation to mathematics and science, then the length of the quotations is irrelevant. To paraphrase remarks made by David Bloor, Sokal and Bricmont are "as it were, coming into the middle of a conversation that has been going on for some time."
> (Michael Harris, unpublished review of *Fashionable Nonsense*)[42]

This completes the first series of case studies. In the next, the focus shifts from hatchet jobs on statements about science or mathematics whose authors are said to be corrupted by relativism or social constructivism to attacks on the two "isms" themselves. In each case, I argue that a charge of nonsense-spouting results from a combination of careless reading and failing to distinguish between denying objectivity (the possibility of context-independent truth) and neither affirming nor denying it. This second series of case studies is prefaced by a thumbnail sketch of the post-*Tractatus* philosophy of Ludwig Wittgenstein, which is offered as an exemplar of the mindset that informs both relativism and social constructivism.

Relativism and social constructivism

> Deny that non-context-dependent assertions [exist and] can be true, and you . . . throw out the Nazi gas chambers.[43]
> (Sokal, *Afterword*)

But to require that the truth about Nazi gas chambers not be context-dependent suffers from as bad a problem. If, after presenting compelling evidence that there were gas chambers at Auschwitz-Birkenau, we still had to prove that the evidence is not context-dependent, we would be "throwing out" not only the gas chambers but also our sanity. A claim that the truth-value of a statement is not context-dependent is too strong for us to get evidence for it, much less proof. Yet many people believe otherwise. When they look around and see no context dependence, that is their evidence. Moreover, the idea of context independence is almost irresistible. When we formulate a statement, a relationship between it and the world is created that is itself in the world independent of us. Or so it seems. There are also counter-intuitions, for example, the constructivism of Kant's *Critique of Pure Reason* and Wittgenstein's discussion of rule following in his *Philosophical Investigations*.

The counter-intuition in the *Investigations* is that language never determines its applications. But language often does seem to determine its applications. Stipulations seem to stick and this impression is probably essential for our cognitive well-being. To illustrate his ideas, Wittgenstein considers the rule for adding two, arguing that no matter what we say or do, we do not seem to determine its application. In support of this, note that we usually do not have a rule for following a rule and, if we do, we usually do not have a rule for following that rule. For Wittgenstein, the problem is not the possibility of multiple interpretations of a statement or rule or a change in its meaning. He does not think that there is even one way of "interpreting" a statement or "following" a rule, even though we seem to do it all the time. Nor is it a matter of vagueness. Some philosophers seem to think that, at least in principle, vagueness can be removed by arbitrary stipulation.[44] But Wittgenstein's view is that we cannot stipulate anything, not even the rule for adding one, although it often seems that we can. If this is right, the idea that we can say things about a reality independent of us runs into trouble—not with the idea of such a reality but because we are unable to endow our statements with meanings that can leave home and make it on their own.

The mindset of the *Investigations* is the irreducible core of social constructivism and its alter ego, relativism. It therefore is not surprising that some readers of it or related writings like *On Certainty* (1972) think that, in them, Wittgenstein frequently comes disturbingly close to a denial of objectivity. Hilary Putnam (1992: 168–179) recalls his dismay on first encountering in *On Certainty* questions like,

§609: . . . Is it wrong for [people] to consult an oracle and be guided by it? If we call this "wrong," aren't we using our language game as a base from which to *combat* theirs?

§610: And are we right or wrong to combat it? . . .

§612: I said I would "combat" [people who consult an oracle]—but wouldn't I give them *reasons*? Certainly, but how far do they go?

Putnam first took this to be a clear denial of objectivity but he revised this view after a closer reading (1992: 172). He now understands it to say[45] that, although we may be right to combat another mindset, argument is unlikely to be effective if it is too different from our own. Moreover, in deciding, from within our mindset, whether it is right to combat another one, we should not be too quick to treat it simply as a stupid or ignorant form of our own. If we resist this and allow ourselves to listen, we may discover that there are fewer mindsets that we want to combat.[46] I agree and invite the reader to consider whether my discussion of "hatchet jobs" provides support for this view. Did Weinberg allow himself to listen to Derrida or did he assume from the start that Derrida was merely posturing? Did Nagel attempt to hear what Irigaray was saying before concluding that her mindset was merely a stupid or ignorant form of his own? And so on. If the hallmark of relativism is sensitivity to considerations of context, is it any wonder that hostility to it often keeps company with a resistance to looking for more generous readings of texts that initially put us off?

Transgressing those conventions

Anyone who believes that the laws of physics are merely social conventions is invited to try transgressing those conventions from the windows of my apartment. (I live on the twenty-first floor.)[47]

(Sokal 1996)

Here Sokal is showing how much he can get away with. A social convention is one thing, a social construction another but "transgressing those constructions" is not funny. Neither Kant, whose view of reality is exactly the kind that Sokal detests, nor the other targets of Sokal's ridicule believe that the laws of physics are social conventions.[48] Once this is understood, the joke is no longer funny. What is funny is the idea that knowledge of the relevant laws of physics has anything to do with why people and goats normally do not jump out of windows. It is dismaying that, in an article allegedly devoted to assuring us of the seriousness of his purpose (Sokal 1996),[49] Sokal prefers being funny to getting it right. Instead of treating the absurdity of his notion of a social construction as evidence that it is not what social constructivists are talking about, he takes for granted that it is, from which it conveniently follows that they are merely posturing. If this is all that it takes to expose them, they clearly do not have good posture. Note also how little it takes for Sokal's remark to stop being a joke and come within sight of addressing a genuine issue. He need only have asked how our normal fear of jumping from a height is consistent with the belief that "reality is a social construction."

A good initial reply is that to say that reality is a social construction does not mean that we can do a damn thing to alter the reality that people normally are killed when they leap from too great a height. More precisely, we believe that this is the reality and our beliefs, together with our attitudes and desires, drive our behavior. Although this tells us only what "reality is a social construction" does not mean, it serves to complicate the discussion in just the right way. If such talk now seems mysterious instead of ridiculous, great progress has been made. In the literature of science studies, talk about social construction is talk about scientific belief formation from a perspective from which rationality appears to have a less decisive role than classical epistemology says it should. To see rationality in this light, the strength of a belief must be rigorously differentiated from the strength of the support provided for it by logic and evidence, notwithstanding the influence of the latter on the former. For a simple illustration of what I mean, consider the following exchange between a traditional realist and two social constructivists in *Physics Today* (January 1997):

> Perhaps some sense of reality could be imparted to Collins and Pinch by putting them on jet planes that lack flaps or spoilers.
>
> (Belver Griffith)

> We agree that we prefer to fly on airplanes with flaps and spoilers, though we have never actually checked with the pilot and cabin crew before taking off.
>
> (Harry Collins and Trevor Pinch)

Griffith thinks that Collins and Pinch wish to deny that facts matter but would admit that they do if their lives were at risk. Collins and Pinch counter that, even at thirty thousand feet, all we have to go on are our beliefs about what the facts are and most of these are based on trust, not anything like rational inquiry. Even when our lives are at risk, we must and do rely on large doses of trust, including trust about what the relevant facts are.

I follow you follow me

On page 87 of *Fashionable Nonsense*, Sokal and Bricmont attribute to Barry Barnes and David Bloor a "radical redefinition of the concept of truth." Here is the passage they quote, followed by their misreading of it:

> The relativist, like everyone else, is under the necessity to sort out beliefs, accepting some and rejecting others. He will naturally have preferences and these will typically coincide with those of others in his locality. The words "true" and "false" provide the idiom in which those evaluations are expressed, and the words "rational" and "irrational" will have a similar function.
>
> (Barnes and Bloor 1981: 27)

But this is a strange notion of "truth," which manifestly contradicts the notion used in everyday life.[50] If I regard the statement "I drank coffee this morning," as true, I do not mean simply that I prefer to believe that I drank coffee this morning, much less that "others in my locality" think that I drank coffee this morning! What we have here is a radical redefinition of the concept of truth, which nobody (starting with Barnes and Bloor them-selves) would accept in practice for ordinary knowledge. Why, then, should it be accepted for scientific knowledge? Note also that, even in the latter context, this definition does not hold water: Galileo, Darwin, and Einstein did not sort out their beliefs by following those of others in their locality.

(Sokal and Bricmont)

For Sokal to regard the statement "I drank coffee this morning" as true is no more or less than for him to believe that he drank coffee this morning. So the idea that Barnes and Bloor are offering "a radical redefinition of the concept of truth" must come from the talk about preferences. One does not have to be very clever to make such talk seem absurd and with the statement "I prefer to believe that I drank coffee this morning" Sokal and Bricmont do just that. But if by the phrase "he will naturally have preferences," Barnes and Bloor mean that the acceptance of a belief is not arbitrary[51] and by "these will typically coincide with those of others in their locality," they mean that most cows agree about most things, especially those who read the *Daily Moos*, then it is not at all absurd. Sokal and Bricmont also turn the observation that our pattern of accepting and rejecting beliefs typically coincides with that of others in our locality into the bizarre claim that we sort out our beliefs by following those of others in our locality—who presumably sort out their beliefs by following ours.[52] I follow you follow me.

A pledge of allegiance to truth

The mistake committed by Sokal and Bricmont is very common. A social constructivist statement that neither affirms nor denies that there is more to truth than consensus is mistaken for a denial. For another example, consider Thomas Nagel's attempt in *The Last Word* (1997: 28) to pin such a charge on Sabina Lovibond. He quotes her reference to

our lack of access to any distinction between those of our beliefs which are actually true, and those which are merely held true by us. No such distinction can survive our conscious recognition that some human authority has to decide the claim of any proposition to be regarded as true—and, accordingly, that the objective validity of an assertion or argument is always at the same time something of which human beings (those human beings who call it "objectively valid") are subjectively persuaded . . . Wittgenstein's conception of language incorporates a non-foundational epistemology which displays the notions of objectivity (sound judgment) and rationality (valid reasoning) as grounded in consensus—theoretical in the first instance, but ultimately practical.

(Lovibond 1983: 37, 40)

Nagel's sole comment about this is that

if one takes [such views] seriously, they turn out to be inconsistent with the very consensus on which they propose to "ground" objectivity. What human beings who form scientific or mathematical beliefs agree on is that these things are true, full stop, and would be true whether we agreed on them or not—and furthermore that what makes that true is not just that we agree to say it!

(Nagel 1997: 29)

Apparently, Nagel expects us to see for ourselves how this queer remark, in which he barrels right through a full stop, refutes Lovibond. The trick, he tells us, is to take her seriously. I did and found that, even if we correct for the fact that Lovibond is talking about reason and judgment, not truth, her remark about objectivity "grounded in consensus" is consistent with his pledge of allegiance to what is true whether or not we agree that it is. "Grounded in consensus" is merely a convenient way of referring to a complex feature of Wittgenstein's conception of language. Where, then, is the alleged inconsistency? Maybe Nagel took Lovibond's first sentence to mean that there is nothing more to being true than being believed. That would do it but it would not be taking her views seriously. For a reading faithful to the rest of her remark, he should take it to say simply that we lack a God's-eye view of our beliefs. Full stop. For the same reason, he should assume that when Lovibond wrote "no such distinction" she meant something like "no belief that there is access to such a distinction," in which case the remark up to the dash is a truism.

Nagel's last chance is Lovibond's carefully crafted remark about the objective validity of an assertion or argument: it is at the same time something of which those of us who call it "objectively valid" are subjectively persuaded. Even without "at the same time," there is nothing here with which Nagel could disagree. Furthermore, if, as he believes, Lovibond denies that there is anything more to the objective validity of an assertion than our being subjectively persuaded of it, why does she add "at the same time"? As I read her, she is being careful not to deny it but also not to affirm it. She also is reminding us of something that we are forever forgetting: that whenever we believe we have an objective justification, we are still in the realm of unjustified belief.[53] So yes, I do see an inconsistency. But it is between Nagel's reading of Lovibond and the one that I get by taking her views seriously.

Reading Roger Anyon

> Postmodernism, in seeking . . . to blur the distinction between [science]
> and "other ways of knowing"—myth and superstition, for example—
> needs to go much further than historicism, all the way to the denial that
> objective truth is a coherent aim that inquiry may have. Indeed, accord-
> ing to postmodernism, the very development and use of the rhetoric of
> objectivity . . . represents a mere play for power, a way of silencing these
> "other ways of knowing."
>
> (Boghossian 1998: 27)

This is part of Boghossian's reading of an account of postmodernism by the
postmodernist scholar, Linda Nicholson (1990: 3–4).[54] I believe that he has
her badly wrong but I will not undertake to prove this here.[55] I wish instead
to evaluate Boghossian's success in catching someone in the act of espousing
the view he takes Nicholson to be describing—one whose ubiquity he tells us
is "a distressingly familiar fact." He writes, "A front-page article in the *New
York Times* of October 22, 1996, provided an illustration." The alleged espousal is attributed to Roger Anyon, "a British archaeologist who has worked
for the Zuni people." It reads, "Science is just one of many ways of knowing
the world . . . [The Zunis' world view is] just as valid as the archaeological
viewpoint of what prehistory is about."

Boghossian asks, "How are we to make sense of this?" (Boghossian 1998:
27). The obvious and surely the best answer is, "Ask Anyon." Remarkably,
the idea seems not to have occurred to him, perhaps because it would have
been inconvenient to let Anyon have a say about what he meant. Boghossian
contends that Anyon's "just as valid" can be understood in three ways, none
of which yields a remotely plausible assessment of the relative merits of the
two views about prehistory.[56] He tries to justify this for "valid" taken to mean
either "true" or "justified." But not only does he ignore the possibility that
none of his interpretations of "valid" is Anyon's,[57] when he comes to the
third, which he describes in terms of serving symbolic, emotional, and ritual
purposes, he says,

> The trouble with this as a reading of "just as valid" is not so much that
> it's false but that it's irrelevant to the issue at hand: even if it were granted,
> it couldn't help advance the cause of postmodernism. For if the Zuni
> myth isn't taken to compete with the archaeological theory as a descrip-
> tively accurate account of prehistory, its existence has no prospect of
> casting any doubt on the objectivity of the account delivered by science.
>
> (Boghossian 1998: 29)

But the issue at hand is not the cause of postmodernism. It is whether
Boghossian can fulfill his promise to show that this interpretation of "just as
valid" produces a postmodernist claim that is not remotely plausible. Not

only does he not do this, he implies that it yields a claim that it is both plausible and not interestingly postmodernist. Perhaps Boghossian meant to say that, on two of his readings, the remark makes an implausible postmodernist claim and that, on the third, it is plausible but irrelevant to postmodernism. But once he has admitted one way of making sense of Anyon's remark on which it is plausible and irrelevant to postmodernism, if he has no evidence that it is not what Anyon meant, Anyon is off the hook. So Boghossian's attempt, to show us one real-life espousal of a view that he says is ubiquitous, fails. However, although it is fair to criticize him for this dreadful argument, I suspect that there is little that Anyon or many others in cultural studies could say that Boghossian would not hear as a denial of objectivity. So in this sense, he is right: for him, this view is ubiquitous.

Reasoning about relativism

A postmodernist dummy about truth

For his interpretation of "just as valid" as "just as true," Boghossian, playing the ventriloquist to a postmodernist dummy, has the latter suggest that contradictory statements can both be true provided that each is true from a different perspective.

> If I say that the earth is flat and you say that it's round, how could we both be right? Postmodernists like to respond to this sort of point by saying that both claims can be true because both are true relative to some perspective or other and there can be no question of truth outside of perspectives . . . But to say that some claim is true according to some perspective sounds simply like a fancy way of saying that someone, or some group, believes it.
>
> (Boghossian 1998: 28)

As a description of real postmodernists, this is fantasy. Boghossian offers no support for it.[58] But for the moment I will ignore this in order to focus on the logic of the argument he uses it to make. He begins by noting that what he says above implies that his dummy is committed to the view that anything is true provided only that someone believes it.[59] As if this were not bad enough, according to Boghossian, the dummy does not always honor her commitment to this view—she does not consider the view itself mistaken merely because somebody else thinks that it is. Boghossian claims that this is not merely an inconsistency but that it reveals a commitment to "truth independent of particular perspectives" (Boghossian 1998: 28). How it reveals this, he does not say—which I take to mean that he trusts the reader to see it.

Here is what I see. The dummy denies the claim that "if someone believes a statement, then it is true" by denying it for a particular statement. This lands her in a contradiction but I see no evidence of a commitment to truth independent of particular perspectives.[60] However, the denial of the claim "If a statement is true, then someone believes it" does express such a commitment. So my guess is that Boghossian mistook his dummy's denial of a claim of the form "If someone believes *S*, then it is true" for the denial of its converse.

However, Boghossian's discussion of this is maddeningly vague, so I have relied on my own unconfident rendering of it. Here is the original:

> If a claim and its opposite can be equally true, provided there is some perspective relative to which each is true, then since there is a perspective—realism—relative to which it's true that a claim and its opposite both cannot be true, postmodernism would have to admit that it itself is just as true as its opposite, realism. But postmodernism cannot afford to admit that: presumably, its whole point is that realism is false.[61] Thus, we see that the very statement of postmodernism, construed as a view about truth, undermines itself: facts about truth independent of particular perspectives are presupposed by the view itself.
>
> (Boghossian 1998: 28)

I am now ready to explain my objection to the statement "postmodernists like to respond to this sort of point by saying that both claims can be true because both are true relative to some perspective." According to postmodernism, a claim is not true because it is true relative to a perspective; it is true in the sense that it is true relative to a perspective. To see the difference this makes, try to repeat Boghossian's argument with "in the sense that" instead of "because." You will not succeed. Also, if a postmodernist were to remark that "The earth is round" and "The earth is flat" can both be true, other postmodernists would probably understand it as a reminder that an apparent contradiction between statements may reflect a difference in the contexts in which their meanings have a home. Boghossian would do well to remember this too.

A postmodernist dummy about justification

For his interpretation of Anyon's "valid" as "justified," Boghossian again plays the ventriloquist to a postmodernist dummy. This one conflates the real postmodernist view that each justification we make is relative to a perspective with the nonsensical claim that a statement is justified if it is justified from some perspective or other. As in the case of postmodernist talk about truth, this conflation renders Boghossian's argument worthless as a refutation against his real target. He also requires his dummy to hold that everyone is free to stipulate what counts as a rule of evidence, as if evidence need have nothing to do with inducing belief. This is used to show that the dummy is obliged to accept that the denial of her belief about justification is no less justified than the belief itself. But Boghossian thinks that she cannot accept this:

The postmodernist needs to hold that his views are better than his opponents; otherwise, what's to recommend them? By contrast, if some rules of evidence can be said to be better than others, then there must be some perspective-independent facts about what makes them better and a thoroughgoing relativism about justification is false.

(Boghossian 1998: 29)

Thus in spite of her postmodernism about justification, the dummy is required to believe that some rules of evidence are better than others, from which Boghossian concludes that she is committed to the existence of perspective-independent facts. As in the case of truth, he offers no argument for this. Presumably he expects the reader not to need one. But this reader does. For one thing, he does not see how Boghossian can rule out the possibility that the dummy believes that there is a universal perspective from which some rules of evidence can be said to be better than others.[62] But even if Boghossian's conclusion is unwarranted, he leaves us with a wonderful question. Forget about the dummy. Do you need to believe that you can give reasons for holding your positions that are good not only from these positions? What bad things will happen to you if you cannot?

This concludes the second series of case studies. For me, they serve mainly as a reminder of how difficult it can be for a believer—in this case, a believer in objectivity, that is, a realist—to tell agnosticism from atheism. In the next and last series of studies, I consider a confusion in realist thought that contributes to this difficulty. Although it is not a necessary feature of realism, it is a predictable consequence of insensitivity to shifts in context—in this case, to shifts associated with the belief/knowledge distinction. So although it is not inevitable, neither is it a surprise.

Reality is hard to talk about

It appears to me that the "real" is an intrinsically empty, meaningless category.

(Albert Einstein)[63]

In "Professor Sokal's bad joke," Stanley Fish (1996) described a sense in which both science and baseball are social constructions, yet no less real for it. The comparison was widely misunderstood. Soon Weinberg countered with his conception of the sense in which the laws of physics are real. It too was misunderstood, even by Weinberg, as I show below.

The laws of physics are real . . . in pretty much the same sense (whatever that is) as the rocks in the fields, and not in the same sense (as implied by Fish 19) as the rules of baseball—we did not create the laws of physics or the rocks in the field, and we sometimes unhappily find that we have been wrong about them.

(Weinberg 1996a: 14)

Contrary to what is suggested here, Fish is not comparing the laws of physics with the rules of baseball. His point is that the statements that we accept as laws of physics help govern its practice, just as the rules of baseball do for our national pastime. Fish is comparing baseball with physics as rule-governed activities. This is a ball. That is a strike. This experiment supports Weinberg's theory, that one does not. As Weinberg notes, the statements that we accept as laws of physics are not stipulative of it.[64] But, as Fish explains in his essay, neither are the rules of baseball stipulative of baseball (Fish 1996). If batters get too many hits, the strike zone might be shrunk or, to think the unthinkable, the rule might be changed to "two strikes and you're out," and it would still be baseball. However, although there is nothing more to being a rule of baseball than being accepted as one by the relevant community, accepting a statement as a law of physics does not make it true. Nor does rejecting it make it false. To accept a statement as a law of physics is to believe that it *is* a law of physics. From inside the belief, there is no belief, only knowledge of how things are. By contrast, when we stand back and reflect upon it, there is the belief but no believing it and, in a queer way, it may no longer seem to be our belief. Indeed, we usually allow that it may be false,[65] which, strictly speaking, is inconsistent with believing that it is true.[66] However, when we stop reflecting on it, we no longer allow this. In the rest of the chapter, I will offer examples of how losing sight of how we oscillate between being inside a belief and standing back from it can lead us to make reasonable-looking statements about the nature of reality that on closer inspection turn out to be gibberish. I begin with Weinberg in the quote above.

Now you believe it

"I always believe stories whilst they are being told," said the Cockroach. "You are a wise creature," said the Old Woman. "That is what stories are for. And after, we shall see what we shall see."

(A. S. Byatt, *The Djinn in the Nightingale's Eye*)

For Weinberg, the laws of physics are real in the sense that sometimes we find that we have been mistaken about whether something is such a law. In each case, the words "we find" mark a report from inside our belief that we were mistaken: it is a discovery, not merely the adoption of a belief. Nevertheless, when we reflect upon it, we are likely to allow that it, too, may be mistaken. Indeed we do sometimes discover that we have been mistaken about being mistaken about whether something is a law of physics. But although, for Weinberg, it is human fallibility that makes the laws of physics real, this potentially infinite source of it should be of no comfort to him. He notes that we believe that we cannot be mistaken about something if we believe that it holds by stipulation. But we also believe that we cannot be mistaken about something if we believe that we have discovered it. True, even if reality bops us into a state of believing that we cannot be mistaken about something, it may then bop us out of it.[67] But so long as Weinberg remains inside a belief that he has discovered a law of physics, he believes also that he cannot be mistaken about it and hence that it is not, in his sense, a law of physics. I doubt that this is what he had in mind.

The correct answer, take one

> The choice of scientific question and the method of approach may depend on all sorts of extrascientific influences, but the correct answer when we find it is what it is because that is the way the world is.
>
> (Weinberg 1996a: 14)

It seems that Weinberg is attempting to say that the correct answer to a scientific question does not depend on extrascientific factors. But this is a tautology. Anything that the correct answer to a scientific question depends on is, for that very reason, scientific even if it was not hitherto recognized as such. The second clause also is a tautology because to be the correct answer just means to be a correct statement of the way the world is. And yet, so long as we do not look too closely, these tautologies seem to be saying something significant. Certainly Weinberg seems to think they are.[68] My guess is that this impression is created by our associations to the words "extrascientific influences" and "when we find it." But by the analysis of the preceding section, the dream of finding the correct answer to some scientific question has a damper. Whenever Weinberg dreams that he has found it, for that very reason, what he dreams he has found is unreal. If this is a disappointment, he can dream instead that he may be mistaken. But then he is no longer dreaming that his answer is correct. It is a dilemma. But even worse, if to escape it, still dreaming or not, he steps back and reflects upon the whole of what from inside the relevant belief is his activity of scientific discovery, he will see only that sometimes he becomes convinced of something and at other times he becomes unconvinced. And contemplation of this barren view of his place in the world may drive him back to dreaming that he has discovered the correct answer to a scientific question.

Is this a fair reading of Weinberg's remark? On the one hand, even if we ignore the loaded use of the words "when we find it," his reliance on fortune cookie philosophy[69] to lecture others on the correct way to talk about our relationship to reality merits scorn. On the other hand, if we wish to be forgiving, we can pretend that it never happened and take him to have merely meant to affirm the traditional realist credo: the truth-value of a scientific statement is independent of social factors.

The correct answer, take two

Weinberg is not alone. In *Fashionable Nonsense*, Sokal and Bricmont use the idea of "the correct answer to a scientific question" to teach Latour how to talk properly about science and reality (Sokal and Bricmont 1998: 92–99). Although Latour talks about settling scientific controversies rather than finding correct answers (Latour 1987: 96–100), to say that a scientific controversy is settled means that there is a shared belief that something is the correct answer to a certain question. Seeing Latour seem to repeatedly insist that facts come into existence only by our recognizing them as such, Sokal and Bricmont accuse him of "playing constantly on the confusion between facts and our knowledge about them." I disagree.[70] However, here I wish only to consider what—with apparently straight faces—Sokal and Bricmont offer contra Latour as the correct answer to what is meant by "the correct answer to a scientific question."

> The correct answer to any scientific question, solved or not, depends on the state of Nature . . . Now it happens that, for the unsolved problems, nobody knows the right answer, while for the solved ones, we do know it (at least if the accepted solution is correct, which can always be challenged).
>
> (Sokal and Bricmont 1998: 97)

I believe that a careful reading will confirm that, as we pass from the idea that "we do know it" to "if the accepted solution is correct," we shift from inside the belief that we know the solution to outside it, where we are able to allow that it may not be correct. Thus the insight that Sokal and Bricmont seem to wish to share with us here—the one that they imply Latour, in his relativistic confusion, missed—is that in science when we believe we have solved a problem, we have, except that maybe we have not.

The infinite regress for evidence

In the previous cases, metaphysical nonsense was produced by failing to notice that one had moved outside a belief or back inside. Here, it is caused instead by failing to notice which relevant beliefs one has entered in the course of moving outside another one. On page 17 of *A House Built on Sand*, Sokal says that how he would evaluate the causes of a man's claim should depend heavily on whether or not the claim is true.[71] He then qualifies this, saying, "more precisely, since I admit that we have no direct, unmediated access to external reality," it should depend on evidence for or against the claim. However, as an assertion about our relationship to external reality, this is crazy.

The problem is not with the idea of looking at evidence. Of course, we should. It is with the conceit that although we do not have direct, unmediated access to the truth-value of an assertion, we do have such access to the truth-value of a claim that something is evidence for an assertion. This is fantasy. The claim that a rabbit test is evidence of pregnancy is itself based on evidence, probably statistical. There is an infinite regress for evidence just as there is for justification. In practice, for one reason or another, the regress stops. I doubt that it is often a matter of conscious choice. Where it does stop, for those like Sokal, who believe that talk about "direct unmediated access" to external reality means something, this *de facto* privileged level seems to become the practical equivalent of a realm to which we do have "direct unmediated access." Maybe this is the source of the blunder.

Science and the study of science

There is a great and, to my mind, fascinating disagreement about the role that the truth of a scientific belief can, should, or even must play in explaining why it is believed. In one camp, which includes many scientists, there are those who find it obvious that in many cases both in science and ordinary life, we can and maybe even must appeal to the truth of a belief to help explain what causes someone to believe it.[72] Like Sokal above, many of those in this camp consider it important to emphasize that to justify such an explanation, which should be thought of as a theory, one must appeal to the evidence for the belief, not to its truth. But they ignore the regress for evidence.

In another camp, in which constructivist sociologists of science figure prominently, there are those who say that such explanations are question-begging, in part because of the regress. They try to position themselves outside any belief whose acceptance or persistence they wish to explain. This is the "Strong Programme" for the sociology of science. For those who pursue it, the regress for evidence is a reminder that the power of evidence to induce belief varies with the state of mind of the jury. Evidence that convinces you may not convince me because a friend whom I trust warned me that it may be a con. The causal irrelevance of authenticity is another consideration. Because we learn to be good cup detectors, normally a belief that there is a cup on the table is pretty good evidence of its truth. Nevertheless we understand, as a fact about our biology, that not only cups trigger our cup detectors. Any good enough imitation will do. Furthermore, a good enough imitation need not be a particularly good approximation to the real thing. It need only be close enough in the realm of appearances. This principle is perfectly general.

Those in the first camp think it is crazy to let such considerations dictate how we study knowledge acquisition. After rolling their eyes, they may explain, "Of course, we don't really know that S is true. What the evidence really shows is that S is highly probable." As if the claim that the evidence shows that S is highly probable were not subject to exactly the same concerns.[73] Yet it is they who insist upon the importance of distinguishing between what does convince people and what should convince them, which is precisely the distinction that grounds these concerns.[74] But they see no contradiction. Indeed, in "Science as a cultural construct" (*Nature*, 10 April 1997), physicists Kurt Gottfried and Kenneth O. Wilson couple severe criticism of the Strong Programme with a defense of this apparent double standard. They contend that although the Strong Programme cannot distinguish between objective knowledge and mere belief, they and other physicists can.[75] They consider it a scandal that the Strong Programme ignores and, in their view, must ignore "the steadily improving predictions of twentieth-century science" (Gottfried and Wilson 1997: 545). How do Gottfried and Wilson support these remarkable claims? On my reading, their whole justification consists of the following remark, supplemented by a reference to two illustrative examples:

> Predictive power, the strongest evidence that the natural sciences have an objective grip on reality, is largely ignored by these commentators. For the question of whether scientific knowledge is contingent on culture, the discovery of phenomena that could not have been foreseen when a theory was invented but which are in accord with that theory are especially germane.
>
> (Gottfried and Wilson 1997: 547)

So they would have us believe. But no matter what the Strong Programme may or may not have been ignoring, there is nothing about even the most spectacular predictive success that puts it out of its reach. Not, at any rate, so long as considerations like the causal irrelevance of authenticity and the infinite regress for evidence retain their cogency. Furthermore, to say that a theory is unlikely to be "contingent on culture" if it holds for phenomena that could not have been foreseen when it was invented is a non-sequitor. How a culture could have spawned scientists that invented such remarkable theories is indeed a mystery. But unless I am badly mistaken it is not one that need concern us here; it is a mystery about the origin of conjectures not the adoption of beliefs.

Elsewhere in their article, Gottfried and Wilson lecture their readers about the bad things that happen when accounts of scientific knowledge acquisition are written according to the Strong Programme. These well-meaning admonishments are, in my view, vivid illustrations of what a world of difference it can make whether one remains inside a belief or stands back from it and takes a long look around before going back inside:

> In 1925 . . . and again in 1933, Dayton Miller announced a positive observation, which contradicts relativity, but was ignored. The authors of *The Golem* see this as proof that what matters is not the quality of an experiment but "what people are ready to believe" because "the culture of life in the physics community meant that Miller's results were irrelevant." When the word "culture" is replaced by "facts," this sentence is no longer misleading, for in the decade following 1909 half a dozen

independent laboratory experiments had confirmed the relativistic relation between velocity and momentum to better than 1 per cent.

(Gottfried and Wilson 1997: 546)

To hear Gottfried and Wilson tell it, it goes without saying that everyone
(except Dayton Miller) saw things as they do. Although they would never say
that "it's a fact because we believe it," they write as if the statement "we
believe it because it's a fact" is a sufficient explanation of at least some cases
of belief formation. The social constructivist authors of *The Golem* want to
study what caused scientists to adopt the beliefs mentioned in the passage. If
Gottfried and Wilson do not understand the relevance for this of what people
are ready to believe, they understand nothing. Their factual claim about what
half a dozen experiments confirmed may be mistaken. Thus their readiness to
believe it is a fact about them, not about a world independent of them. In this
respect, the authors of *The Golem* have it exactly right. However, readiness is
one thing, believing is another. It was reality, not a vote of the American
Physical Society, that bopped a ready to be bopped physics community into
believing the experiments.[76] How did reality do it? God only knows.

So. Ve may now perhaps to begin. Yes?[77]

Notes

1 Supporting materials are posted at the website http://math.bu.edu/people/nk/rr.
2 I thank Phil Baringer, Susan Carey and Nancy Kopell for a wealth of constructive
   criticism that it was a pleasure to receive. And I thank Keith Ashman for his
   patience and understanding.
3 They say, "The Einsteinian constant is, of course, the speed of light in *vacuo*"
   (Gross and Levitt 1994: 79). Of course? Also, the surface contradiction in "The
   Einsteinian constant is not a constant" is *prima facie* evidence that the two senses
   of "constant" are different. For example, if one is numerical, the other is not. The
   authors need to prove that the two senses are the same but they don't even attempt
   to do this.
4 See "What's this, Polus?" below.
5 See "A philosopher experiments with scholarly discourse" at my website. Below,
   see "I am not a reference frame" and "The correct answer, take two."
6 For a trivial but telling example, Boghossian is so confident that Sokal's "But this
   framework is grossly insufficient for a liberatory mathematics, as was proven long
   ago by Cohen 1966" is not a pun that he bases one of his main arguments on it.
   Nevertheless, it is a pun on Cohen's proof of the independence of the axiom
   of choice. Although the argument is easily repaired and Boghossian privately
   admitted the mistake after his essay first appeared, it appears again, unacknowledged and uncorrected, in Koertge's volume. See also note 12.
7 In one, on the evidence of a sentence stripped of its context and first clause, Paul
   Gross (p. 104) concludes that Andrew Ross wants his readers to think that Gerald
   Holton is the author of a famous apocalyptic remark by his *bête noir*, Oswald
   Spengler! For the full story, see "Selective quotation" at my website. For another
   example, see "Masculine channels and feminine flows," below.
8 See "The hoax according to Weinberg" at my website. Here see "The oracle of
   deconstruction," "Now you believe it," and "The correct answer, take one," below.

9 A skeptical reading is a suspension of trust, a refusal to cut any slack. We don't normally read this way.

10 There are many appalling examples but, to my mind, nothing beats the philosopher Thomas Nagel's "The sleep of reason" (1998), a review of *Fashionable Nonsense* by Sokal and Bricmont (1998). The first part reads as if the reviewer was taking dictation. See "Professor Nagel's *Fashionable Nonsense*" at my website and "What's this, Polus?" below.

11 A generous reading is not necessarily a more accurate one. But in these cases, it is.

12 This is the main brief of Boghossian's chapter of *A House Built on Sand*. Like Weinberg's "Sokal's hoax," on a non-skeptical reading, Boghossian's chapter is clear and convincing. Yet, on a skeptical one, the reasoning is sloppy and the interpretation of the evidence lacks credibility. See "Reading Roger Anyon" and "Reasoning about relativism," below, and the essay "An unphilosophical argument," at my website.

13 Or at least our beliefs about it.

14 For views of which these are parodies, see especially "Transgressing those conventions" and "Science and the study of science," below.

15 Almost always, those who call themselves or are called relativists or constructivists are agnostics not deniers, but the conventional wisdom is that they are deniers. I use the term "relativist" here only for these agnostics—"good" relativists. But some agnostics (who are called relativists/deniers by others) use it only for deniers—"bad" relativists. *Caveat lector.*

16 See, for example, *Philosophical Investigations*, *On Certainty* and *Remarks on the Foundations of Mathematics*.

17 Victor Brudney's exhortation to his beginning students about how to read a legal text. He is alluding to *How to Read a Book* (1940: 14), where the author, Mortimer Adler, writes, "When [men and women] are in love and are reading a love letter, they read for all they are worth. They read every word three ways; they read between the lines and in the margins; they grow sensitive to context and ambiguity . . . Then, if never before or after, they read."

18 "Yet the effect of a hatchet job like this, if it succeeds [is a] shift in the climate of opinion . . . outsiders who have grumbled privately to one another for years have something concrete to which they can point" (Nagel 1998: 34).

19 See "What's this, Polus?" below.

20 In my unscientific poll, three physicists and a physics teacher disagreed with Nagel's claim that special relativity is beyond the intuitive grasp of a layman. One physicist agreed with it.

21 He and I read Latour differently. My Latour understands relativity much better than his does.

22 Before concluding that I am wrong, note that this is the spatial distance between events, not points.

23 In fact, it is gibberish offered by a layman to laymen as evidence that a layman cannot intuitively grasp Einstein's theory, even roughly! Yet for a similar claim about quantum theory, which is far stranger than special relativity, Nagel uses an analogy to weather prediction that one physicist awarded an "A+."

24 I thank David Mermin for calling this to my attention.

25 For our purposes, it suffices to note that they offer no support for this implausible idea, a consideration that does not seem to trouble Nagel. Also, like Sokal mocking Derrida on the radio, Sokal and Bricmont are silent about what, if anything, their "comically patient" (I would say "hare-brained") remark has to do with Irigaray's speculation about gender coding. Whatever their intention, the effect is to treat Irigaray as an idiot and encourage their readers to do the same. Indeed, this is exactly the word Nagel uses to describe Irigaray elsewhere in his review. See "Professor Nagel's *Fashionable Nonsense*" at my website.

26 Editors' note: Sokal's contribution to this volume is essentially the same as his chapter in *A House Built on Sand*.

27 The ellipses are Sokal's.

28 Sokal seems oblivious to the implausibility of anyone confusing these two things.

29 See "Reading Latour reading Einstein" in "A physicist experiments with scholarly discourse" at my website.

30 How can Sokal square talk about an observer being delegated to an electron with his unargued claim that, for Latour, an observer has to be human? In fact, for Latour, any recording device is an observer—even a stick that records a fire by being consumed.

31 Hayles seems unsure whether she wants to talk about fluids in general or only nearly incompressible ones, like water.

32 This is why God said, "Let there be editors." What went wrong here?

33 For Frege, see, for example, *The Basic Laws of Arithmetic* (1893: xix). I thank Warren Goldfarb for this reference.

34 Executing a mathematical rule requires both computation and observation.

35 I assume she means "with the flow."

36 In its interior? Every undergraduate physics student should know that, in many cases, the center of mass of a body is not in its interior. Imagine if Hayles had made this slip, not Sullivan.

37 Does he seriously think that Hayles does not know this?

38 So far as I know, the first attempt to brand Derrida a physics faker was made by Ernest Gallo in the *Skeptical Inquirer* in 1991. Gallo was read by Gross and Levitt, who inspired Sokal, who made Derrida's "Einsteinian constant" remark a centerpiece of his hoax, which brings us to Weinberg, whose efforts I discuss here. For a debunking of Gallo's reading of the remark and also of more recent ridicule of it in *Fashionable Nonsense* and the second edition of *Higher Superstition*, see "The invention of Jacques Derrida, physics faker" at my website.

39 Levine's objection and Weinberg's reply are in "Sokal's hoax: an exchange," *New York Review of Books*, October 3, 1996, 54–56.

40 For example, "It is a constant in the game? It is *the* constant in the game" (Derrida 1970: 267).

41 For example, "Successively, and in a regulated fashion, the center receives different forms or names. The history of metaphysics, like the history of the West, is the history of these metaphors and metonymies" (Derrida 1970: 249).

42 The title of Harris's review is "I know what you mean!"

43 This is part of a response to a remark by Andrew Ross that Sokal first correctly calls "epistemological agnosticism" but then misrepresents as a denial of objectivity. See Sokal and Bricmont (1998: 274).

44 See, for example, Paul Boghossian (Koertge 1998: 30) on stipulation in baseball. For my critique of this, see "An unphilosophical argument" at my website.

45 This is my reading of part of Putnam's discussion of *On Certainty* §§608–612 and Wittgenstein's notes on Frazer's *Golden Bough*. I use "mindset" where Putnam, following Wittgenstein, says "language game."

46 On my unscholarly reading, §612 also acknowledges that, even for us, our reasons go only so far.

47 Merely social conventions? Tell it to the women of Afghanistan.

48 In his unpublished essay *The Sleep of Reason Produces Monsters*, the philosopher Simon Blackburn notes that Kant was not in the habit of jumping out of windows.

49 This is the article in which Sokal revealed his hoax.

50 In a footnote, Sokal and Bricmont admit that Barnes and Bloor may merely be noting that what people believe, they label "true." But they manage to make even this into a complaint!

51 It makes sense that they do. Their project is to explain, in cases of interest, what makes people believe one thing rather than another.

52 However, there is some truth to this. Even if Einstein did not follow any other scientist, which I doubt, plenty of them followed him.

53 I am referring to the regress for justification. A belief that we have an objective justification of something itself stands in need of objective justification. If we provide what we believe is one, then that belief stands in need of objective justification, and so on. See also "The infinite regress for evidence," below.

54 Boghossian seems unaware that Nicholson is a postmodernist. Why else would he say that she gives her description of postmodernism, on which he relies, "without necessarily endorsing" it?

55 Nicholson does not say that postmodernism seeks to blur distinctions or to either affirm or deny that objective truth is a coherent aim of inquiry. She says that postmodernists think that the criteria for distinguishing true from false and science from myth are "internal to the traditions of modernity." See Nicholson's contributions to *Feminism/Postmodernism* (Nicholson 1990) and *Social Postmodernism* (Nicholson and Seidman 1995). See also note 58 and, at my website, "An unphilosophical argument."

56 However, the question is not only whether what Anyon said is implausible but whether it is postmodernist.

57 My guess is that Anyon thinks in terms of coherence not correspondence—assessing a belief in terms of how well it serves within a particular world view to help explain whatever those who hold it need explained, and does not find either belief about prehistory to be superior in this respect.

58 I have already noted that it can be difficult to tell "good" relativism (non-affirmation of objectivity) from "bad" (denial of objectivity), offering as an example Putnam's initial difficulty doing this for Wittgenstein. But Boghossian does not even attempt to make the distinction. How then can he defend his reading of how postmodernists like to respond? Does he think Nicholson—a postmodernist he seems to respect—likes to respond this way? I doubt it. Yet, on his reading of her description of postmodernism, she does.

59 The word "because" does all the work. A claim is true because it is true from some perspective—that is, because some person or group believes it. Hence everything anyone believes is true!

60 Indeed, it is compatible with the claim that a statement is true if and only if the dummy believes it.

61 A real postmodernist could have a good time deconstructing this use of the word "presumably." Also, note the crucial role played here by an alleged denial of objectivity: "Its whole point is that realism is false."

62 Such a belief does not seem to imply a commitment to perspective-independent justification, except in the sense that everything can be seen that way. This surely is not Boghossian's claim.

63 Quoted in Beller (1998: 31).

64 Derrida puts this nicely when, on a reading I find plausible, Hyppolite calls Lorentz invariance "the rule of the game." Derrida replies, "It is a rule of the game that does not govern the game . . . When the rule of the game is displaced by the game itself, we must find something other than the word rule" (Derrida 1970: 267).

65 Such skepticism may be more difficult in some cases than in others.

66 When people grant that a statement they believe may be false they sometimes try to remove the appearance of a contradiction by saying that they really believe only that it is highly probable. However, when they reflect upon the claim that it is highly probable, they usually grant that it too may be false.

67 Reality makes a rat expect a food pellet that it may or may not get and it makes people believe, rightly, or not, that there is chaos in the solar system or a ghost in

the closet. Reality is always bopping us into different states of mind and even into forming new states of mind into which we may then be bopped. But it operates by selection, not instruction. It cannot teach a chicken Chinese until the chicken is ready to learn it. Which state we go into depends not only on the bop but also on particulars of our cognitive structure and the state we currently are in.

68 They are his rejoinder to a remark by Sandra Harding.

69 "The correct answer is what it is because that is the way the world is."

70 I say why at my website in "A physicist experiments with scholarly discourse."

71 The claim is that there is a stampeding herd of elephants in a nearby lecture room! The passage in which this is discussed is repeated almost verbatim on page 91 of *Fashionable Nonsense*.

72 For example, I might explain why I believe there is a cup on the table by saying that there is one on it and I see it. I might also say that part of the reason contemporary physicists believe that Newton's laws of motion are true to within a relativistic correction is that because they are, whenever competent scientists tried to confirm this, they eventually succeeded.

73 See note 66 and the preceding section.

74 The regress for evidence stops when we are convinced but, logically, its existence implies that we never should be convinced. Similarly, the causal irrelevance of authenticity implies that whenever we are convinced we should not be.

75 This looks like a substantive claim. But if we insert "what Gottfried and Wilson believe is" before "objective knowledge," and "that something is objective knowledge" after "mere belief," then Gottfried and Wilson seem to be saying that although the Strong Programme cannot distinguish between Bugs Bunny and a wabbit, they and other physicists can. Yet for everyone except them—and maybe even them—the insertions do not alter the meaning.

76 See note 67.

77 Dr. Spielvogel to Portnoy in the last line of *Portnoy's Complaint* by Philip Roth.

Bibliography

Adler, Mortimer (1940) *How to Read a Book*, New York: Simon and Schuster.

Barnes, Barry and Bloor, David (1981) "Relativism, rationalism and the sociology of knowledge," in Hollis, Martin and Lukes, Steven (eds) *Rationality and Relativism*, Oxford: Blackwell.

Beller, Mara (1998) "The Sokal hoax: at whom are we laughing?" *Physics Today* September.

Blackburn, Simon *The Sleep of Reason Produces Monsters* (unpublished).

Boghossian, Paul (1998) "What the Sokal hoax ought to teach us," in Koertge, Noretta (ed.), *A House Built on Sand: Exposing Postmodernist Myths about Science*, New York: Oxford University Press.

Bork, Robert (1996) *Slouching Towards Gomorrah: Modern Liberalism and American Decline*, New York: Regan Books.

Derrida, Jacques (1970) "Structure, sign, and play in the discourse of the human sciences," in Macksey. R. and Donato, E. (eds) *The Structuralist Controversy*, Baltimore: Johns Hopkins University Press.

Fish, Stanley (1996) "Professor Sokal's bad joke," *New York Times*, May 21, A23.

Frege, Gottlob (1982) *The Basic Laws of Arithmetic: Exposition of the System*, translated and edited, with an introduction, by Montgomery Furth, Berkeley: University of California Press.

Gallo, Ernest (1991) "Nature faking in the humanities," *Skeptical Inquirer* (Summer), 371–374.

Goode, Erica (2000) "Among the inept, researchers discover ignorance is bliss," *New York Times* January 18.

Gottfried, Kurt and Wilson, Kenneth O. (1997) "Science as a cultural construct," *Nature* 85(11), 545–547.

Gross, Paul and Levitt, Norman (1994) *Higher Superstition*, Baltimore: Johns Hopkins University Press.

Harris, Michael, "I know what you mean!," unpublished review of *Fashionable Nonsense*.

Hayles, N. Katherine (1992) "Gender encoding in fluid mechanics: masculine channels and feminine flows," *Differences: A Journal of Feminist Cultural Studies* 4(2), 16–44.

Kant, Immanuel (1998) *Critique of Pure Reason*, translated and edited by Paul Guyer and Allen W. Wood, Cambridge, UK, New York: Cambridge University Press.

Koertge, Noretta (ed.) (1998) *A House Built on Sand: Exposing Postmodernist Myths about Science*, New York: Oxford University Press.

Latour, Bruno (1987) *Science in Action*, Cambridge, Mass.: Harvard University Press.

Latour, Bruno (1988) "A relativistic account of Einstein's relativity," *Social Studies of Science*, 3–44.

Levine, George (1996) "Sokal's hoax: an exchange," *New York Review of Books*, October 3, 54–56.

Macksey, R. and Donato, E. (eds) (1970) *The Structuralist Controversy*, Baltimore: Johns Hopkins University Press.

Lovibond, Sabina (1983) *Realism and Imagination in Ethics*, Oxford, UK: B. Blackwell.

Nagel, Thomas (1997) *The Last Word*, New York: Oxford University Press.

Nagel, Thomas (1998) review of *Fashionable Nonsense* in the *New Republic*, October 12, 32–38.

Nicholson, Linda J. (ed.) (1990) *Feminism/Postmodernism*, New York: Routledge.

Nicholson, Linda J. and Seidman, Steve (eds) (1995) *Social Postmodernism*, Cambridge, New York: Cambridge University Press.

Norris, Christopher (1996) *Deconstruction: Theory and Practice*, revised edn, London, New York: Routledge.

Norris, Christopher (1997) *Against Relativism*, Oxford, Malden, Mass.: Blackwell.

Plato (1994) *Gorgias*, translated by Robin Waterfield, New York: Oxford University Press.

Putnam, Hilary (1992) *Renewing Philosophy* Cambridge, Mass.: Harvard University Press (paperback edition).

Sokal, Alan (1996) "A physicist experiments with cultural studies," *Lingua Franca* 6(4) (May/June), 62–64.

Sokal, Alan (1998) "What the *Social Text* affair does and does not prove," in Koertge, Noretta (ed.) *A House Built on Sand: Exposing Postmodernist Myths about Science*, New York: Oxford University Press.

Sokal, Alan and Bricmont, Jean (1998) *Fashionable Nonsense*, New York: Picador USA.

Sullivan, Philip A. (1998) "An engineer dissects two case studies: Hayles on fluid mechanics, and MacKenzie on statistics," in Koertge, Noretta (ed.) *A House Built on Sand: Exposing Postmodernist Myths about Science*, New York: Oxford University Press.

Weinberg, Steven (1996a) "Sokal's hoax," *New York Review of Books*, August 8, 11–15.

Weinberg, Steven (1996b) "Sokal's hoax: an exchange," *New York Review of Books*, October 3, 54–56.

Wittgenstein, Ludwig (1968) *Philosophical Investigations*, 3rd edn, translated by G. E. M. Anscombe, New York: Macmillan.

Wittgenstein, Ludwig (1972) *On Certainty*, edited by G. E. M. Anscombe and G. H. von Wright, translated by Denis Paul and G. E. M. Anscombe, New York: Harper and Row.

5 Pure objects and useful knowledges

Barry Shank, Shari Speer, Alan Thompson, and Sarah Wayland

At this very moment, we are all falling from the twenty-first story of an apartment building in lower Manhattan. Having stepped outside of Alan Sokal's window, we are confronting the full force of gravity and are speeding towards a certain, rather concrete, doom. We have been encouraged to take this step by a statement made by Alan Sokal in his second most notorious article, his announcement in *Lingua Franca* (1996b) of the parodic nature of his most notorious article "Transgressing the boundaries," which originally appeared in *Social Text* (1996a). While making clear that he meant nary a word in the first piece, Sokal insists on the seriousness of this second one by quoting himself. He declares that his earlier statement, " 'physical reality' . . . is at bottom a social and linguistic construct," is easily and obviously negated by his later statement, "anyone who believes that the laws of physics are mere social conventions is invited to try transgressing those conventions from the windows of my apartment." Disregarding the significance of the word, "mere," we are taking the physicist at his (second) word and, at this moment, are falling.

Why are the sciences and the humanities at war?

The content of Dr. Sokal's much-discussed gesture to *Social Text* might be paraphrased as a denial of the possibility of a useful dialogue between workers from disciplines whose language, perspectives, and practices diverge as sharply as cultural studies and physics. It suggests that the gulf between science and the humanities has grown so wide that concepts developed on either side can do nothing to inform work on the other. This hyper-extension of C. P. Snow's concept of two cultures (1962) also appears in *Higher Superstition* by Paul Gross and Norman Levitt (1994), the work that inspired Sokal's prank. For Gross and Levitt, the use of scientific concepts in a literary or cultural criticism context demonstrates that those who use these terms outside of their scientific field of origin do not understand them. According to Gross and Levitt, the only legitimate meaning for such terms is the meaning that developed for them within the specific theoretical and experimental contexts where they were initially elaborated—within the laboratory or in the mathematical notebook. No other use of scientific theories, concepts, labels, or terms, no recognition of their metaphorical allusiveness, or even their ability to illustrate and specify complex relationships in a different manner in a different field, is considered appropriate. The scientists' claim to epistemological authority and methodological autonomy can be seen with even greater clarity when Gross and Levitt discuss certain critics of science, in particular those who practice the "Strong Programme" of the sociology of scientific knowledge. According to these defenders of scientific autonomy, the belief that scientific practice is a subset of social life and, therefore, that it is governed by the general rules of social life is either an outrageous falsehood or an insignificant triviality.

Both Sokal's prank and Gross and Levitt's attack on the possibility of hybrid forms of knowledge that cross the boundaries between science and the humanities were executed for the explicit purpose of protecting the theoretical and methodological autonomy and authority of scientists. These border conflicts have created grand philosophical arguments about objective reality and the way to achieve knowledge. We believe that the ontological and epistemological debates that have produced so many fireworks and have attracted so much attention are simply a sideshow, a secondary effect of an acute struggle over power. This struggle is so intense because it is not concerned with some abstract power but with the specific power to direct and shape basic research and the construction of knowledge in both the sciences and the humanities. The question of whether or not there is an objective reality that can be truthfully known is asked for different reasons and the answers to it take on different meanings for different purposes in these two general areas of scholarship. Only when such boundaries are crossed does it begin to matter whose understanding of the real will control the rules of evidence and argument.

It must be the economy

Perhaps the most fiercely contested borders are created in the fight over the distribution of resources. Social support for basic research is faltering in both the sciences and the humanities. The actual places where people's primary work is basic research are disappearing. This is undeniably the case within academe, for researchers in colleges and universities (Kolodny 1998). It is true as well for those working in institutions of cultural production (for example, museums, symphonies, and public libraries) and the basic research units of corporations and state and federal governments. Workers in each of these institutions face increasing pressures to make their work pay off immediately—museums and symphonies must generate ticket sales, public libraries and basic research units must get money via federal grants, or they must create a product that will pay off in the stock market. Just as there are fewer basic research positions, there is reduced funding and increased oversight and workload for those that remain. To quote from Dorothy Nelkin's article in the much-discussed but little-read "science wars" issue of *Social Text*,

> The social contract between science and the state . . . included a set of both tacit and open agreements about the autonomy of science . . . The government, for its part, has not been able to fulfill its side of the contract . . . Just when the costs of cutting-edge research have escalated, economic support for research has declined. It is more and more difficult for scientists to win grant support from government agencies, and those who are grant-funded face greater oversight.
>
> (Nelkin 1996: 95–96)

Although some humanities research is paid for by government agencies and private foundations (such as the National Endowment for the Humanities or the Guggenheim Foundation), the vast majority of research in the humanities is funded indirectly through university salaries. Nevertheless, researchers in the humanities are experiencing many of the same challenges to their authority and processes of peer review as are researchers in science. State legislatures are beginning to insist that faculty members at public research universities spend more of their time and energy in teaching and community service and significantly less in research. Public figures from politicians to journalists isolate particularly complicated or even obscure phrases from their proper context solely in order to hold them up for ridicule, casting doubt on the legitimacy and usefulness of humanities research. According to Nelkin and Kolodny, religious groups not only declare the uselessness of most humanities research but claim that most of it is fundamentally wicked. Steve Fuller (1992) has described these conditions as "scientific management," where the workers in knowledge production are coming increasingly under the intense and occasionally hostile supervision of managers who do not understand the work that is being performed. In these anti-intellectual circumstances, the profound appeal of the desire for autonomy, authority, and the ability to manage one's own work can be readily understood.

There are many reasons, therefore, for researchers in the sciences and the humanities to develop jointly a process that will allow us to argue for the value of principled intellectual work. We suggest the notion of "useful knowledge" as an organizing concept around which such a process could develop. We want to take pains to make clear that by useful knowledge we certainly do not mean profitable knowledge, nor do we simply mean immediately practicable knowledge. We want to develop a useful concept of useful knowledge that can provide a starting point for the evaluation of research and for democratically determining the areas in which knowledge will be produced, while still retaining enough methodological and conceptual autonomy for workers in science or the humanities to be able to follow their trained intuitions (and their noses) through the effective, if bumbling, processes of knowledge production. As a side effect of our efforts, we hope to encourage a more humble and honest vision of these processes.

As a group of authors we are unusual in that our collaboration spans three disciplines (American studies, physics, psycholinguistics) and three types of employing institutions (the state university, the federal government, and high-tech industry). As a group of friends, we have discussed many of the issues that arise among and within our disciplines and we have found that dialogue among physical sciences, social sciences, and humanities is not at all impossible. This is not to say that we have found this easy, or a simple matter of finding a shared language that enables transparent translation. In fact, we believe that the hope of transparent translation is utopian. But we equally believe that the insistence on complete autonomy for knowledge production is equally utopian. Despite the impossibility of translation, dialogue must take place. Intervening as we are in a debate characterized by polemic, we hasten to admit that the claims and proposals we are presenting are rather modest. We are advocating communication and cooperation across the boundaries that define and separate most fields of intellectual work. In the process of establishing our own cross-disciplinary means of communication, we found it necessary not only to tone down any polemical edge to our comments, but also to rely on a shared lexicon, avoiding the more specialized languages that add a pungent vigor to most entries in the science wars.

How can we have an interdisciplinary dialogue?

The production of useful knowledge requires the blending of perspectives, languages, and values from within the specific fields, laboratories, and libraries where basic research occurs and from the less specialized social and cultural contexts where their significant effects will be experienced. What is required is not necessarily a translation, but perhaps the slow creation of a creole, a hybrid blend of values, perspectives, and languages within which dialogue can occur. The significance of basic research derives from the physical and philosophical effects it eventually has on human lives; it lies in the way it changes the world for humans. Pure knowledge of objective reality is a field-specific goal, useful for the directing of basic research in certain areas. It is not a requirement for useful knowledge; in fact, such pure knowledge rarely says anything of the messy worlds that humans actually live in. In their everyday lives, humans do not deal with field-specific versions of objective reality. Useful knowledge helps humans deal in relatively predictable ways with the immediate world(s) in which they find themselves. For most people most of the time, these worlds are what is real. As philosopher Ian Hacking neatly puts it, "We shall count as real what we can use to intervene in the world to affect something else, or what the world can use to affect us" (1983: 146). This is a useful version of the real; it is based on experience. In this view, a hypothetical construct like a "neutron" was not "real" until the first nuclear bomb based on the construct exploded, at which point it became all too real. Likewise, a hypothetical construct like "oppression" was not real until the society that used the term was willing to declare that fundamental inequalities among groups should not exist.

An example dialogue

In this paper, we are advocating a hybrid process of networking between disparate intellectual fields, but we will begin by demonstrating some of the difficulty we have had in simply trying to explain our differences to each other as we tried to create such a network among ourselves. We encountered what seemed to us to be an almost inevitable clash in perspective when we began simply trying to establish common ground. Our example of the conceptual incommensurability that separates our fields comes from our attempts to understand the differences between historical knowledge and scientific knowledge. These attempts took the form of two questions: first, did the neutron exist before 1932? Second, did oppression of native peoples exist before 1969 (an admittedly random date chosen for the purposes of provocation)? These were questions that Alan (the physicist employed by the United States Government, whose opinions were formed on his time and are solely his own) came up with in order to help clarify the relationship between history and scientific knowledge. We had all agreed that yes, science takes place in time and that, therefore, scientific understandings of the world change; it is possible to write a history of these changes. But we could not agree on what those changes meant. Did they represent simply a change in knowledge about a world that remained fundamentally unchanged? Or did the change in knowledge result in a more profound change in the interactive and mutually determining relationships between humans and their world? Did it make sense to say that changes in scientific understanding changed the world? Or had the world always been this way, and it was only human beings who had changed?

While it seemed obvious to Alan that neutrons had always existed or otherwise we humans (made up of cells, made up of organic compounds, made up of atoms with nuclei that contain neutrons) would not have been having this conversation, it seemed equally obvious to him that oppression of native peoples had taken place well before it became the motivation for the development of a political movement (at whatever date that actually occurred, whether it be fixed at 1680 and the Pueblo Revolt, or 1969 and the founding of the American Indian Movement, or any date in between). To Alan's consternation, Barry (a university-employed specialist in American studies) had no difficulty declaring that the neutron had not existed before 1932.[1] But he refused to answer the second question in a similar yes or no fashion. "Oppression," he insisted, was a difficult concept. Certainly violence against native peoples had taken place well before political movements of the second half of the twentieth century came to focus on them. But violence was not the same as oppression. Oppression requires a recognition of fundamental inequalities in the political treatment of one group by another. It also requires an even more basic belief that such inequalities ought not to exist. Once a charge of oppression has been levelled, the moral landscape has changed (Cudd 1998). This change in the moral landscape changed our society's interpretation of past (and future) violent acts against native peoples. Thus our ideas of the history of the world changed because the meaning we assigned to violence changed. It was this understanding of the relationship between meaning, history, and the world that Barry brought to the conversation. While Alan could see the relevance of this system of reasoning for issues of culture or history, it seemed nonsensical to him when brought to objects of scientific knowledge. Once neutrons had been "discovered" or hypothetically conceived of and experimentally observed and verified, then it was obvious that such entities had always been there. The understanding of humans had changed in an irrevocable fashion, but the world had not. While it might have been possible to say that there had been a period of New World contact and violence between Europeans and Native Americans before this contact took the form of oppression, it was simply impossible to say that there had ever been a time with no neutrons. For Alan, that distinction marked the fundamental difference between scientific knowledge and historical knowledge, the difference between knowledge about nature and knowledge about culture. Barry, on the other hand, had never actually experienced a neutron and was much more willing to think of them as hypothetical constructs that were quite handy in the production of a certain kind of laboratory effect. He was certainly willing to call that knowledge, but he was not so confident of the ubiquitous universal and eternal nature of the neutron. What we could agree upon was our different understanding of the object of knowledge. For Alan, the object was a distinct entity that knowledge was about. For Barry, the object was constructed in the act of knowing. In this conversation, then, Alan was a realist and Barry was a constructionist. Alan could agree with a statement like "the concept of the neutron did not exist before 1932." Barry could live with the compromise position that the neutron existed before 1932 but not until after the concept of the neutron was introduced in 1932. Even with these compromises, the ontological and epistemological differences remained unresolved. But we have come to believe that it is completely unnecessary to resolve them. We want to claim, in fact, that the collective project of producing useful knowledge is better off for the tension. For the moment, then, let the concept of the object of knowledge remain fuzzy, allusive, polysemic.

Cultural influences on knowledge production

When is a concept like "objective reality" useful?

Rather than trying to solve fundamental philosophical questions, we want to describe the conditions within which the concept of pure knowledge of objective physical reality can function as a useful metaphysical conceit that promotes research and governs scholarly debate. For example, not all theoretical physicists agree with Steven Weinberg (1993) that a unified theory of everything is just around the corner, but enough agree that such a theory is an important goal to allow it to partially organize the internal evaluation of competing explanations, hypotheses, and facts within the field itself. A grand unified theory can only be constructed within a conceptual framework that holds that what is scientifically true now has always been scientifically true and always will be scientifically true. In this sense, the fundamental reality of the universe has no history; it is truly an object. Objective reality serves a different but equally important function for experimentalists. Experimental physicists "stub their toes" against reality constantly. Experiments turn out differently than expected. Often the best designed and most carefully executed experiments produce surprising results, or (even worse) fail to produce meaningful results at all. These results (and failures) are explained by reference to objective reality. To the experimentalist, objective reality seems like a glittering jewel swirling in a vat of seething acid: parts of it are driving us to grasp it, while other parts are making it almost impossible to do so. Objective reality is both what inspires research and that which disrupts and frustrates our efforts to make sense of the world. The possibility of achieving a pure knowledge of absolute objective reality, therefore, can then be seen as something like a foundational belief that structures both the successful and unsuccessful attempts at the production of knowledge within physics. It could operate in a manner similar to all such structuring beliefs not only in that it sets the basic terms within which debate can take place (marking the boundaries of the field) but also in that one of its main effects is to allow the participants in this field to "deny the social world" (Bourdieu 1993: 87).

When is "acknowledging the social world" useful?

Historians cannot operate in their own field with such a concept of absolute and pure knowledge. Their goals are not promoted by a belief in the absolute nature of truths about an objective physical reality; their explanations, hypotheses, and facts are not better evaluated within a framework organized by such a belief. As in physics, debate in history is a debate about causes, but it is about specific causes in nearly unique cases. In fact, understanding the process of historical change requires a certain methodological relativism— not an absolute relativism, but a recognized ability to empathize with, understand, and describe a different way of living. This is what it means to write history the way it actually was—"*wie es eigentlich gewesen,*" in the words of the German historian Leopold von Ranke (Novick 1988: 28). Curiously, to write history in the way it actually was requires that the historian also "deny the social world" that she or he lives in. The worst methodological sin of the historian is to be presentist, to evaluate the past by the standards of the present. The historian must, therefore, attempt to escape his or her social and cultural context. Where research in the field of physics is organized by a belief in immutable objective physical reality, research in history is organized by a belief in a discrete past that can be described "as it actually was." In order for each field to effectively produce its explanations, hypotheses, and data, it must limit its engagement with its current social context. Whether or not research in physics actually operates free from social influence, its practitioners must believe that they have, in certain crucial aspects, succeeded in the diffi-cult task of eliminating social influence from their research results (see Ashman, this volume). Equally, whether or not historians actually escape their current cultural conditioning, they are professionally obligated to attempt to do so. For both, if other practitioners in the field do not believe that they have succeeded, their knowledge is rejected. The evaluation of evidence, the valid-ity of logical inferences, and the persuasiveness of arguments are all shaped by their accordance with or deviance from these basic structuring beliefs.

Neither of these basic beliefs is in itself very useful. Their relationship to useful knowledge is distanced and attenuated. The specific explanations, hypotheses, and facts that are directly produced as a consequence of these beliefs tend not to be particularly useful—with the notable exception of their use to professional participants. Useful knowledge is specifically produced and then evaluated elsewhere—in arenas where those structuring denials of the social are not so powerful. But we want to insist that useful knowledge cannot be produced without the specific explanations, hypotheses, and facts that are created in the pursuit of these abstract metaphysical organizing prin-ciples. Or, rather, while it might be created in some other way, in our world, it is not.

Knowledge is produced in a cultural context

We are proposing that we think of both physics and history as discrete exam-ples of what Pierre Bourdieu calls a "field of cultural production" (1993: 31 and *passim*). We hope that by thinking of knowledge production as a cultural activity we can recognize the ultimate cultural context within which knowl-edge is produced and evaluated, the sociological mechanisms that motivate and limit the actions of individuals in a group, and the legitimate demand for autonomy that is so powerfully expressed and experienced within these fields. We hope also to be able to suspend the questions about the objective truths produced within these fields by recognizing that these sociological mechan-isms provide a powerful structure for creating knowledge but also that this structure may not be as effective outside of the field creating the knowledge.

A field of cultural production is an organized social group that establishes its own organization by agreeing more or less about the basic purposes of their collective endeavors and the basic rules of what counts as a legitimate claim or statement within the field (in our case, an academic discipline). It can be helpful to think of cultural production as a game, albeit a very serious game, but also a game whose rules are under constant revision. Bourdieu's conceptualization of cultural production thus escapes some of the problems associated with Kuhn's paradigms (1962). In Kuhn's discussion of scientific revolutions, there seems to be no mechanism whereby individual actors (that is, scientists) come to change their minds. If they are not changing their minds because the new paradigm is better than the old one—that is, it pro-vides a better understanding of the underlying physical reality, for instance (an interpretation that Kuhn specifically dismissed)—then what could possibly be causing them to change their minds (Weinberg 1998)? Bourdieu's understanding of fields provides a sociological explanation. Not only are the rules of the game under constant revision, the evaluation of the effectiveness of the rules is also under constant revision. And what is at stake in these revisions is of absolute sociological significance: the power and the prestige of the participants as well as the very legitimacy of their claims to be real participants in this field (to be a physicist or historian, which means to be recognized as such by other physicists or historians). In order to be as clear as we can about how this works, we will begin by quoting Bourdieu, and then we will go on to try to explain what we think this means for our argument. We are afraid that we must begin with an abstract description; to facilitate understanding, we are going to avoid introducing specifics about the ostensible object being produced—whether it be knowledge of the historical past or of physical reality. But we will be introducing examples from time to time in order to aid clarity.

According to Bourdieu, any field of cultural production is made up solely and totally by the positions taken by the actors in the field.[2]

> Every position [in the field], even the dominant one, depends for its very existence, and for the determinations it imposes on its occupants, on the other positions constituting the field; and . . . the structure of the field . . . is nothing other than the structure of the distribution of the capital of specific properties which governs success in the field and the winning of the external or specific profits . . . which are at stake.
>
> (Bourdieu 1993: 30)

This is Bourdieu's description of the sociological operations within the field, which he understands to be relations of power and determination. Dominant positions in the field, in any field, exert their power through their influence on what count as meaningful and significant statements. For example, the field of psycholinguistics is currently dominated by two main poles of thought, with successive versions of Chomskyan rule-based grammar competing with connectionist network-based models. Theorists and experimentalists phrase their arguments so that they can be recognized and positioned with relationship to these dominant theoretical perspectives. This is not simply Kuhn's normal science, as it acknowledges competing paradigms operating simultaneously and provides a sociological mechanism that shapes the actions of individual participants. A psycholinguist risks the possibility of being completely misunderstood if she refuses to state her arguments in terms that one pole or another can recognize. If she desires her work to be significant and meaningful, it will be less risky to investigate some of the hypothetical consequences of one dominant position or the other (or perhaps bring together predictive consequences from both). Each incidence of such position-taking participates in the ratification of the dominance of the current poles.

What happens if our renegade psycholinguist persists in stating her position in isolation from the dominant poles? While it is more likely that her work would not be recognized as psycholinguistics, it is possible that this new position would gain adherents and would come to challenge the dominance of the other two poles. If this does occur, then the relationships of power and determination within the field would be completely reorganized. If, for instance, she finds herself suddenly championed by actors occupying already powerful positions (say, Steven Pinker or David Rummelhart), then this will legitimize the relative value and significance of her position. And the much greater risk assumed by her rather radical position-taking will have paid off quite handsomely. With the coming to dominance of this new position, other actors in the field will find it necessary to position their work in relationship to hers. What is important about this simplified fable for our purposes is that the entire system, the specific field of cultural (or knowledge) production, operates by virtue of the value accorded to the positions taken by actors in the field by other actors in the field. Yet each actor's ability to evaluate is determined by the relative dominance of other positions in the field. This is a sociological model that values the internal autonomy of the participants in the field without making each of them into atomistic disconnected individuals. Science operates like a field of cultural production, but recognizing the cultural basis of scientific practice does not strip science of its autonomy, rather it indicates the conditions of knowledge production that create that autonomy.

Bourdieu's sociological understanding of cultural production contributes more to our argument for useful knowledge than this ratification of field-specific autonomy. Another aspect of his formulation is the fact that each field is situated in a larger context that Bourdieu calls "the field of power." The significance of this renaming of what has traditionally been called the social or political context is that it enables a clear statement of the relative power of the intellectual fields within this larger field. Bourdieu points out that intellectuals are "a dominated fraction of the dominant class." By this he means that the educational advantages gained and the prestige and power that intellectuals occasionally achieve, while not insignificant, are actually quite limited forms of power that are fundamentally subject to the material domination of other forms of power, particularly those of the state and of the market (1990: 145). Bourdieu's analysis encourages us to focus constantly on these relations of power. Within the specialized fields of cultural or intellectual production, a certain limited autonomy from the explicit and immediate demands of the state and the market is possible. This limited autonomy is achieved through a variety of mechanisms. The most important means is acceptance by each participant of the structuring belief that enables the field to effectively "deny the social," that is, the field of power. Whether by declaring allegiance to the "absolute conception," the purity from anthropomorphisms demanded by science (Taylor 1989: 56), or by insisting on the actual pastness of the past in order to comprehend history, intellectual fields effectively police their boundaries by insisting that all who would have an impact on their internal operations must believe in the field's self-defined conditional autonomy. The second most important mechanism for realizing relative autonomy is the field's ability to institutionalize itself, thereby accruing resources and achieving control of the internal distribution of these resources. Once the field has created enough internal structure, it can organize the internal distribution of prestige and financial awards, both of which are crucial to its ongoing viability. The relative autonomy internal to each field is an effect, therefore, of that field's ability to maintain its fundamental structuring belief and of its ongoing capacity to accrue resources to it from the external field of power for its own internal redistribution. This combination of dependency and denial obviously creates considerable tension at the borders of each field, at the lines that mark the difference between legitimate participants and interlopers.

Cross-cultural communication

Science studies has located itself precisely on this mark. When we called it a hybrid form of knowledge earlier, this was precisely what we meant. From Donna Haraway to Andrew Pickering, from Sarah Harding to Bruno Latour, practitioners of science studies insist on the significance of scientific practice even while emphasizing the limits to science's claims to autonomy. Science studies, like cultural studies, creates networks across the boundaries that separate traditional fields of knowledge production. It is, therefore, an interdisciplinary intellectual project operating in an increasingly interdisciplinary age and benefiting subtly from the increased desire for relative immediate payoffs from intellectual work that partially motivates support for these hybrid fields. It is no wonder that some scientists have reacted with hostility. Similarly violent reactions occur in the humanities when their own boundary-marking procedures are not respected. Discipline-oriented English professors insist on the relative autonomy of literature and ask pointed questions about the loss of aesthetic criteria in some versions of cultural studies (Scholes 1998).

   But, to return to a theme we introduced earlier, such boundary crossings are occurring with increasing frequency, particularly at the highly charged moment when the larger social or political context—the field of power—is engaged in evaluating the worth of a particular field and determining the extent of future funding. We believe that to turn our backs on this process in a loud and dismissive insistence on the autonomy of our work would be to abandon the unavoidable processes of networking and evaluating to the mechanisms of the market and the state. We believe that useful knowledge is created when objects of basic research have been stabilized to the extent that they survive the transition outside of their basic fields, beyond the boundary created by the basic structuring belief that denies the social world. We further believe that useful knowledge cannot be created without the work that goes on under the relatively autonomous conditions that hold within those fields. Finally, we insist that professional intellectuals must collaborate in the collective articulation and evaluation of useful knowledge. When Donna Haraway says that "our problem" is "how to have simultaneously . . . a critical practice for recognizing our own 'semiotic technologies' for making meanings, and a no-nonsense commitment to faithful accounts of a 'real' world" (Haraway 1991: 187), she is making a demand that the specialized knowledge produced in field-specific basic research be linked in useful and productive ways, at specific and localized moments, to the field of power, the social and political context. Field-specific truths must become useful knowledge and the usefulness of this knowledge must be both professionally responsible and democratically recognizable.

But who should have the right and the ability to determine what is useful knowledge? We believe that scholars across multiple disciplines must not simply be engaged with but must in fact direct this process. So far, we in the United States rely on two primary mechanisms for this evaluation: Government funding and private investment. Government funding has been traditionally guided by peer review, and scientists have seen the ability to obtain Government funding as an implicit statement about the legitimacy of a line of research. Increasingly, political pressures are being brought to bear on this process. Private investment is made with the understanding that the resulting competitive commercial advantage will allow the investor to market a profitable product. If the true goal of both science and the humanities is the production of socially useful knowledge, not knowledge that accommodates the relatively immediate needs of profit or state policy, then we as a society must come up with alternative mechanisms for determining what is socially useful knowledge. In our current anti-intellectual and intensely politicized environment, professional intellectuals have the obligation to articulate as clearly as possible and advocate as forcefully as possible the need for a public and systematic process of linking the objects of basic research to the real needs of diverse peoples living in, for all intents and purposes, different worlds. This project needs hybrid networking forms of knowledge such as cultural studies and science studies, just as it needs the rarefied fields that produce basic research. It will require that scholars from the humanities who specialize in describing and evaluating the culturally specific moral frameworks of different societies be able to speak and work with scholars from the sciences whose conceptual frameworks require an absolute insistence on objective knowledge that transcends the shaping force of human needs. It will demand the courage to recognize that most theories are wrong and that most experiments fail, but that the social and financial support for basic research must be maintained. It will require the wisdom to insist that field-specific autonomy continue to direct and shape knowledge production in basic research. Finally, it will insist that this support be earned, democratically and publicly, through the articulation and demonstration of useful knowledge.

Notes

1　The neutron, a component of most atomic nuclei, was discovered by Chadwick in 1932 (Chadwick 1932).
2　In Bourdieu's sociology, "position" is a multivalent word. Its primary meaning involves an attempt to spatialize the relationships among differing legitimate intellectual statements in a specific field. But the metaphorical resonances of the word are also intended to suggest both "point of view" and "social status." One of the most important aspects of Bourdieu's theoretical system is that point of view and social status are not extricable from each other. In addition, the value or significance of an intellectual position within a particular field is both a reflection of and reflects back on the social status and point of view of the actor holding the intellectual position. Finally, it is important to emphasize that the terms "social status" and "point of view" are simplified versions of the more nuanced concepts that Bourdieu uses in his analysis.

Bibliography

Bourdieu, Pierre (1990) *In Other Words: Essays Towards a Reflexive Sociology*, Palo Alto: Stanford University Press.

Bourdieu, Pierre (1993) *The Field of Cultural Production*, New York: Columbia University Press.

Cartwright, Nancy (1983) *How the Laws of Physics Lie*, Oxford: Oxford University Press.

Chadwick, James (1932) *Proceedings of the Royal Society A* 136: 692–708.

Cudd, Ann E. (1998) "Psychological explanations of oppression," in Willett, Cynthia (ed.) *Theorizing Multiculturalism: A Guide to the Current Debate*, Oxford and Malden, MA: Blackwell Publishers.

Fuller, Steve (1992) "Social epistemology and the research agenda of science studies," in Pickering, Andrew (ed.) *Science as Practice and Culture*, Chicago and London: University of Chicago Press.

Gross, Paul and Levitt, Norman (1994) *Higher Superstition: The Academic Left and Its Quarrels with Science*, Baltimore: Johns Hopkins University Press.

Hacking, Ian (1983) *Representing and Intervening: Introductory Topics in the Philosophy of Natural Science*, Cambridge and New York: Cambridge University Press.

Haraway, Donna (1991) *Simians, Cyborgs, and Women: The Reinvention of Nature*, New York: Routledge Press.

Harding, Sandra (1986) *The Science Question in Feminism*, Ithaca, NY: Cornell University Press.

Kolodny, Annette (1998) *Failing the Future: A Dean Looks at Higher Education in the Twenty-First Century*, Durham, NC: Duke University Press.

Kuhn, Thomas (1962) *The Structure of Scientific Revolutions*, Chicago: University of Chicago Press.

Latour, Bruno (1993) *We Have Never Been Modern*, Cambridge, MA: Harvard University Press.

Nelkin, Dorothy (1996) "The science wars: responses to a marriage failed," *Social Text* 46–47: 93–100.

Novick, Peter (1988) *That Noble Dream: The "Objectivity Question" and the American Historical Profession*, Cambridge: Cambridge University Press.

Pickering, Andrew (ed.) (1992) *Science as Practice and Culture*, Chicago and London: University of Chicago Press.

Pinker, Steven (1994) *The Language Instinct: How the Mind Creates Language*, New York: HarperCollins.

Rumelhart, D. E., McClelland, J. L., and the PDP Research Group (1986) *Parallel Distributed Processing*: Vols 1 and 2, Cambridge, MA: MIT Press, Bradford Books.

Scholes, Robert (1998) *The Rise and Fall of English: Reconstructing English as a Discipline*, New Haven: Yale University Press.

Snow, C. P. (1962) *The Two Cultures and the Scientific Revolution*, New York: Cambridge University Press.

Sokal, Alan (1996a) "Transgressing the boundaries: toward a transformative hermeneutics of quantum gravity," *Social Text* 46–47: 217–252.

Sokal, Alan (1996b) "A physicist experiments with cultural studies," *Lingua Franca* 6(4) (May/June 1996): 62–64.

Taylor, Charles (1989) *Sources of the Self: The Making of the Modern Identity*, Cambridge, MA: Harvard University Press.

Weinberg, Steven (1993) *Dreams of a Final Theory: The Search for the Fundamental Laws of Nature*, New York: Pantheon Books.

Weinberg, Steven (1998) "The revolution that didn't happen," *New York Review of Books* 45(15) (October 8): 48.

6   Objectivity and ethno-feminist critiques of science

Ann E. Cudd

Introduction: objectivity, science, and scientists

In the conference which generated this paper, the word "objectivity" was used often by the participants. Many of the scientists there claimed that scientists believe in "objective truth." They believe in the existence of an objective reality, and "if you don't," one of them added, "then you are welcome to take a step off my highrise balcony to test the hypothesis." Meanwhile, some of the "critics of science" attending the conference were saying things like "science is not objective," "truth is relative to a social practice," or "scientists are simply the high priests of modernism." Clearly there was disagreement; on what, however, was not so clear. It was equally clear that the two groups were often talking past one another. So let me begin to try to help clarify where we philosophers tend to begin: with some definitions.

Philosophers typically distinguish sharply between metaphysical claims— claims about what there is—and epistemic claims—claims about what we can know or have some warranted beliefs about. The claim that there is a real world apart from our individual ideas of the world is a metaphysical claim known as "realism." There are two main ways to be a realist. One can hold that reality consists in the ideas that are independent of any particular mind (thus my thinking something does not make it so), but are accessible to different minds, provided that they are in the right perceptual circumstance. This is an odd form of realism, known as "idealism," that has been held by only a relatively small number of philosophers, most importantly Bishop George Berkeley, an Irishman from the eighteenth century, but also by a few scientific luminaries, such as Ernst Mach. The scientists represented at our conference were more likely to be realists of the materialist stripe, however, materialists holding that there exists a material world apart from any observer of the world. Realism, whether of the idealist or materialist stripe, is a metaphysical position. Opposed to realism is relativism or anti-realism. Metaphysical relativism is the view that what there is depends on the observer. The more common term for this view these days is "anti-realism," probably to avoid the confusion that I am trying to explain away right now. With either term, there are many ways to be a metaphysical relativist or anti-realist. One might hold one's ontology relative to one's language, or one's scientific or religious theory, for example.

"Objectivity" is a confusing term because it is sometimes construed as a metaphysical claim and sometimes as an epistemic one. Metaphysical objectivists posit the existence of real objects. In this use "objectivity" means realism. "Objectivity" construed as an epistemic term, on the other hand, concerns the nature of our knowledge or possible knowledge of the world. (It also has an ethical connotation, but let us set that aside for the moment.) To have objective knowledge is, minimally, to go beyond one's subjective perception of the world, to reach outside, somehow, to a broader understanding of the world, more true to reality. Now if one could claim to know the nature of the material world, then that knowledge could be objective in both senses: it could be a realistic account of the world beyond one's senses. But given the human condition of uncertainty of the nature of the reality beyond one's senses, that claim is generally held by philosophers to be unwarranted. An alternative to understanding objectivity as grounded in the correspondence of theory to the world is to see it grounded in the process by which knowledge is pursued.

In the debate (or confusion) between the scientists and the critics of science, "objectivity" is usually meant in the metaphysical sense by the scientists and in the epistemic sense by the critics. Not to side with either one from the beginning, but merely for the sake of clarity, I shall use "realism" for the metaphysical claim that there exist real (and, I will assume, material) objects independent of all observers, and I shall use the term "objectivity" in its epistemic sense to characterize knowledge that somehow goes beyond the perception of the subject. With this distinction in hand, then, the scientists claim that there exists a real, material world, and the critics claim that science is not the only (or best or infallible) way to come to know that material world in a way that goes beyond their subjective prejudices. This is not to say that everything in the apparent disagreement can be chalked up to a semantic misunderstanding—there is still some real disagreement; we just have not located it yet.

I share with the scientists the realist metaphysical faith in the material world apart from us observers; I won't argue for it in this paper, but I won't be stepping off any balconies. I also agree with the critics that science is fallible, systematically, in its pursuit of objectivity, and this is the point I shall argue. By charging "systematic fallibility" I mean to claim that because science is practiced by human beings who must bring to their pursuits systematic prejudices and biases of various sorts, the science they produce will be systematically biased, and so, fallible. My focus in this chapter is to clarify and illustrate the ways that the social systems of race and gender impact science and bias its pursuit of the truth. (Other cognitive biases based on the physical limitations of human sensory apparatus, or on political, cultural, or religious differences among people also exist, but are beyond the scope of this chapter[1]). Perhaps this claim of fallibility is not threatening or surprising to scientists. That would be great news; controversy is not what I aim for. I hope to help to clarify the ways that race-, sex-, and gender-generated cognitive errors can infect the objectivity (in the epistemic sense of the term) of science. I hope thus to inspire better science, on science's own grounds, as well as on moral grounds. Feminist philosophers of science have already done much of the work in this direction. I shall mainly be reporting and illustrating what I see as the most defensible critique that emerges from this vast literature. If there is novelty here it is in the analogy I draw between the cognitive mistakes based on sex and gender biases on the one hand, and those mistakes that stem from racial biases on the other.

In this chapter I shall argue that science cannot be objective unless its practitioners seek constantly to uncover cognitive biases, such as those caused by the cognitive mistakes related to sex, gender, and race that I will examine here. Objectivity, in the sense that I mean the term, characterizes the processes of science when they are open to continual, and well-intentioned, scrutiny. Objectivity, in this view, is never a finished product, but only a characterization of the process, a process that is to be challenged constantly by both scientists and by the non-scientist critics of science, provided that they can show how the assumptions that they criticize science for make a difference, or could make a difference, to the outcome of scientific research. On this understanding of objectivity, then, it makes sense to talk in terms of degrees of more and less objectivity. A theory or a science is more objective if it is more open to considering criticisms of its assumptions or if the scientists in that branch of science are less biased than some other set of scientists. I have argued elsewhere that only the open, fair, social practice of science can secure objectivity for science; simply having chosen individuals adhere to rigorous hypothesis-testing will not do it, for such privileged scientists are likely to miss the ways that background assumptions skew their reading of the evidence (Cudd 1998). For science to be objective with respect to its race and gender biases, it will need to constantly challenge those biases by bringing in scientists from race and gender minorities.

The argument of the chapter runs as follows. First, I discuss the sex/gender distinction in order to introduce the feminist critique of science, and show how there is an analogue to race as a biological versus social category. Next, I continue the analogy between race and gender by showing how the cognitive mistakes based on sex and gender have analogues with those based on race. The heart of the chapter comes in the fourth section, where I illustrate these cognitive mistakes with scientific theories. I then conclude with remarks about how science might be pursued more objectively.

The analogy between sex/gender and race as biological/ social categories

The sex/gender distinction

Feminism begins with the distinction between sex and gender, so if we are to be clear on the feminist critique, we must begin here as well. Let us begin by drawing the distinction in the sharpest way possible, recognizing that we will have to dull the borders a bit upon further reflection.

Sex is a biological category. Males and females are the two sexes, though some have argued that there need to be a few more sex categories to include all the varieties of intersexed individuals. Basically, females are the sex that provides the eggs and males provide the sperm. But what counts as an egg or a sperm tends to be circularly defined in terms of whether the sex providing that gamete is female or male. Generally speaking, however, sperms are identified as whatever are the more numerous gametes in the species and eggs as the less numerous gametes. There are few other commonalities concerning characteristics of maleness and femaleness across species: in some species the males are larger while in others the females are; in some species the males are the aggressors while in others the females are; in some species the males bear the young inside their bodies, in some the females do so, and in some neither do so; in some species the males rear the young, in some the females do so, in some both do so, and in some neither do so. If we confine the distinction to humans, then we can say that there are some clear biological sexual differences. Nonetheless, while there is a lot of scientific work on human sexual difference, much of it is confused by another main way to categorize humans: by gender.

Gender is a social category. Men and women are the two genders that are normally found in societies, but many argue that large numbers of people do not neatly fit into one of them, or they fit into both, and some societies are said to have more than two. When we look closely at that division of the human species we find quite a wide range of meanings and overlap between the genders across societies. As Margaret Mead once put it, in some societies the men fish and the women weave, and in other societies the women fish and the men weave. But one nearly universal fact has been this, that in every society men are politically, religiously, and economically dominant and women subordinate. One of the main social functions of the category of gender has been to divide labor or social roles. As Mead added to her claim about gendered division of labor, whatever men do is seen as the more valuable activity. All societies practice some segregation by gender in division of labor. Most societies, including our own at present, practice a great deal of gender segregation in division of labor (Anker 1998).

Sex and gender do not match up one to one. That is, not all females are women and not all males are men, unless we dogmatically conflate the categories. For instance, if a woman is someone who wears clothing that is

socially classified as women's clothing, walks in a way that is socially classified as a woman's walk, performs labor that consists in caring for the physical
and emotional needs of others, is generally unaggressive, and has intimate
sexual relationships with men, then there are males who are women.[2] More
often, though, people do some things that are coded as masculine and some
that are coded as feminine, that is, they represent a mix of genders even
though they have one sex. For example, I am in a male-dominated profession, like to play and talk sports, wear men's clothing whenever I can get
away with it, and never wear makeup or carry an object that is classified as a
woman's purse. But I also take primary care of a child, clean the toilets in my
house, and identify with the oppressed condition of women around the globe.
I am clearly female (having given birth a couple of times, I am fairly certain
that scientists would classify me that way, even though I am now rendered
surgically sterile), but I am socially a mannish woman. I suspect that most
academic females are also mannish, otherwise we probably would not survive
in academia, as it is a workplace with masculine norms.

Does sex cause gender? I think that is an interesting question whose answer
is quite complex. Here is a possible scenario for how sex could have caused
gender initially.[3] Primitive conditions of survival and the sexual difference in
reproduction and lactation provided an economic incentive for human societies to invent gender. That is, because of the likelihood that any adult woman
would be pregnant or lactating at any given time, it was advantageous for
these societies to organize their labor activities by female/male categories,
since this provided a close approximation to reproducer/non-reproducer
categories, and one's reproducing status was highly correlated with the kinds
of subsistence activities one could otherwise engage in. It would not have
been necessary; they could have divided exactly between reproducer/non-
reproducer, or swift/slow, or large/small, or some other classification relevant
to their survival needs. That is, I suspect that sex does not necessarily cause
gender. But it was surely a salient, and efficient enough, way to categorize
persons, and so our ancestors chose to endow great social significance to
sexual difference and thereby invented gender. Since gender just was and is
the norms that socially classified sexual difference, sex and gender must have
started out to be very closely connected. But even from the beginning there
must have been those individuals for whom the gender categories chafed.
There were the females who were sterile or particularly strong, aggressive and
swift. Or the males who were slow, or nurturing, or not aggressive. So to
maintain the link with sex, gender must have been enforced with strong coer-
cive measures, as we find even now in many cultures. The need for such
coercion is more evidence for its being socially constructed. Now that there is
no survival need for this sharp distinction between the sexes, gender has
strayed farther away from its connection with sex. The prevalence of gender
norm violations is evidence for this, thus it is not clear that sex causes gender
any more. Whether or in what form gender will survive the next millennium
is an interesting question, indeed. What vital social function could it serve

that would preserve it in the face of pressures from individuals to violate its norms?

Race as biological / social categories

We can draw an analogy between sex and gender categories on the one hand and race on the other in the following sense. Like sex, race has some biologically rooted characteristics. There are some, relatively trivial, biological differences among peoples whose descendants came from, or perhaps stayed for a very long time on, various parts of the earth. Some groups of people have dark skin, black hair, and brown eyes, others have light skin, blonde, red, or light brown hair, and blue, green, or brown eyes. Some are shorter on average and some taller on average; some are slighter and some more muscular on average. In some groups genetic diseases of one sort or another are common and in others unheard of. In some groups one blood type is common and another rare. We think of race as categorizing people by clusters of these traits, and therefore assume that there are clear biologically marked necessary and sufficient conditions for group membership in one or another race. But this common assumption is wrong: the groupings by "race" cut across these differences, and there is more variation within races than between them for each of these traits. Unlike for sex, there is no single genetic marker for race; race is a loosely defined cluster of traits, a mere "family resemblance" concept as Wittgenstein used the term in a quite different context.

Biology is not all there is to race. In fact, as many race theorists have argued, biology is very little of what there is to race. Like gender, race is primarily a social category that people identify with styles of dress, mannerisms, ways of talking or being intimate with others, family structures, religious beliefs, and many other things besides skin color, hair texture, or blood type. Race is an identifiable feature of us; we classify each other by race immediately upon meeting one another, and our initial classifications are almost always consistent with those of others, including the classified. Many societies use racial categories to divide labor; many societies still practice segregation of racial groups to a greater or lesser extent. Race is a real, materially consequential fact about us. But it is rooted in our cultures, our families, and our social institutions and practices more than in our genes.

There are many ways to show that race as a biological category does not link up with race as a social category. In our society some very light-skinned persons are racially classified as Black and some very dark-skinned ones as White. There is the so-called one-drop rule: one drop of so-called "black blood," that is, a single black ancestor, makes a person Black (although approximately 6 percent of Whites have Black ancestry—somehow they have skirted the rule) (Zack 1998: 20). It is possible for people who descend from many different ethnic groupings to "pass" as white, and the fact that there are incentives to "pass" show that race is more a social than a biological category. Furthermore, while non-White categories are finely divided in our society, by such race-producing institutions as the US Census, "White" is presented as a univocal category covering a wide variety of European ethnicities.[4] Meanwhile, the category "Hispanic" covers a wide range of ethnicities and skin colors, and is intended to comprise persons from, or descended from, persons from Central and South America. The point of differentiating Hispanics but not various categories of Whites must surely be to keep tabs on immigration patterns that we, as a nation, would like to control. Racial categories as we commonly and formally use them are clearly more socially and politically than biologically grounded.

Unlike sex, race as a biological category is disappearing. As groups migrate and interbreed, they have become and will continue to become more and more mixed biologically. There is no longer a set of distinct biological racial characteristics that set groups apart. The only way to maintain the distinctions is through the social categorization, by membership of other family members and memberships in other social institutions that mark race. Meanwhile, the category of "other" on the Census forms becomes more and more heavily populated. However, just because race disappears as a coherent biological category, this will not mean that race ceases to exist as a category. As long as race retains its social meaning and significance, that is, as long as people divide and are categorized by "race" (meaning some aspect of skin color, hair color, or ethnic descent) in ways that have political, economic, and religious significance, race as a social category exists. Whether race as a social categorization system will survive the next millennium is another interesting question.

Three categories of race and gender-related mistakes that can infect science and scientific theory[5]

Sexism and racism

Sexism is the denigration of one sex or gender, typically females and women. Racism is the denigration of one race, whether biologically or socially defined. The most familiar type of sexism and racism is a normative judgment of inferiority of a race or a sex. For example, "women are intellectually inferior." This is not to be confused with purely descriptive claims, such as, "women on average score lower on the Quantitative section of the GRE." It is also sexist to mistake a social fact about, or construction of, sex or race for a natural or essential feature of that sex or race, for example, to infer from the fact that women on average score lower on the Quantitative section of the GRE that there is some natural or genetic basis for these scores. There may be some natural or genetic basis for this fact, but that cannot be directly inferred. The social effects of gender (like those of race) contribute enormously to the perceived differences among human capacities, and that fact makes any easy inference from a perception of difference to an attribution of natural or essential difference illegitimate.

My definitions of the terms "racism" and "sexism" focus simply on the effect of the phenomena, and do not attribute a cause. I do this to avoid needless controversy here;[6] whatever the cause, I claim that sexism and racism are cognitive mistakes. Minimally, they are mistakes for science because they mix the normative judgment of inferiority into theories that are supposed to remain descriptive. Both sexism and racism can be unconscious, as well as conscious. Sexism and racism can be part of the unstated and unrecognized assumptions of a theory. In fact, this is the place where they are most likely to be, although most difficult to find, prove, and change. That sexism and racism can have pernicious social consequences, is, I hope, a point that requires no argument. As I have defined them, the first type of sexism and racism always involves normative moral, social, or political judgments, that is, it involves value judgments. As such, the official scientific method rules them out as illegitimate assertions or assumptions. But that does not mean that they do not continue to affect science, as I shall show in the next section of this chapter. The second type of sexism and racism, however, does not necessarily involve normative value judgments. The problem here, rather, is the reckless willingness to believe in innate or essential differences. In these cases science would also seem to be self-correcting: scientists just have to pursue every possible cause of difference. But again, as we shall see, scientists can be blinded by their essentialist presuppositions for a long time.

Sexism infects a scientific theory when it asserts that women are inferior to men, that women are properly subordinated to men, or that women should be confined to gender-stereotyped roles, or when it asserts a double standard for judging men and women. Some scientific theories assert the inferiority of females intellectually and physically.[7] These theories are premised on the social inferiority of women economically, politically, and in the public institutions of the arts and sciences. Science, as an institution, is sexist. It is harder for equally qualified women to earn the same authority, or conduct their research as easily and with as much support, as men.[8] Racism infects a scientific theory when it asserts that one race (biologically or socially defined) is inferior to some other(s), that some race or races are properly subordinated to others, or that some race or races should be confined to racially stereotyped roles, or when it asserts a double standard for judging persons of different races. In the next section of this chapter, I discuss a famous example of biological theories of the racial inferiority of non-White "races." Science as an institution is also racist in that scientists who are racial minorities face barriers to equal opportunity (Pearson 1985; Guthrie 1997).

Androcentrism and ethnocentrism

Androcentrism infects a scientific theory when the theory assumes that the experiences, biology, and social roles of males or men are the norm and that of females or women a deviation from the norm. Ethnocentrism infects a scientific theory when it assumes that the experiences, biologically based or socially created physical attributes or medical problems, and social roles of people of a particular ethnic or racial background are the norm and those with other backgrounds are deviations from the norm. Like sexism and racism, androcentrism and ethnocentrism may be explicit or implicit, conscious or unconscious. Androcentrism and ethnocentrism reflect the interests of scientists, most of whom, in part because of the sexism and racism of science, are White men. But they are not necessarily moral, political, or social values. They might well be characterized as epistemic values, that is, as assertions of what is most interesting to study. And this kind of value judgment is not ruled out by the official scientific method. After all, scientists, funding agencies, and journal editors make judgments all the time about whether a line of research is interesting. Such judgments are sometimes completely internal to the scientific theory, but many other times they have subtle or not-so-subtle external motivations. Research that meets a recognized social need is interesting by that fact alone. Funding agencies motivate such research explicitly, through requests for proposals that require it explicitly and that then require the agency referees to judge the proposals by the degree to which they meet that interest. There are also more subtle motivations to finding some subject interesting. Until women entered the economics profession in significant numbers, the gender wage gap and the value of domestic unpaid labor were not considered topics of general economic interest and there were almost no economists working on these topics.

If the full range of genders and races were represented in the sciences in roughly equal numbers, and if women and racial minorities had roughly equal financial and social power in society generally, we might expect that there would be enough gender- and race-related interest in each sort of grouping so that science as a whole could not be seen as androcentric or ethnocentric. But as this is not the case, that is, as science is dominated by the dominant gender and race in our society, science is often androcentric and ethnocentric.

There are both epistemic and social consequences to androcentrism and ethnocentrism. The epistemic consequence is that for some kinds of scientific theories, particularly biological and social scientific theories, the questions and focus of research are on only part of the phenomena and the answers are thus only partial. The social consequence is that, because of science's close relation to and influence over technological development and public policy formation, these in turn are biased in whatever ways the relevant scientific theories are partial.

Gender symbolism and racial symbolism

We often code our ideas, theories, and methods as masculine or feminine, White or ethnic, and this is true of scientific ideas, theories, and methods as well. What I mean by saying that we "code" ideas with gender or race is that we associate them with the experiences and values that are likewise thought to be somehow raced or gendered. This coding is clearly hierarchical. Whatever is coded masculine is better than that coded feminine; what is coded White is better than that coded non-White or ethnic.

Some methodologies for data-gathering are coded as feminine or ethnic. Interviewing, participant observation, and the use of orally transmitted stories as sources of scientific data are considered informal and less credible sources of knowledge. Personal knowledge, the kind of information that is gained by virtue of lived experience, is considered to be an inferior kind of knowledge than theoretical knowledge, the kind of information generated by theory, mathematical model, and controlled experiment (Collins 1990). Theoretical knowledge, knowledge gained through the scientific methods of hypothesis formation, experimental test, and statistical sampling, or through logical deduction and mathematical proof, is thought to be masculine and White, precisely because it avoids the personal and claims therefore to be objective and impartial.

Theoretical knowledge is valued over personal knowledge by the sciences. Thus information gained through theoretical methods trump personal experiences in the search for and justification of scientific knowledge. For much of what the sciences do, it makes sense to hold theoretical knowledge above personal knowledge. Yet there is information that can be gained only through personal knowledge, and so for science to close itself off from or denigrate this source is a cognitive mistake.

The coding goes both ways, however, and this is perhaps the greater mistake in science. That is, the interests pursued or knowledge gained by women and non-Whites is suspiciously viewed, as if it must be based on "mere" personal knowledge, which is held to be epistemically inferior. Meanwhile, the interests pursued and knowledge gained by men and Whites is assumed to be objectively, impartially generated. Worse, residual and typically unconscious sexism in the minds of scientists, whether male or female, leads to women scientists' ideas being less initially credible and hence less likely to be accepted or as readily accepted despite their purely cognitive scientific merits. The geneticist Barbara McClintock's work on transposition is a good example of a discovery which, because it was by a woman, was denigrated and overlooked for many years. Thus when women or non-White scientists employ conventional scientific methodology their results are still suspect.

Gender and racial or ethnic symbolism also affects the content of theories. Evelyn Fox Keller has done a great deal of work illustrating the gender symbolism in mathematical biology, where models of genetics as a field of competition and self-interest have dominated to the point of excluding models that postulate cooperation. Keller illustrates this with McClintock's theory, which Keller likens to modeling a conversation within the organism between the DNA and its cellular environment, rather than DNA as the master molecule dominating the rest of the organism and ordering all the other cells around. Keller attributes the difficulties McClintock had in getting her theory accepted in part to the masculinist urge to see dominance relations in nature (Keller 1985).

The point of noting gender symbolism in scientific models is not to suggest that the models ought not to incorporate sexist, racist, Eurocentric, or patriarchal images—whatever leads to good, fruitful science is legitimate epistemically. There should be no *a priori* limits about what can be a good model of some phenomenon. The point is rather that the models then tend to borrow their cognitive authority from the political ideology that they endorse, and then competing models that do not endorse a dominant political ideology have a more difficult time being accepted, even when they are scientifically better models.

Examples

I now discuss three examples of scientific work that has been clouded by the mistakes that I have described above. The first comes from biology, the second from economics, and the third from archeology and paleontology.

Biological theories of intelligence

In his book *The Mismeasure of Man*, Stephen Jay Gould examines and debunks the wide range of attempts in the past three centuries to discover a link between race and intelligence. His careful attention to the detail of the experiments and measurements makes his book an impressive chronicle of scientific failures. Gould argues that most of these scientific theories were widely accepted during their time because of the ways that they reflected the cultural beliefs about race. Had any one of these intelligence scientists come up with the conclusion that African-descended peoples were the most intelligent of all humans, the theories would never have been accepted.

Some of the theories were clearly motivated by blatant, conscious racism; others seem to have been legitimate, that is, scientifically motivated, attempts to inquire about the origins of the human races, without any conscious attempt to fix the outcome of the inquiry in advance. For example, Gould repeated the measurements of Samuel George Morton, who, in the mid-nineteenth century, measured hundreds of human skulls from around the world, both contemporary and ancient, including American Indians, "Negroes," "Hindus," "Mongolians," and "Caucasians." Replicating the social beliefs at the time concerning the relative intelligence of the groups, the Caucasian skulls came out largest, followed by the Mongolians, followed by the Negroes, followed finally by the American Indians. What Gould learned by repeating the measurements was that Morton "fudged" and "finagled" the data in myriad ways. First, Morton failed to weight the various subgroups by the relative numbers in the actual population, so that a group with a small number of persons but for which he happened to have a large number of skulls would have an unusually large effect on the outcome of the population's number as a whole. Second, he failed to consistently include equal numbers of both sexes. Since overall body size is highly correlated with skull size, a group for which he happened to have a large number of female skulls would appear to have smaller skulls on average. These errors might have washed out; after all, they are not necessarily going to favor the Caucasians and disfavor the Negroes. But the third sort of problem that Gould noted with the data is that Morton systematically excluded the larger-stature subpopulations from the groups where he expected a smaller skull and included a disproportionate number of skulls from subpopulations of smaller-stature people. He left out some of the larger Asian Indian skulls from the Mongolian grouping, and included a disproportionate number of the smaller Peruvian skulls from the American Indian grouping. Now this mistake might be chalked up to blatant, conscious racism. But that would miss the more significant implication for science, I think. As Gould points out, the fact that Morton so meticulously recorded his data shows that he did not think of himself as committing scientific fraud. In choosing among skulls I would suggest that he thought he was getting a "more representative" value for the various populations. First, we must remember that Morton and his contemporaries held a highly Eurocentric view of the relative value of European culture. Second, they reasoned, fallaciously, that since European culture was the "most highly developed," Europeans must be the most intelligent people. So, if one "knows" that Mongolian people are less intelligent than Caucasian people (and thinks that brain size is a good proxy measure of intelligence), then it must be the case that the largest (skull-wise) subpopulation of the Mongolians must be at the outer edge of Mongolianism and nearing Caucasianism in the racial continuum of the species. In other words, those with larger—more Caucasian-like—skulls would not be central examples of the race. Hence a true picture of the race can only be gleaned by eliminating those marginal examples. Or so one might reason in the grip of an unquestioned ideology of Eurosupremacy.

Gould reports that when the corrections are made there are "no significant differences among races for Morton's own data" (Gould 1996: 67). But, more importantly, I hasten to add (as a small-stature female) there is no reason to believe that intelligence correlates with skull size to begin with. Throughout his book Gould chronicles the search of scientists for a single measure of intelligence, a search which goes through an amazing array of different contortions and which would be highly amusing if it were not so horrifically linked to the attempt to rationalize the subordination of non-Whites and women.

This example, and the other intelligence studies that Gould investigates, reveal all three of the race-bias cognitive mistakes that I have discussed above. Clearly the studies are racist in claiming, falsely (not to mention circularly), the inferiority of non-Whites to Whites in terms of skull size and the many other proxies for intelligence that have been devised. They are Eurocentric in their assumptions that Europeans must be the smartest because European civilization is the best. And the theories, despite their obvious obtuseness in hindsight, were given an enormous amount of credibility because they reinforced the common view of the order of the races (not to mention the sexes).

Economics of the family

Even though "economics" comes from the Greek *oikonomikos*, meaning of or pertaining to household management, the family has been much neglected by economic theory in the past. Today we still see textbooks in which the family is overlooked in lists of important social institutions. In the history of the discipline we can see two basic models of the family: the "household as individual (and father as head of it)" model, and recently, under the influence of feminist economics and the women's movement generally, the "competing-but-unequal-agent model." The first of these we can trace at least to Hobbes, but perhaps is best summarized by the words of the early nineteenth-century economist James Mill:

> One thing is pretty clear, that all those individuals whose interests are indisputably included in those of other individuals may be struck off without inconvenience. In this light may be viewed all children, up to a certain age, whose interests are involved in those of their parents. In this light also, women may be regarded, the interests of almost all of whom is [*sic*] involved either in that of their fathers or in that of their husbands.
>
> (Quoted in Folbre and Hartmann 1988: 188)

This model assumes that women are under the protection of sovereign men, either husbands or fathers, and that men would provide this protection without undue selfishness. It made attention to the family unnecessary theoretically; economic theory could assume that the only individuals that existed might or might not come attached with wife and family, but that data would be irrelevant to the theory. Modeling the economy of the household would be like modeling the economy of the individual—uninteresting.

In the 1960s economic theory began to take a look at the family with what is called the "new home economics." The 1992 Nobel Prize in Economics was awarded to the founder of the new home economics, Gary Becker of the University of Chicago, "for having extended the domain of microeconomic analysis to a wide range of human behavior and interaction, including non-market behavior." Becker's motivation was to try to apply economic theory to all sorts of areas of behavior that had been overlooked by mainstream economics: crime, animal behavior, and drug use, to name but a few. Becker uses the same basic model of the family as Hobbes and Mill, however. He models the family as acting to maximize total utility (that is, as an individual), with an altruistic head of the family (Becker 1981). He first endows each member of the family with an individual utility function that she or he tries to maximize. Then he shows, in what he terms the "Rotten Kid Theorem," that if there is an altruistic family member, by which he means a member whose utility function has other family members' utilities as arguments, then it is rational for the selfish members of the family to act to maximize total family utility as well. Thus rational families have male heads who lead by example, persuading their naturally selfish charges to do what is in the best interest of the family as a whole.

Well, there is no arguing with mathematics. Somewhat concealed by the mathematics, however, are three other critical assumptions: (1) wealth or control of income is unequally distributed so that the altruist is able to redistribute income to maximize his utility function (I use "his" here because Becker quite explicitly assumes that the altruist is the father); (2) the egoists in the family (including the altruist's wife) have no better option than the one that the altruist gives them, such as leaving the family; (3) the use of the pejorative term "altruist" presumes that his utility function ought to be maximized, without regard to what he wants; the "altruist" might think it in the best interests of the family to move a thousand miles away, and that counts as altruistic simply because it is the aim of the one in control of the wealth and income of the family. Becker thus understands the family as an altruistic institution led by a benevolent dictator. In such a situation, there is no need for the intrusion of law since there is no competition for resources. The father's paternalistic wishes are to be fulfilled; the legal status quo of the 1960s is justified; inequality within the family is not an issue. Becker speculates, then, that marriage must have evolved as a deal to protect women.

Becker's analysis thus makes the following mistakes: first, like economists before him, he continues in the androcentric view that intrafamily economics is uninteresting. There are no separate preferences being considered here, and no outside options that could constitute a strategic threat to the "altruist's" aims. Second, he makes the sexist assumption that the "head of the family" is male and altruistic, while the other spouse is female and, like the children, egoistic. Third, he fails to model the full range of options for the spouses by assuming that they cannot leave the family, and this reinforces his sexist assumption that families maximize a single utility function, which in turn reinforces the androcentric idea that what happens within families is devoid of economic interest. We can see how great his errors are in modeling by testing his conclusions against empirical experience. His conclusion that marriage is a deal to protect women is refuted by the empirical evidence that women have been exploited and oppressed by marriage, for instance, by longstanding and even legally sanctioned spousal abuse, by the fact that married women were until relatively recently prohibited from owning property, by unequal divorce laws, and by countless other laws and norms that constitute the double standard for married men and women. Economics as a science, especially the economics of the family, is used not so much for precise predictions, but rather as a rough guide for predicting how individual motivations could be influenced by social policy. It is true that which gender the head of the household is assigned does not matter to the mathematics. But it does matter to the perceived usefulness and subsequent influence of the theory. If Becker had called the head of household the wife, and the outcome of his theory had been to recommend that wives be given complete control over family resources in order to maximize family welfare, then the theory would not have made the impact it did. Thus Becker's mistaken sexist and androcentric assumptions are both especially (morally) egregious and especially (from the perspective of gaining cognitive authority) effective.

If his work is so mistaken, how do we explain his Nobel Prize? Here is where the mistake of gender symbolism infected the judgment of his peers. His theory is just the kind of thing that economists love: it extends the neoclassical economic approach to a new area, the family, yet appears to vindicate the longstanding tradition of overlooking intrafamily economic issues, while justifying the political status quo concerning gender relations. Economics is a highly male-dominated profession. Women comprise only 13 percent of the economics faculty in America.[9] Thus the comfortable, sexist, and gendered political ideology of the theory for economists lent cognitive authority to the theory that it did not warrant scientifically.

Paleontology and theories of human origins

It is easy enough for us to be amused by the errors of nineteenth-century scientists, and chalk them up to preposterous racial prejudices. But before we conclude that such prejudice does not affect the sciences today, let us consider another plausible scenario for how race-based cognitive mistakes may be invading contemporary science. In *Red Earth, White Lies*, Vine Deloria, Jr. criticizes the Bering Straits theory of the migration of peoples from Asia to the Americas via a land bridge that was supposed to have existed between thirteen and twenty-three thousand years ago between those continents (Deloria 1995: Chapter 4). Deloria argues that although this theory is taken to be simply common knowledge by most White or non-American Indian people, including scholars and scientists in a wide range of disciplines, it is a highly dubious theory with very little evidence to support it. (Indeed, I myself was very surprised to learn that there were any questions about this theory— I thought it was well-established fact until I read this book.) However, the Bering Straits theory is supported by many cultural assumptions and prejudices that non-Indians have about American Indians.

Deloria first discusses the evidence put forward in favor of the theory that a land bridge existed in the time period stated above. This basically consists in a deduction from the fact that American Indians exist on the North American continent and the theory that they migrated from Asia. If people migrated from Asia, they could either have come by land or by sea. Ruling out sea travel as implausibly complex for these people, this leaves the land bridge option. So the evidence in favor of the land bridge consists in showing that it is possible that there was a land bridge at about the right time. The only plausible time period for the land bridge to have existed is the glacial period that occurred between thirteen and twenty-three thousand years ago, when glaciers might have covered the expanse between what are now Alaska and Siberia, the area now called the Bering Straits.

Deloria then asks the following questions about this evidence. First, what evidence is there that any Paleo-Indians crossed a land bridge at the Bering

Straits? The answer is none, other than the indirect inferences alluded to above. Second, there is reason to be dubious about the nature of the trip across the bridge. There was nothing to eat on the bridge, and no guarantee that it would lead somewhere with something to eat. Deloria argues that there are formidable mountain ranges between the place in Siberia that the Paleo-Indians must have been coming from and the hypothesized land bridge. Then there are some forbidding mountain ranges in Alaska between the land bridge and anywhere that the people would want to settle. Why would they make the trip, and what makes it logistically easier than a sea voyage? Third, there seems to be little motivation for making the trip. The conditions in Alaska were boggy and severe, and therefore did not provide much of an incentive to migrate. Again, what would have been the motivation for people to cross the land bridge or, once over, to stay? Finally, Deloria suggests that the premise upon which the whole theory is predicated might be flawed if there is evidence, as he believes there is, that Paleo-Indians did not originally migrate from Asia. What makes us so certain of the migration and its supposed direction?

Deloria believes that there are several background assumptions that keep the otherwise poorly supported Bering Straits land bridge theory afloat. These assumptions commit or transmit the race-based cognitive errors that I have identified. One is the assumption that the American Indians must have migrated, and must have migrated from Asia. This assumption is in turn supported by the comfortable (Eurocentric) view for European Americans that the American Indians are immigrants to this land, too; they just came a little earlier than the Europeans. Another is the assumption that the migration must have occurred by land, because the logistics of sea travel would have been beyond the technical knowledge of the people involved. But this is based on nothing but either a racist denigration of their intelligence, or a dubious theory about the chronology of discovery—that it must somehow mirror the chronology of Western science and technology another piece of Eurocentrism. Meanwhile, the work done by Thor Heyrdahl to recreate long sea passages by other ancient peoples suggests the real possibility of migration by sea. Lastly, Deloria discusses what I would call the negative evidence against the Bering Straits land bridge theory that is completely ignored by most contemporary scientists working in related fields: that the American Indian creation stories make no reference whatsoever, no matter how metaphorical or glancing, to any such migration. This is where I want to argue that the racial coding of theories plays a role: because such orally transmitted knowledge cannot count as scientific, the creation stories of American Indians cannot be counted even as evidence against a theory, even one as poorly supported as this one. Yet this seems to me to be clearly a mistake. The myths of the American Indians are surely full of metaphor and entertaining aspects, but as this is the major way that entire groups of people transmitted their collective knowledge, there must also be some truth-value in them. To ignore them as a possible source of evidence about the history of the peopling of the Americas is to make a cognitive mistake.

Conclusion

These examples reveal how recognizing the influences of race and gender on science makes science better on science's own terms, namely the openminded pursuit of truth. By looking out for gender- and race-based cognitive mistakes we are better able to spot the influences in the directions scientific theorizing takes, the mistakes in theory construction, and the mistakes in the assignment of empirically unwarranted cognitive authority to particular scientific models. As a result of scientists' identification of these errors, new and better theories, models, and methodologies can be created. Furthermore, recognizing that scientists are under these influences and make these mistakes does not impugn the objectivity of science, properly understood. Recall how I characterized objectivity: a theory or a science is more objective if it is more open to considering criticisms of its assumptions or if the scientists in that branch of science are less biased than some other theory or set of scientists. Clearly, then, if criticism of science on the grounds that it is gender biased or racially biased is allowed free and open discussion and investigation, then science is more objective. These remarks suggest that we, both scientists and the public who will be subject to the technology and public policy informed by science, will be better off with more feminist and racially conscious scientists.

Notes

1 Although political, cultural, and religious differences appear to be quite similar to differences based on sex, gender, or race, there is a crucial difference for the arguments of this paper. Namely, the former associations are voluntary, while the latter are, for all intents and purposes, inborn and involuntary. Different issues arise concerning discrimination against these two types of group membership. For example, while it may be appropriate scientifically to discriminate when hiring or funding biologists against people who hold religious creationist theories, it is not appropriate scientifically to discriminate against women biologists.
2 It should be noted that this is a culturally specific description of femininity. Gender differs radically across culture, including across racial and ethnic subcultures.
3 Since there is no empirical evidence on the matter, I hope that the reader will indulge (but not put too much store in) my *a priori* speculations a little.
4 On the complexities and historical idiosyncrasies of race categorization by the Census, see Goldberg (1997, especially Chapter 3).
5 In this section I owe much to the feminist analysis of Anderson (1995).
6 Goldberg (1997: Chapter 2) characterizes this controversy as one between whether hate (racial animus) or a desire to maintain social power (group self-interest) is the root cause of racism (and by extension, sexism). I would agree with Goldberg that it is more the latter than the former, but that is irrelevant to the argument of this chapter.
7 Fausto-Sterling (1985) selects and debunks a number of theories that purport to show the biological inferiority of women.
8 A Swedish study, for example, recently showed that women applicants for biomedical research grants in that country have had to be 2.5 times as good as men, as judged by objective measures of quality and quantity of publications, to get the same funding. See "Shameful," *The Economist*, May 24, 1997: 79. A recent discovery by

women professors at MIT found that women were required to raise twice the amount in grant funding to receive equal treatment in terms of tenure and promotion, office and lab space, and salary. See Zernike (1999).

9 Committee on the Status of Women in the Economics Profession, 1998 Annual Report, table 1; http://www.denison.edu/economics/cswep/annual/1998ar.html

Bibliography

Anderson, E. (1995) "Feminist epistemology: an interpretation and a defense," *Hypatia* 10: 50–84.

Anker, R. (1998) *Gender and Jobs: Sex Segregation of Occupations in the World*, Geneva: International Labour Office.

Becker, G. (1981) *A Treatise on the Family*, Cambridge: Harvard University Press.

Collins, P. H. (1990) *Black Feminist Thought*, New York: HarperCollins Academic.

Cudd, A. E. (1998) "Multiculturalism as a cognitive virtue of scientific practice," *Hypatia* 13: 43–61.

Deloria, V., Jr (1995) *Red Earth, White Lies*, New York: Scribner.

Fausto-Sterling, A. (1985) *Myths of Gender*, New York: Basic Books.

Folbre, N. and Hartmann, H. (1988) "The rhetoric of self-interest: ideology and gender in economic theory," in Klamer, Arjo, McCloskey, Donald N., and Solow, Robert (eds) *The Consequences of Economic Rhetoric*, New York: Cambridge University Press.

Goldberg, D. T. (1997) *Racial Subjects*, New York: Routledge.

Gould, S. J. (1996) *The Mismeasure of Man*, revised edn, New York: W. W. Norton.

Guthrie, R. V. (1997) *Even the Rat was White*, Upper Saddle River, NJ: Prentice Hall.

Keller, E. F. (1985) *Reflections on Gender and Science*, New Haven, CT: Yale University Press.

Pearson, W., Jr (1985) *Black Scientists, White Society, and Colorless Science*, Millwood, NY: Associated Faculty Press.

Zack, N. (1998) *Thinking About Race* Belmont, CA: Wadsworth.

Zernike, Kate (1999) "MIT women win a fight against bias," *Boston Globe*, March 21, A1.

7 Measuring the Hubble constant
Objectivity under the telescope

Keith M. Ashman

The value of disagreement

In the sixteenth and seventeenth centuries, there was a heated debate concerning the motion of the heavenly bodies and the place of the Earth in the universe. Some advocated the Ptolemaic model, in which the Sun, Moon, planets, and stars all traveled on circular orbits around a stationary Earth. Others held that the Copernican model, in which the Earth and other bodies revolve around the Sun on circular orbits, was correct. Both models were heavily influenced by considerations that seem, to modern-day scientists, to be unscientific. Most notably, the assumption of circular motion of the heavenly bodies stemmed from astrological and religious concepts originating in Babylonia and Egypt and adopted by the Greeks. The Earth was regarded as the corrupt realm of humankind, whereas the heavens were supposed to be perfect. For the Greeks, this perfection equated to circular motion. These ideas were first formalized by Aristotle and later developed by Ptolemy into what became known as the Ptolemaic model. Copernicus made the intellectual leap of moving the Earth from the center of the universe, but retained the idea of circular motion.

The two models predicted the positions of the Sun, Moon, planets, and stars with comparable accuracy, so additional observational tests were required in order to distinguish between the two models.[1] Empirically, the planet Venus is always observed to be fairly close to the Sun in the sky. In the Ptolemaic model, this observation is explained by tying down Venus to a line between the Earth and the Sun, so that Venus is always physically positioned on the near side of the Sun relative to Earth. In contrast, the Copernican model predicts that Venus spends some of its time on the far side of the Sun. This difference in the range of relative positions of the Sun, Earth and Venus in the two models leads to different predictions for the observed phases of Venus. (It was generally understood at this time that the Moon and planets "shine" through reflected sunlight. The "phase" of a planet is thus directly analogous to the phase of the Moon: it is that portion of the body illuminated by the Sun as seen from Earth.) Specifically, in the Ptolemaic model Venus only shows a crescent phase, whereas in the Copernican model Venus exhibits a full range of phases. The phases of Venus are not visible with the naked eye, but are easily detected with a small telescope. Galileo carried out such observations and found that Venus does go through a full range of phases. This effectively ruled out the Ptolemaic model.[2]

While this episode is more commonly remembered for the friction it produced between Galileo and the Roman Catholic Church, it also illustrates that disagreement between researchers is often the catalyst that produces a deeper understanding of physical systems. For example, a leading advocate of an Earth-centered universe, Tycho Brahe, spent many years measuring the positions of the planets to a high degree of precision. These data were subsequently used by Johannes Kepler to show that the Copernican model was also faulty, and that the Earth and planets travel around the Sun on elliptical rather than circular orbits. There are many other examples in the natural sciences in which these kinds of disagreements have ultimately led to theoretical advances.

The so-called "science wars" represent, to a large extent, a disagreement about the nature and process of science. As discussed elsewhere in this volume, a key element of this disagreement is the assertion by natural scientists that science is in some sense objective, and a range of positions held by some philosophers and sociologists of science that in different ways reject this notion of objectivity. Can we anticipate that the disagreement between scientists and their critics will lead to theoretical advances in the understanding of science? There are several reasons to be pessimistic. As Shank *et al.* (this volume) emphasize, simply finding a common language for scientists and their critics is a challenge. An issue which may be related, and which motivated much of this chapter, is that most scientists find it extremely difficult to connect the work that is emanating from many science studies programs to their experience of carrying out scientific research. (I make this statement not on the basis of a scientific poll of scientists, but from conversations with many colleagues in the sciences who have some familiarity with these issues.) For example, it is difficult to imagine how a scientist could accept any analysis of science that claims that the nature of the physical world is of little consequence in the formulation of scientific theories (see Sokal, this volume, and references therein).

Since few natural scientists are also philosophers or sociologists, it seems inevitable that many scientists will miss some of the subtleties of research in science studies. However, it strikes me as extremely unlikely that ignorance alone explains the gulf between scientists and the critics of science. There is a genuine disagreement here, with the question of the objectivity of science being one of the key elements. Further, when sixteenth-century astronomers were debating the nature of the solar system, the scientists involved agreed on the rules of the debate. The issue would be decided by empirical evidence. As I discuss in "Bridging the gulf," below, present-day scientists and their critics do not agree on the rules of the debate.

In this paper I focus on the claim that scientific knowledge is objective in the sense that it transcends the potentially subjective viewpoints of individual scientists. (In other words, the epistemic meaning of "objectivity" discussed by Cudd in this volume.) I support this claim using a recent disagreement among astronomers that persisted for almost two decades concerning a measurable quantity known as the Hubble constant. During this period, it appeared that the value of this quantity depended on the group of scientists measuring it. Since astronomical constants are assumed, at least by scientists, to reflect the nature of the universe rather than the members of a research group, this disagreement was quite troubling. However, to the satisfaction of nearly everyone in the field, this disagreement has now been resolved and, in the view of astronomers, we have a more accurate understanding of the universe as a result. My primary goal in presenting this account is to show, through a specific and contemporary example, how the process of science operates. I claim that the scientists involved in this research were, to a degree, influenced by sociological and cultural factors, but that despite these influences, the self-correcting nature of the process of science ensured that such influences were eventually purged. This example also illustrates the value of disagreement in advancing scientific knowledge. Having presented this admittedly restricted evidence that science is objective, I return to the debate between science and its critics and the prospects for future resolution. My attempts at sociological and philosophical commentary are necessarily those of an amateur, but I feel that one way of bridging the gap between scientists and their critics is for scientists to present their experience of the process of science.

One final comment on the content of this chapter. I have given quite a detailed discussion of some of the technical issues involved in determining the Hubble constant, particularly in the following section. Many of these details can be skimmed without losing the main thrust of my argument. However, I chose to include this discussion because I felt that it might provide an interesting contrast to the contributions of sociologists and philosophers of science presented elsewhere in this volume. I have found marked differences between research papers and popular articles written by natural scientists and those written by some members of the science studies community. I believe it is important to recognize and understand these and other operational differences between practitioners of different disciplines if we genuinely hope to bridge the gap between them.

The Hubble constant controversy

The Hubble constant is an observable measure of the expansion rate of the universe. For many years, empirical determinations of the Hubble constant produced controversy, with one research group repeatedly obtaining a value a factor of two higher than that found by a second group. In order to explain fully the nature of this controversy and its relevance to the question of the objectivity of science, it is useful to provide some historical background and a description of what the Hubble constant is and how it is measured.

Hubble's law

It has been nearly four hundred years since Galileo provided the crucial evidence that placed the Sun rather than the Earth at the center of the solar system. During this time, technological and theoretical advances have led to a deeper understanding of the physical universe. It is now known, for example, that the Sun is a rather ordinary star located in a galaxy containing roughly one hundred billion stars. Our home galaxy, the Milky Way, is visible to the unaided eye on clear, dark nights as a band of fuzzy light stretching across the sky. Astronomers have observed a vast number of other galaxies, many of which are similar to our own.

Astronomy is an observational rather than an experimental science. For the most part, astronomers do not set up controlled experiments in the laboratory to investigate phenomena. Instead they are restricted to observing the constituents of the universe. In the case of galaxies, it is relatively straightforward to measure their "radial velocity." This is simply the speed at which a galaxy is moving towards or away from an observer on Earth. The technique takes advantage of a phenomenon known as the "Doppler shift." If a source of light, such as a galaxy, is moving towards an observer the light waves get squeezed together, thereby causing a reduction in the wavelength of the observed light. Since blue light has a shorter wavelength than red light, this is referred to as a "blueshift." Conversely, for light sources moving away from an observer the light waves are stretched out producing a "redshift." The situation is analogous to the effects of motion on sound waves. If an observer is standing by the side of a road as a police car goes by, siren wailing, the pitch of the siren is higher as the police car approaches and drops to a lower pitch as the car passes the observer and moves away. Sound waves with a short wavelength have a higher pitch than those with longer wavelengths. The important point in the case of both sound and light is that there is extensive empirical evidence that the Doppler shift provides an accurate measure of radial velocity.

In the early part of the twentieth century, astronomers began measuring the radial velocities of galaxies through their Doppler shifts. In 1912 Slipher noted that the majority of galaxies exhibited redshifts. In other words, most galaxies were found to be moving away from our own galaxy. This is not a cosmic snub of Earth. Further investigations revealed that all galaxies are, on average, receding from one another in a universal expansion. Of central importance was the finding that the speed of recession of galaxies increased with distance (Hubble 1929; Hubble and Humason 1931). In other words, the greater the distance to a galaxy, the faster it moves away from us. Specifically, the speed of recession of a galaxy, v, is related to the distance to that galaxy, r, by the simple relation:

$$v = H_0 r \tag{1},$$

where H_0 is a constant of proportionality now known as the Hubble constant. This relationship is referred to as Hubble's law. For readers who break out into a cold sweat at the first sign of an equation, all this mathematical statement says is that recession velocity is directly proportional to distance. Thus if galaxy A is twice as far from us as galaxy B, galaxy A is moving away from us twice as fast as galaxy B. However, to determine the absolute recession speed of a galaxy at a certain distance, one needs to know the value of H_0. (It is all very well knowing that Brand X is twice as expensive as Brand Y, but without knowing the cost of Brand X one cannot determine the cost of Brand Y.)

The importance of the Hubble constant

Before discussing how the Hubble constant is measured, it is first helpful to discuss why astronomers were so keen to determine its numerical value. In particular, I argue below that the physical interpretation of the Hubble constant and its relation to the age of the universe is one of the factors that contributed to the Hubble constant controversy.

As discussed above, the recession speed of a galaxy is measured fairly easily through the Doppler shift. However, determining the distance to a galaxy is, in general, quite difficult (see the following section). This is extremely irritating since without knowing the distance to a galaxy we can say little about its size, the amount of radiation that it emits, and a host of other physical properties of interest to astronomers. The situation is similar to that of observing the silhouette of a boat at dusk. Without a knowledge of the distance to the boat, it is hard to say whether it is a small tug or a massive ocean liner. An accurate determination of the Hubble constant gets around this difficulty. All one has to do is to measure the recession speed of a galaxy and apply Hubble's law (equation (1)) and one has an estimate of the distance to that galaxy.[3] More generally, one can think of the value of the Hubble constant as a measure of the scale of the universe.

Perhaps of even greater interest is the relation of the Hubble constant to the age of the universe. The Hubble law is interpreted as indicating that the universe is expanding, with the value of the Hubble constant essentially measuring the rate of that expansion. A large Hubble constant means that the universe is expanding rapidly. The observation of universal expansion is also one of the cornerstones of the Big Bang model, which asserts that at some time in the finite past, the universe was compressed into an extremely small volume and thus the material of the universe was at an extremely high density. If we can determine the rate of expansion of the universe by measuring the value of the Hubble constant, we can mentally run the expansion backwards to determine when the expansion began. In other words, we can estimate the age of the universe from the Hubble constant.

To explain how this works, consider a friend who is coming over to dinner.[4] The friend lives four miles away and is very fond of walking just before dinner. At seven o'clock, just as you are setting the table, you observe your friend walking towards your door at four miles per hour. You might reasonably conclude that your friend walked from his or her house to your own and has maintained a speed of four miles an hour for the entire journey. Since the distance traveled is four miles and the speed four miles an hour, your assumption leads you to conclude that the journey took one hour. In other words, through a knowledge of speed and distance, you have determined when your friend left home. The same is true with the speed and distance of galaxies, as related through the Hubble constant, but rather than calculating the time taken for someone to walk between two houses, one is calculating the time taken for the universe to expand from the Big Bang to its present configuration: the age of the universe.

There is clearly a rather large assumption here. In the case of the friend walking to dinner, the journey described above only takes exactly one hour if he or she maintains a constant four miles per hour for the entire journey. You only measured this speed at the end of the journey as your friend approached your front door. It is quite possible that your friend left home late and drove most of the way at a speed far in excess of four miles per hour. In this case, it is apparent that the journey would have taken considerably less than the hour that you calculated. Alternatively, your friend may have started walking at a leisurely two miles per hour or so, admiring the scenery and contemplating whether or not science was objective, and only increased the pace to four miles per hour towards the end of the journey on realizing that he or she was about to be late for dinner. In this case, the journey would have taken more than one hour.

The universe can behave in a similar way. Until recently, the conventional view was that the expansion rate of the universe is slowing down. All objects in the universe exert a gravitational force of attraction on every other object. This has the effect of reducing the rate of expansion, just as the gravitational force of the earth slows, and eventually reverses, the velocity of a ball thrown vertically upwards. It is also possible (and perhaps likely: see "The controversy resolved," below) that the rate of expansion of the universe is increasing. This will arise if there is a repulsive force (a sort of universal pressure) that acts with the universal expansion causing the expansion rate to speed up.

Since the Hubble constant measures the rate of expansion of the universe, these possibilities show that the Hubble constant need not be a constant. In a universe in which the expansion is slowing down, for example, the Hubble constant had a higher value in the past. However, our measurements of the Hubble constant are, for the most part, confined to fairly local regions of the universe, just as your observation of your friend arriving for dinner was confined to the very end of the journey. Thus most measurements of the Hubble constant are not affected by the possibility of a varying expansion rate, but determinations of the age of the universe based on the Hubble constant do require some assumption (or, ideally, another measurement) of how the expansion rate has varied with time.

Measuring the Hubble constant

I suspect the previous discussion may upset some people. How do we know that the universe expands? Is the idea of an expanding universe meaningful? Do we even know that there is a universe? It is certainly true that there is a good deal of interpretation of observation, particularly in the connection between the Hubble constant and the age of the universe, and, yes, the Big Bang model is just that: a model. The point I want to emphasize is that for the purposes of measuring the Hubble constant these concerns simply do not matter. As I discuss below, the connection between the age of the universe and the Hubble constant plays an important role in the Hubble constant controversy, but the heart of the controversy, and the reason that the controversy was ultimately resolved, is simply the measurement of observable quantities.

To illustrate this point, notice that we can rearrange equation (1) to obtain:

$$H_0 = \frac{v}{r} \tag{2}$$

In other words, the Hubble constant is just the ratio of the recession speed of a galaxy to the distance to that galaxy. In principle, all we need to do to obtain a value for the Hubble constant is to measure the recession speed and distance of a single galaxy and divide the first number by the second. In practice, this would give a very uncertain value of the Hubble constant for a variety of reasons (some of which are discussed below). A far better approach, and one that is common in science, is to measure the recession speeds and distances of a large number of galaxies and determine the Hubble constant by a process analogous to taking an average. This has the added bonus of determining whether the relationship in equation (1) is indeed linear; that is, whether the recession speed of galaxies is directly proportional to distance.

While recession speeds can be easily and accurately measured using the Doppler shift, there is an annoying complication when one attempts to determine the Hubble constant. The first part of the problem stems from the fact that all galaxies exert gravitational forces on one another. This leads to "peculiar velocities" of galaxies. The terminology is a little misleading since the origin of these velocities is well understood. The problem is that the Hubble constant is a measure of universal expansion and these peculiar velocities are essentially deviations from the universal expansion speed. A crowd of people leaving a sports stadium will, on average, tend to expand outwards from the gates at a roughly constant rate. One could stand at one of the gates and measure this "expansion" using the Doppler shift. However, if such an observer focuses on particular individuals in the crowd, he or she will detect peculiar velocities: someone stops to tie a shoelace or veers in another direction to meet up with a friend.

Although peculiar velocities of individual galaxies do constitute something of a problem, this is mitigated by studying large numbers of galaxies. In this way, the average behavior dominates over the behavior of individual objects.

However, the second part of the problem is that observers on Earth also have a peculiar velocity. Since the Doppler shift measures relative velocities (technically relative "radial" velocities either directly towards or away from the observer), this means that we must "subtract out" the peculiar velocity of observers on Earth if we are to measure the cosmological recession velocity of galaxies and thus the Hubble constant.

Many of the contributions to the peculiar velocity of Earth observers can be accounted for fairly easily. They include the motion of the Earth around the Sun and the motion of the Sun around the center of the Milky Way. Unfortunately, a significant contribution is less well understood. The gravitational effects of relatively nearby galaxies on the Milky Way produce a peculiar velocity of our galaxy relative to the universal expansion. Accurate determinations of this peculiar velocity are difficult and this leads to a source of uncertainty when determining the Hubble constant.

The second element in determining the Hubble constant is to obtain accurate distances to galaxies. On Earth, and within our local corner of the Milky Way, distances can be measured using simple geometry. If one takes a geographical bearing on a distant object from two positions that are a known distance apart, the distance to that object can be easily calculated. Primarily because of the huge distances involved, such methods cannot be used to measure the distances to individual galaxies. Instead, the majority of methods use some kind of "standard candle." If one knows the intrinsic luminosity of an object (the amount of light it is emitting), it is a simple matter to calculate its distance. This is because the amount of light received by an observer decreases in proportion to the square of the distance to the light source. If we imagine two identical flashlights, one at a distance of one meter and the second at a distance of two meters, then the amount of light from the more distant flashlight will be one-fourth that of the closer flashlight. We can turn this argument around to measure distances. For example, if we observe another identical flashlight that is producing one ninth the amount of light relative to its twin one meter away, we can conclude that this flashlight is at a distance of three meters. A standard candle is simply an astronomical object that emits a known amount of light, or which has some other observable property which is related in a known way to the amount of emitted light.

In order to measure the distance to a galaxy, all one needs to do in principle is to measure the observed brightness of a standard candle in that target galaxy. In practice, however, there are several subtleties in this process. To give one example, the so-called vacuum of space is actually made up of low density gas and dust. The dust is a particular nuisance since it can dim the light from distant astronomical objects. In the case of distance determinations, the result is that a standard candle is observed to be fainter than it would be if its light passed through a true vacuum. If the effects of dust are not accounted for, one would therefore conclude that the galaxy containing the standard candle in question is further away than its true distance. In the context of the flashlight discussed above, one can imagine observing a very dim flashlight and concluding it is a long way away, whereas in reality the flashlight is quite close but a heavy fog is reducing its observed brightness. If one knew the distribution of fog and its effects on light, one could account for its presence and derive the correct distance to the flashlight. A similar procedure is required to derive astronomical distances from standard candles.

A full discussion of all the possible complications in distance determinations is beyond the scope of this chapter. A detailed technical treatment is given by Jacoby *et al.* (1992) and a slightly easier account is provided by Rowan-Robinson (1985). The point I want to emphasize is that the process of determining the Hubble constant is understood, but difficult, and that many of the necessary "corrections" (such as that required to account for dust) introduce uncertainty into the final result. Let me emphasize that these corrections are not made arbitrarily in an attempt to obtain a desired answer. In some cases they are little more than the kinds of math we all do when "correcting" our gross income for taxes in order to determine our net income. A scientist who did not pay attention to these kinds of effects and attempt to do something about them would be grossly negligent.

The nature of the controversy

The clearest statement of the Hubble constant controversy of which I am aware is provided by Rowan-Robinson (1985: vii; also quoted in Jacoby *et al.* 1992: 601):

> Gerard de Vaucouleurs on the one hand, and Allan Sandage and Gustav Tammann on the other, arrived at estimates of the size of the universe, as measured by the Hubble constant, differing from each other by a factor of two. Moreover, when I asked the protagonists what was the range outside which they could not imagine the Hubble constant lying, these ranges did not overlap. Given that they were studying more or less the same galaxies with rather similar methods, often using the same observational material, I found this incredible.

To expand upon this quote, two major research groups had been attempting to measure the value of the Hubble constant for many years at the time Rowan-Robinson made the above statement. These two groups came up with different answers. In itself, this is not particularly surprising. Two roofing companies may look at the same house and come up with different values for the square footage of the roof. One would hope, however, that the values arrived at by the two companies would not be wildly different. Yet in the case of the Hubble constant determinations, the two principle research groups came up with numbers that could not be reconciled, even allowing for the uncertainties quoted by each group for their results.

In order to quantify this discussion, it is helpful to give the actual numbers these researchers found for the Hubble constant. The group led by de

Vaucouleurs repeatedly obtained values of around 100 km/s/Mpc whereas Sandage and co-workers obtained a number half as big, around 50 km/s/ Mpc. The units after the numbers are read as "kilometers per second per megaparsec." A megaparsec is a unit of length used by astronomers and is roughly equivalent to three million light years. One can convert the unit to meters or miles, but frankly there are so many zeros that the procedure is not particularly enlightening. If the value of the Hubble constant is 100 in these units, it means that a galaxy one megaparsec away will have a cosmological speed of recession of one hundred kilometers per second (this assumes the peculiar velocity of the galaxy and an observer on earth have been taken into account). For the same value of the Hubble constant, a galaxy ten megaparsecs away will have a recession speed of one thousand kilometers per second, and so on.

Both research groups quoted typical uncertainties on their results of about 10 percent. As described in the above quote, this led to the conclusion by members of both groups that their value of the Hubble constant was incon- sistent with that derived by the other. It is also worth noting that the numbers derived by the two groups were not simply the result of a single experiment or set of observations. For many years, these researchers continued in their efforts to pin down the Hubble constant and each consistently obtained results similar to their earlier values, and still at odds with the other group. Further, although the groups led by de Vaucouleurs and Sandage were the most notorious for obtaining this dichotomy, other researchers, particularly in the 1980s, tended to obtain either high or low values for the Hubble con- stant. Thus it appeared at this time that the value of the Hubble constant depended on the research group measuring it.

To avoid the last sentence being used as evidence for the subjectivity of science, let me emphasize here that my conclusion is not that the value of astronomical parameters depends on the observer. I will shortly argue the reverse. However, this peculiar state of affairs did produce some rather non- scientific statements and interpretations throughout the 1980s and into the early 1990s. I first became aware of the controversy as a student in 1984 during an extragalactic astronomy course. My professor, an expert in the field of extragalactic astronomy, made the following statement during one of his lectures: "Methods that give values of H_0 around 100 km/s/Mpc appear to be more sound, but H_0 probably has a value around 50 km/s/Mpc." In other words, my professor (and many others in the field) concluded that the analyses that produced high values of the Hubble constant were superior, but that the value of the Hubble constant was nevertheless likely to be low.

I found this statement most bothering. To understand its origin, recall that the value of the Hubble constant is related to the age of the universe. A large value of H_0 corresponds to a rapid expansion rate and consequently, when one "runs the clock backwards," to a low age of the universe. For the tradi- tional picture of an expansion that slows with time, a value of H_0 of around

100 km/s/Mpc implies that the universe is no older than about ten billion years. This presents something of a problem since there are objects in the universe that have estimated ages of around thirteen billion years.[5] Making the not unreasonable demand that the universe must be older than objects within it led many to conclude that the low value of H_0 must be correct, despite qualms about the analyses used to obtain it.

This prejudice for a low value of H_0 was not unreasonable. In the view of most scientists, the solution to a scientific problem proceeds first through a reductionist phase in which small, tractable problems are addressed, and then through a synthesis in which individual results are brought together to form a bigger picture. This bigger picture, at least eventually, needs to be self-consistent. If it is not, the conclusion is that one or more of its elements are in error. This led many astronomers and astrophysicists to conclude that there must be an error in the analyses that led to high values of the Hubble constant.

The controversy resolved

Perhaps the strangest element of the Hubble constant controversy is that, at least in the 1980s, derived values of H_0 seemed to fall into one of two groups, either around 100 km/s/Mpc or 50 km/s/Mpc. As noted above, it is normal for different studies to obtain different values for an observable quantity, particularly when such measurements are pushing the technology of the day to its limits, but one would expect a range of values rather than a dichotomy. A related issue is that differences between determinations of H_0 were consistently larger than the errors quoted in individual studies.

The situation began to change significantly in the 1990s when derived values of H_0 between the traditional extremes began to appear more frequently in the literature.[6] This reflected a growing number of researchers joining the field and an increase in the number of available techniques for measuring the Hubble constant. At the same time, information required for the various corrections required to derive H_0 from galaxy distances and recession velocities became more reliable. This information included more accurate estimates of the peculiar velocity of the Milky Way and the distribution of dust that dims light from astronomical objects.

Perhaps the most important development for this field was the launch of the Hubble Space Telescope in 1990. One of the primary missions of this satellite was to obtain a precise value for the Hubble constant. Its principal advantage over existing technology at the time of launch was its ability to detect a reliable standard candle—a type of star known as a Cepheid variable—in galaxies at appreciable distances. This mission has now been completed and a value for the Hubble constant of 70 ± 7 km/s/Mpc obtained (Freedman 2000). The "plus or minus" symbol indicates an error estimate on the value of 70 km/s/Mpc and means that there is a 67 percent probability that the Hubble constant has a value between 63 and 77 km/s/Mpc. This value appears to be accepted by the majority of workers in the field. Notice that the value falls between the traditional high and low values of H_0.

The above results demonstrate that the Hubble constant is a well-behaved observable quantity that does not depend on the particular scientists attempting to measure its value. So how did the Hubble controversy arise? First, in the 1980s the majority of papers on the topic were published by the research groups of de Vaucouleurs and Sandage. The two groups used different corrections in deriving H_0 from galaxy velocities and distances which tended to act in opposite directions. That is, errors in the corrections used by de Vaucouleurs and collaborators tended to increase the derived value of H_0, whereas errors in the corrections used by Sandage's group had the reverse effect. Consequently, when more reliable information for these corrections became available, the dichotomy eased. Further, the fact that other research groups in the 1980s also derived H_0 values that were either high or low is largely attributable to their using the corrections of either de Vaucouleurs or Sandage.

A second critical element is that many workers in the field underestimated the errors associated with their derived values of H_0. To draw an analogy, if one student measures the time for a pendulum to swing back and forth to be 10.07 ± 0.03 seconds and a second student measures the same phenomenon to take 10.34 ± 0.03 seconds, one might conclude that one of them has made an error. On the other hand, if these two students quote times of 10.1 ± 0.2 seconds and 10.3 ± 0.2 seconds, there is no problem: the two times are consistent within the quoted errors. In the case of Hubble constant determinations, there is compelling evidence that many groups underestimated errors, thereby adding to the perception of a dichotomy between high and low values.

Rowan Robinson (1985) analyzed existing Hubble constant determinations when the controversy was at its peak. By combining results in refereed journals and arguing that errors quoted by the original researchers were, in general, too small, he obtained a value of the Hubble constant of 66 ± 10 km/s/Mpc, consistent with the value recently obtained using the Hubble Space Telescope. A similar result was obtained several years later by Jacoby *et al.* (1992), again from published data. It seems that the Hubble constant controversy was primarily the result of bad luck (corrections used by the two principle groups acting in opposite directions) and unrealistic error estimates. The fact that this natural conclusion was not accepted much earlier may be partly a consequence of the prominence of de Vaucouleurs and Sandage and their deserved reputations as excellent scientists.

One final note on the Hubble constant and the age of the universe. The modern value of 70 km/s/Mpc along with information about the amount of material in the universe (which slows down the universal expansion) still produces an estimate of the age of the universe that is uncomfortably young. That is, depending on the precise age of globular clusters (see note 5), it may suggest that the universe is younger than objects in it, if one assumes that the universal rate of expansion is decreasing. There is no such problem if, contrary to the traditional view, the universal expansion is speeding up. (Remember the hypothetical dinner guest who took the longest to walk over to dinner was the individual who dawdled for the first part of the journey.) Recently, astronomers have presented tentative evidence that the universal expansion may indeed be increasing, thereby leading to a greater derived age for the universe (Riess *et al.* 1998).

Implications for the objectivity of science

In this section I attempt to draw some conclusions about the objectivity of science from the Hubble constant controversy and its resolution. Generalizing from a specific case has its limitations, but I believe that the Hubble constant controversy provides interesting insights into how the process of science is carried out and how subjective factors tend to get removed.

The High Priests decide it is time to agree?

Skeptical readers may have reached the conclusion that the account in the previous section above is "too good to be true." If scientists are really the "high priests of modernism" (or of anything else, for that matter), would it not be natural for them to protect the credibility of their field (religion?) and ensure that embarrassing incidents like the Hubble constant controversy are patched up? After all, the objectivity of natural science demands that a measurable quantity must have the same value irrespective of the individual doing the measuring.

To illustrate why I regard the account in the previous section as credible, let me present the non-scientific "social" and "cultural" factors that I have experienced in astronomy and astrophysics and relate them to the Hubble constant controversy. First, who is in charge here? Who drives the scientific process? Are there high priests (tenured faculty) handing down The Word to their initiates (graduate students)? To some extent, the answer is "yes." Part of the responsibility of a thesis adviser is to ensure that his or her students work on tractable, interesting problems. It is inevitable that such an adviser will regard problems as "interesting" if they are related to his or her own research work. Moreover, it would be a less than responsible thesis adviser who suggested a thesis project outside of that adviser's field: one requires a knowledge of a subject before one can teach it or supervise a thesis on that topic.

A more problematic issue is whether a thesis adviser communicates his or her own biases to graduate students. In an ideal world in which "the scientific method" is both clearly defined and universally followed, the only such bias would be the research areas of interest to an adviser discussed above. In practice, the situation is less clear. In the context of the Hubble constant controversy, many of the researchers in the field had graduate students who carried out thesis work on the topic. There is evidence that these students tended to use similar prescriptions for the various corrections required to derive values for the Hubble constant once they had graduated, although there are exceptions to this trend. This is hardly surprising, particularly when one considers that early in a researcher's career letters of recommendation from a thesis adviser are important in obtaining subsequent academic positions. (This in itself is something of a departure from objectivity: one would hope that a young researcher's future career is determined by merit rather than the fame of his or her thesis adviser.)

In addition to the adviser–student relationship there are several other situations where human foibles may come into play. The refereeing of research papers and, perhaps more importantly, grant proposals means that individual scientists have the power, if they choose to so abuse it, to adversely affect the careers of their colleagues. Astronomer A sits on a grant review panel and has the task of reviewing a proposal by Astronomer B. Astronomer B made the mistake of sleeping with Astronomer A's spouse a few years back and consequently has his or her grant proposal turned down. The point to note here, however, is that while social and cultural factors can lead to such abuses, it is not the process of science that is flawed. Indeed, if we were all better scientists, the frequency of such incidents would decrease.

Can these and other "human" factors provide an alternative explanation for the resolution of the Hubble constant controversy? To link this question more directly to the issue of the objectivity of science, the following syllogism may be useful. Either the Hubble constant controversy was solved by astronomers objectively (in the epistemic sense) measuring this parameter and gradually eliminating uncertainties and biases, or astronomers have, through social and cultural pressures, mutually agreed on a value of a parameter. (In the latter case, I suspect we have to throw out "measurable," since if science is nothing more than a process by which scientists agree on certain results, I see no sense in measuring anything.)

One approach to assessing the likelihood of a non-objective explanation to the resolution of the controversy is to establish the possible motivation of astronomers in simply "agreeing" on the answer. As mentioned above, the credibility of the field, and thus of its practitioners, demanded that a resolution to the controversy be found. While this is a powerful motivation, it is difficult to see how such collusion might occur in practice. The fact that different astronomers can initially disagree about the answer to an astronomical question is clearly illustrated by the protracted disagreement between the research groups of de Vaucouleurs and Sandage. More generally, there is little to be gained in research science by simply agreeing with what everyone else is saying. Personal advancement in research astronomy, as measured by the ability to secure an academic position, tenure, and funding, is more readily attained by discovering something new. Considerable prestige would be bestowed upon an individual who demonstrated convincingly that the Hubble constant had a "surprising" value; say 35 or 120 km/s/Mpc. Either value would have interesting implications for other areas of extragalactic astronomy and would further, by necessity, have shown that one of the two "traditional" values was badly wrong. Thus if we assume that individual astronomers are primarily motivated by a desire for personal gain, whether measured by job security or by the recognition of their peers, there does not appear to be a mechanism whereby this motivation could act for some kind of "greater good." Specifically, I find it hard to imagine how such a motivation would lead to a mutual agreement on the value of the Hubble constant.

Let us take a rather more paranoid approach and suppose that scientists are so concerned with the credibility of science and its alleged primacy in modern society that they discard thoughts of personal advancement. This seems closer to the "priesthood" scenario in which scientists jealously guard their specialized knowledge and techniques in order to preserve their authority. Is it possible in such a scenario to find an alternative explanation for the resolution of the Hubble constant controversy? The history of the problem does not appear to reveal any evidence for such a collusion. However, there is evidence to refute this proposition. The animated debates at conferences and in the astronomical literature between the leading protagonists in the field are in sharp contrast to the "closed ranks" of a scientific community claimed by some critics of science. Research papers on the topic frequently include a discussion of why the methodology of, and thus the value of the Hubble constant obtained by, the authors are more reliable than those of other researchers.

The competitive nature of scientific research, particularly in a system such as that of the United States in which securing grants is of such importance, makes the likelihood of community collusion extremely remote. Scientists simply do not work like that. Ironically, a system in which personal advancement is sacrificed for a larger "cause" (such as a more rapid solution to scientific questions) may be closer to the scientific ideal of a community of dispassionate scientists whose only concern is to understand the physical universe. In the current system, one can imagine reasons why individual scientists may sacrifice their objectivity in order to claim a more impressive result and obtain greater prestige. This strikes me as a fascinating topic that might be addressed by sociologists of science. However, my interpretation of the Hubble constant controversy, and many similar episodes in the history of the natural sciences, is that scientific methodology eventually overcomes the non-scientific pressures and vanities that influence individual scientists.

Bridging the gulf

The conference that led to this volume had the stated goal of promoting dialogue between scientists and the critics of science. In this final section I speculate on where such a dialogue may be profitable and where, in my view, the disagreements between scientists and some of their critics are insurmountable. I concentrate on ideas that generally fall under the umbrella of postmodernism and more specifically those of cultural constructivism since this is where the gulf between scientists and their critics appears to be the widest. It is important to emphasize that not all practitioners in the field of science studies are cultural constructivists, nor do all cultural constructivists share identical views on the process and nature of science. My goal is simply to high-light problem areas and develop the claims made in the preceding sections that science is objective.

Cultural constructivism and relativism

Advocates of the more extreme positions in science studies can be thanked, to some degree, for raising the awareness of many scientists to current fashions in this field. However, the so-called "science wars" indicate that a significant number of scientists are less than thrilled with what they have discovered. The considerable e-mail and internet traffic on the subject suggests that there are three main areas of contention that are also delineated in Gross and Levitt's *Higher Superstition*. The first stems from the claim made by certain critics of science that scientific knowledge is predominantly (even exclusively) a "construction" that is independent of the physical universe. Thus socially or culturally constructed ideas are somehow responsible for our understanding of the natural world, rather than the natural world possessing phenomena that can be observed and hopefully understood to produce scientific knowl-edge (for example, see Sokal, this volume, and references therein).

Does the cultural constructivist position make sense? Could it be that the filter of perception through which we sense the universe is so colored with culturally based values that scientific theories are purely cultural constructs? The first problem that I have in addressing this question is that I am a product of the same culture that produced science (and, incidentally, cultural con-structivists). Thus even if I provide arguments against the cultural constructivist position, this method of addressing the issue can itself be viewed as a cultural construct. (Deductive and inductive reasoning are, after all, part of what is generally understood to be the "scientific method.") This demonstrates the simultaneous cleverness and emptiness of the cultural constructivist stance, as well as the fact that it is essentially traditional relativism with some added bells and whistles (see Cudd, this volume, for a discussion of relativism).

It is necessary for constructivists to throw out "Western" methods of argu-ment and reasoning since the techniques are so effective at undermining cul-tural constructivism. For example, consider the debate between the advocates of the Ptolemaic and Copernican models. The originators of both models can be classed as "Western" although there are marked cultural differences between Ancient Greece and Renaissance Europe. Further, there were clearly cultural factors that influenced the two models, as discussed in the opening section. It can be argued that dominant religious ideas at the time made it natural for Aristotle and Ptolemy to place the Earth at the center of the universe, while the gradual development of skeptical inquiry allowed

Copernicus to move the Earth from this privileged position.[7] Cultural constructivists would presumably suggest that the Ptolemaic and Copernican models provide equally valid representations of the material world. While it may be possible to produce interesting linguistic arguments that support some kind of equality between the two models, I see no way of escaping the rather fundamental observation that the Earth travels around the Sun. I am also convinced that if every sentient being on Earth believed that the Earth was stationary and at the center of the universe this would not make it so.

The above argument implicitly assumes the existence of a material world. I acknowledge the well-known problem that I cannot prove the existence of the material world. For scientists, this is simply a useful working hypothesis (without which there would be very little point in carrying out scientific research). I suppose that if there is no material world, the cultural constructivist position is valid in the sense that people have somehow constructed the appearance of one. However, in the absence of a material world, there would also appear to be an absence of sentient beings other than myself. If I am the only sentient being, the material world is purely the product of my imagination, and since I am not a cultural constructivist there are no cultural constructivists. These kinds of problems convince natural scientists that the existence of a material world is the only sensible, if unprovable, assumption.

I find it extremely unlikely that scientists will ever come close to accepting extreme cultural constructivist positions, particularly when applied to science, but also more generally. This is because any form of relativism is anathema to scientists. We believe that we can discover truths, or approximate truths, about the universe. This conviction is built on the experience that science works. A pendulum on Earth with a string of a certain length will swing back and forth with the same period no matter who is observing the pendulum. Indeed, we can predict its period before the pendulum has even been set in motion. Further, the methodology of science appears, at least to scientists, to succeed. Central to this methodology is the practice of asking questions, constructing experiments, and using reasoning to reach the "right answer" to a physical problem. Relativism does not allow for right answers, just a bewildering array of equally valid perspectives.

Science and scientists abused?

In terms of intellectual content, I believe the extreme cultural constructivist positions outlined above constitute the greatest difficulty for a productive dialogue between scientists and science critics of this particular hue. However, the open hostility between the two "sides" in this debate has two other notable causes: the misuse of scientific terms and concepts by some postmodernists and science critics and their assertion that "Western science" is by nature reactionary. It is not my intention to apportion blame for the hostility, but while it persists it seems likely that it will compound the difficulties in communication. These issues are treated in detail by Gross and Levitt

(1994) and Sokal and Bricmont (1998) among others (see also Sokal, this volume).

As in any academic discipline, obtaining a doctorate in the natural sciences requires a great deal of work and periods of poverty. Most of us who go through the process find that the rewards are well worth the hardship. However, it is hardly surprising that natural scientists react negatively when the cornerstones of their disciplines appear mangled and maligned in postmodernist texts. Before I am accused of some form of elitism, let me emphasize that as a scientist I am delighted when natural science proves useful in other disciplines. Indeed, I am attracted to Wilson's (1998) vision that the natural sciences will expand into non-traditional fields (see my closing remarks in "The future," below). The point is that any researcher has a responsibility to use the results from other fields with understanding and accuracy, whether it be a linguist employing physics or an astronomer employing semiotics. Further, if the purpose of one's work is to criticize, say, the theory of quantum mechanics, a rudimentary understanding of the topic is in order.

Many postmodernist critics of science do not seem to be overburdened with a desire to familiarize themselves with the subject matter of their criticism. To be fair, there is a degree of self-consistency in this approach, since postmodernism places a greater emphasis on the techniques of criticism and analysis than on the content of the field under study. This is apparent in the literary criticism technique of deconstruction which asserts that the meaning of any text is known only to the author. If one accepts this premise, there is no possibility for an author to communicate his or her meaning and thus no prospect of an author having anything communicable to say about objective reality. More pertinently, if we are all doomed to live in intellectual isolation, unable to share the meaning of our ideas, one can argue that there is no objective reality (in the epistemic sense), just a huge number of subjective realities.

I am not qualified to comment on the effectiveness of deconstruction in the analysis of works of fiction, but it strikes me as extremely unlikely that one will learn much about natural science through such an approach. Communication of ideas and a mutual understanding of concepts between scientists is fundamental to the scientific process. In order to lessen ambiguity, scientists frequently cast their ideas into mathematical equations which have the additional benefit of economy. The prose of research articles is typically terse, again to communicate ideas swiftly and accurately. If the basic premise of deconstruction is correct, there is no point in reading scientific research articles and no apparent chance of a productive exchange of ideas between scientists. Indeed, if the premise is correct, I see little point in reading anything. The whole idea is profoundly depressing.

While deconstruction is not the only weapon in the postmodernist and cultural constructivist arsenal, the above discussion prompts the question of whether techniques that are allegedly useful in fields such as literary criticism have any applicability to the natural sciences. A sociological analysis of the effects of the tenure system on dual-career astronomers makes perfect sense. A sociological analysis of the effects of comets on planetary atmospheres does not. One does not need to read too many pages of the *Astrophysical Journal* to realize that astronomical research papers are not literary works. More generally, and as stated earlier, postmodernist analyses of science do not appear to scientists to be related to their own experience of their field. This is somewhat ironic given the emphasis on different "ways of knowing" in cultural studies. In the light of this perspective one would think that an important, if not necessarily scientific, element in analyzing the sociology of science would be to gather anecdotal evidence from scientists themselves. For the most part, this does not appear to be a priority of the critics of science.

Not all scientists are troubled by postmodernist theorists misinterpreting science, but many have been irritated by the assertion that the natural sciences, and by implication scientists, are reactionary. The argument is simple although it has a multitude of different forms and advocates. By postmodernist hypothesis, science is a cultural construction, specifically one constructed by Western culture. Western culture is bad because it is capitalist, reactionary, conservative, bourgeois, sexist, racist, oppressive, and so on, therefore science is also bad because it is capitalist, reactionary, conservative—you can insert your favorite complaint. Through further guilt by association, some critics of science extend this to criticize scientists for the same sins.

The main problem with this argument is that it contains a rather glaring fallacy. (It may have survived because it is not entirely clear how anything is demonstrated to be false within the premises of postmodernism.) Even if one accepts the claim that science is a cultural construct, it does not follow that the natural sciences, much less scientists, carry within them the perceived flaws of that culture. There are certainly cases in which scientific research has been perverted by sexist and racist views (see, for example, Cudd, this volume), although I would argue that the self-correcting nature of science eventually removes such biases. There are scientists who claim, with some justification, that the process of career advancement in the sciences discriminates against women. These issues are frequently debated by professional societies and individual faculties. But to charge that science also contains all the biases and flaws of Western culture and that it is by nature politically conservative constitutes an unsupported extrapolation. A car license plate manufactured by convicted criminals has no greater proclivity for criminal behavior than does a license plate made by anyone else.

Science is both a body of knowledge and a method of acquiring that knowledge. If the individuals carrying out the process of science do so in the spirit of science, in which empirical evidence is paramount and the prejudices and feelings of the individual are minimized, I do not believe it can be characterized in political terms. This strikes me as another case of using a system of analysis in a field where it is inapplicable. The irony is that this political criticism of science and scientists has annoyed and alienated a significant number of scientists who have left-of-center to left-wing views.

The future

Given the obstacles to a dialogue between scientists and their critics described above, is there hope that these obstacles may be overcome? I think it is important to stress some of the areas of agreement, since they may act as seeds for further dialogue. Few scientists would have difficulty with the weak form of cultural constructivism. Science is clearly a social activity and as such it is susceptible to the weaknesses of human individuals and institutions. There are many areas in which sociological analyses would be of great benefit to science and scientists in order to better eliminate these weaknesses. The Hubble constant controversy provides one example where such an analysis might produce useful reflection within the astronomical community. It might even lessen the chances of such a situation developing in the future. However, I predict that the strong form of cultural constructivism as applied to science will never be accepted or even influence scientists for the simple reason that it reduces science to a series of badly written works of fiction.

My personal hope is that a stronger bond will develop between scientists and their critics through the expansion of the natural sciences into other areas. Wilson's recent (1998) book *Consilience* offers a remarkable picture of how this development might occur. It also illustrates that one of the primary strengths of science is that it stays within its limits and pushes out slowly and cautiously. In this sense, science is indeed conservative. This may be another reason why many scientists have reactions from dubiousness to outright hostility when postmodernists take analysis methods developed in the humanities and social sciences and apply them to the natural sciences. There have been some scientists who have embarked on unfortunate projects to link, for example, results in quantum mechanics to the question of free will, but for the most part we avoid such speculations. This does not stem from a lack of interest. There are some questions for which natural science is not (yet) the appropriate tool.

As science, through technology, affects an increasing number of this planet's citizens, individuals need to be scientifically literate. I make this claim not because I envision billions of people wearing laboratory coats and staring into test tubes, but because without scientific literacy people will be unable to participate in the decisions that will affect their lives. Empowerment of individuals will not come about by propagating the notion that all theories are equally valid, or that if one believes that certain crystals will bring good luck or health then it is so. I do not regard science and scientific literacy as a panacea. Like most natural scientists, I am acutely aware of the destructive products of science and the despicable acts carried out in the name of science. I do believe that denigrating science will lead to the promotion of a host of superstitions and a more credulous public. And I believe that the rejection of bigotry and oppression is more likely to occur in a society comprised of people who ask questions than in a society in which people will believe anything.

Acknowledgments

I am grateful to Jill Baringer, Phil Baringer, Lydia Diebolt and Donald Hatcher for reading an earlier draft of this chapter and suggesting many improvements.

Notes

1 It is worth noting in this context that the majority of scientists from the seventeenth century onward would balk at the idea of proving a model correct. Irrespective of more general philosophical questions of whether a model or theory can ever be regarded as "true," it is generally accepted that theories can only be disproved.
2 A complete discussion of Galileo's refutation of the Ptolemaic model is given in most introductory astronomy texts. The discussion by Seeds (1999) is particularly good. Galileo's observations of Venus were not the only observations that contradicted the Ptolemaic model, but in some ways they were the most definitive refutation of the model. That is not to say that Galileo's results were immediately accepted. There are several accounts of people refusing to look through one of his telescopes at these phenomena for fear that the instrument might "mislead" them. Others hypothesized that Galileo's telescopes had been taken over by demons.
3 I argue below that in order to observationally measure the Hubble constant one must determine distances to galaxies. It may therefore appear somewhat circular to claim here that one of the main uses of Hubble's law is the determination of galactic distances. The point is that to obtain a distance to an individual galaxy without appeal to Hubble's law invariably requires repeated observations of the galaxy over many nights. In contrast, with a reliable value of the Hubble constant one can obtain distances to hundreds of galaxies with a few hours of observing time by measuring their recession velocities.
4 I am grateful to the novelist Philip Kimball for his input in developing this analogy.
5 The oldest objects for which ages are fairly well determined are star clusters known as "globular clusters." While age determinations for these objects have varied somewhat over the last two decades, they have consistently remained above ten billion years. See Ashman and Zepf (1998) for a detailed discussion.
6 Kennicutt *et al.* (1995) give an excellent summary of published values of the Hubble constant as well as a more technical treatment of other issues discussed in this section.
7 One could also argue that Aristotle and Ptolemy were more heavily influenced by the apparent motion of the heavenly bodies around the Earth once a day and the fact that humans do not "sense" the motion of the Earth.

Bibliography

Ashman, K. M., and Zepf, S. E. (1998) *Globular Cluster Systems*, Cambridge: Cambridge University Press.

Freedman, W. L. (2000) "Determination of cosmological parameters," in *Particle Physics and the Universe*, in press, New York: World Scientific Press.

Gross, P. R. and Levitt, N. (1994) *Higher Superstition: The Academic Left and Its Quarrels with Science*, Baltimore: Johns Hopkins University Press.

Hubble, E. P. (1929) "Distance and radial velocity among extragalactic nebulae," *Proceedings of the National Academy of Sciences, USA* 15: 168.

Hubble, E. P., and Humason, M. L. (1931) "The velocity–distance relation among extragalactic nebulae," *Astrophysical Journal* 74: 43.

Jacoby, G. H., Branch, D., Ciardullo, R., *et al.* (1992) "A critical review of selected techniques for measuring extragalactic distances," *Publications of the Astronomical Society of the Pacific* 104: 599.

Kennicutt, R. C., Freedman, W. L., and Mould, J. R. (1995) "Measuring the Hubble Constant with the Hubble Space Telescope," *Astronomical Journal* 110: 1476.

Riess, A. G., Filippenko, A. G., Challis, P., *et al.* (1998) "Observational evidence from supernovae for an accelerating universe and a cosmological constant," *Astronomical Journal* 116: 1009.

Rowan-Robinson, G. M. (1985) *The Cosmological Distance Ladder*, New York: Freeman.

Seeds, M. A. (1999) *Foundations of Astronomy*, 4th edn, New York: Wadsworth.

Sokal, A., and Bricmont, J. (1998) *Fashionable Nonsense: Postmodern Intellectuals' Abuse of Science*, New York: Picador USA (published in the British Commonwealth under the title *Intellectual Impostures: Postmodern Philosophers' Abuse of Science*, London: Profile, 1998).

Wilson, E. O. (1998) *Consilience: The Unity of Knowledge*, New York: Knopf.

8 Above, beyond, and at the center of the science wars

A postcolonial reading

Ziauddin Sardar

Just as America existed before Columbus, science wars have existed for much longer than the nascent discipline of sociology of knowledge. Surprisingly, Columbus and science wars have a great deal in common. Columbus globalized a world view: the world view of modernity. Science wars, in their current manifestations, represent a last-ditch effort to defend that world view. But the science wars themselves have their origins in the formative phase of modernity. The first, pre- and post-Columbus, science wars have two—one visible and one invisible—strands. The visible strand is the post-Columbus warfare of science and Christian theology in Western civilization; the invisible strand is the war of modern science against the sciences of all other civilizations and all other notions of science. The new science wars are a consequence, in a dialectical fashion, of the victory of science in that earlier conflict.

The sciences that existed before the emergence of Western civilization were not all that different from science as it exists today. The sciences that thrived in such civilizations as China, India, and Islam were, within their own framework, just as "rational," "objective," and "universal" as contemporary science claims to be. The mathematics of Brahmagupta (*c.* 568) in India, acupuncture in Chinese science, and Ibn al-Haytham's experiments in optics or ar-Rhaze's observations of smallpox, are all empirically verifiable and are equally valid across time and cultures. What is different between the sciences of non-Western civilization and modern science is that non-Western sciences are products of cultures and civilizations which emphasize the unity of knowledge. Physics is not separated from metaphysics, and science is seen both in terms of a social function and as an integral part of the value structure of the culture within which it thrives. Thus science and religion, or science and values, were or are perceived as two sides of the same coin of knowledge. In other words, the metaphysical assumptions of the culture and civilizations within which non-Western science flourished were openly acknowledged. Of course, these assumptions shaped the style and emphasis of these sciences; sometimes they even shaped the contents of these sciences leading to culturally specific, or tacit, knowledge. However, the emphasis on the unity of all knowledge did not mean, as is sometimes suggested, that all differences of opinion or plural perspectives were precluded. It would be much too simplistic to assume that a civilization like Islam, India, or China contains only one, single point of view and that scientific activity and its products were not contested within each civilization. But in the history of these civilizations, there has been no such thing as a pitched battle between science on the one hand and religion on the other. In Islam, for example, such a war would be inconceivable given the emphasis placed in the Qur'an on reason and empiricism and the praise heaped on scientific knowledge by the Prophet Muhammad. The nearest thing we have is the long-running debate between Greek philosophy and classical scholasticism in Islam; a controversy that lasted over four hundred years and ended with the victory of traditional Islamic thought.

The Europe of Columbus owed most of its science and learning to Islam. From Islam, Europe learned how to reason logically, acquired the experimental method, discovered the idea of medicine, and rediscovered Greek philosophy. Most of algebra, basic geometry and trigonometry, spherical astronomy, mechanics, optics, chemistry, and biology—the very foundation of the scientific renaissance in Europe—came from Islam.[1] But while Islam furnished Europe with its intellectual apparatus, it also presented a series of problems. The main problem, which dates back to the very origins of Islam, was the theological issue of the very existence of Islam as a new post-Christ religion. What need was there for a new Arabian prophet when God's own son had died on the cross to redeem all humanity? The rapid expansion of Islam also presented a military problem. The cultural and scientific advancements of Islamic civilization were perceived as an intellectual problem. Western civilization solved the "problem" of Islam not just by war and conquest, going back to the Crusades, but also by a very specific representation of Islam as the Darker side of Europe. Islam was the evil, infidel Other that forever menaced Christendom and personified everything that Europe was not. While Europe was civilized, Islam was barbaric; while Christianity was peaceful, Islam was inherently violent; while Europe was clean, orderly, and law-abiding, Muslim lands were unclean and inferior, lawless, and chaotic. It followed that Islamic science and Muslim learning, which Europe borrowed, plagiarized and otherwise appropriated freely for over seven centuries, was more than tainted with unsavory colors. 1150—1900 ?

The Islamic intellectual inheritance was a pervasive presence in Europe right up until the end of the sixteenth century. Clearly, a Europe perceived to be far superior to Islam could not admit a deep intellectual debt to the inferior, barbaric civilization of Islam any more than it could acknowledge the existence of an Islamic science that was on a par with anything that Europe produced. Thus began the first and the original science wars: the war of European science against the science and learning of Islam. This war had three main functions: first, to sever the Islamic roots of European science and learning. Second, to make the history of Islamic science all but invisible. Third, to deny the very existence of science in Islam. In the initial stage, this was done consciously as an integral part of the Orientalist scholarship.

Orientalism, as I have stated elsewhere, is "the scholarship of the politics of desire: it codifies Western desires into academic disciplines and then projects its desires onto its study of the Orient" (Sardar 1999: 5). When the sixteenth- and seventeenth-century Orientalists looked at Islamic science they found it to be trivial and, in many cases, not to be science at all, but simply a rag-bag of superstitions and dogma. The fiction was created that Muslims did little more than translate the works of Greeks and were themselves unable to add anything original to them. Thus was born what I call the "conveyer belt" theory: the Muslims preserved the heritage of Greece and, like a conveyer belt, simply passed it on to its rightful heir: Western civilization. Islam was bypassed, and the intellectual roots of the West were reconnected to Greece. The seven-hundred-year history of Islamic science became a dark, blank hole. At later stages, the denial became so total and so pervasive at every level that it became unconscious, and it was extended to other civilizations. Indian and Chinese science also came to be seen as non-science, insignificant and irrelevant when compared to the European achievements. This was the invisible strand of the early science wars.

The visible struggle for the domination of science took place in Europe itself. The myth that relegated non-Western sciences to the dark ages and edges of Europe had a corollary: true science was created by and belonged to the West. But this true science had to be radically different from the non-sciences of other civilizations. In non-Western cultures, several different sources of knowledge are recognized and respected equally. Islam, for example, gives equal emphasis to empirical as well as to intuitive knowledge; reason and revelation are legitimate sources of knowledge and truth. Moreover, new knowledge comes about from the interaction between a whole array of different branches of knowledge, and society itself plays an important part in both shaping and directing that knowledge. Since all cultures and civilizations have equal access to reason and revelation, knowledge can come from anywhere, any civilization, any methodology—no particular culture or civilization has a monopoly over knowledge. Such ideas of science were the unthought of Europe: perceived as dark and unworthy notions, but ever-present, if deeply suppressed, in European consciousness. The reconstruction of science in Europe, as the science and the only way to truth, during the seventeenth and eighteenth centuries, was partly an outcome of this unthought and partly a product of the European colonial project. The unthought found its expression in science's war against Christianity.

If we look at the writings of the founders of the scientific revolution, the militant proclamation of the truths of science is quite clear. Galileo (1953: 63) made a classic statement, which established the hubris of science for centuries afterwards:

> If this point of which we dispute were some point of law, or other part of the studies called the humanities, wherein there is neither truth nor falsehood, we might give sufficient credit to the acuteness of wit, readiness of

answers, and the greater accomplishment of writers, and hope that he who is most proficient in these will make his reason more probable and plausible. But the conclusions of natural science are true and necessary, and the judgement of man has nothing to do with them.

Galileo's stance contrasts sharply with the position of a Muslim scholar like ibn Hazm, who saw law, science, and humanities as equally valid modes of inquiry and truth and accorded them equal respect. "Intellectual inquiry," ibn Hazm suggested, is "useless if it is not supported by the good fortune of religion and by that of sciences of the world" (Chejne 1982: 64). Ethics and empiricism go hand in hand, argued ibn Hazm, for whom the conclusion of science had no meaning without the judgment of community. Prudently, Galileo chose not to include Christian theology in his attack; but Descartes was more direct. In speaking of his humanistic education, in which he first praised and then murdered the whole syllabus, he commented,

> Our theology I revered, and was as eager as anyone else to gain heaven; but having learned that the way thither is open to the most ignorant no less than to the most learned, and that the revealed truths, which guide us on our way, are above our understanding, I should not have dared to submit them to the weakness of my understanding. Indeed, a man who undertook to investigate these truths and who succeeded in his task, would need, in my judgement, to be favoured with some special aid from heaven, and to be himself more than a man.
>
> (Descartes 1960: ii: 41)

In other words, theology declares itself to be impossible as a learned discipline. This, despite the fact that both Descartes and Galileo were (to all intent and purposes) believers. Indeed, the humanism that Descartes was so proud of was itself based on a theology—the theology of Islam. Europe did not invent humanism; as George Makdisi demonstrates so powerfully in *The Rise of Humanism in Classical Islam and the Christian West* (1990), humanism began in Islam and was transferred, almost intact, to Europe.[2]

The self-confidence of natural science, in the tradition of Galileo and Descartes, increased steadily after their lives. Criticisms of its claims to truth came only from outside. The first serious attempt was by Bishop Berkeley, who attacked the mechanics of Newton (who was a not-very-secret Unitarian), and (with greater success), the foundations of mathematics. As a committed defender of the truths of religion, he was outraged by the pretensions of the irreligious scientists to be the bearers of clarity and enlightenment. Ironically, Berkeley became a freethinker in his criticism not of Newton's mechanics but of the calculus. He was concerned with the reasoning whereby the differential calculus is explained, raising the question "does the increment actually reach zero, or not?" The answers he received were totally unsatisfactory, and in his reply he produced this classic analysis of dogmatism in science:

Men learn the elements of science from others; and every learner hath a deference more or less to authority, especially the young learners, few of that kind caring to dwell long upon principles, but inclining rather to take them on trust; And things early admitted by repetition eventually become familiar; And this familiarity at length passeth for evidence.

(Berkeley 1951: 117)

With these words, he explained the phenomenon of explanation by the principle of "every schoolboy knows" that something is obvious, when in fact it is totally obscure. The pamphlet in which he published this was entitled *A Defence of Freethinking in Mathematics*, an ironical accusation that the mathematicians themselves were the dogmatists, who treated any criticism as scandalous. But in the eighteenth century Berkeley was a lonely voice; and even those mathematicians who took his criticisms seriously were sure that there was a simple answer to something so clear as the calculus.

There were later attacks on mechanistic science from what is called the "Romantic" school, which for a while was quite influential in chemistry. This flourished most strongly in Germany, as in Goethe's (unsuccessful) theory of colors and the (successful) drive by the *Naturphilosoph* scientists to demonstrate the unity of electricity and magnetism. But we had to wait until the end of the nineteenth century before the first genuine self-conscious criticisms of basic science emerged from within. It is to be found in the works of Ernst Mach, who was a physicist of some distinction. Mach demonstrated that Newton's Laws of Motion, hitherto accepted as very nearly "synthetic a priori" truths, were in fact quite confused. Their concepts were unclear and their scientific status obscure. Mach went on to analyze the foundations of scientific knowledge, including truth and error, and came up with his own solution to the problem of how scientific knowledge can be considered as genuine: a principle of economy of effort.

After Mach, others made similar critical analyses, notably Karl Pearson in Britain and Pierre Duhem in France. But in all cases the intent was to find a more secure basis for the scientific knowledge which all knew to be genuine. This was a large part of the motivation of the Vienna Circle, which flourished through the 1920s and 1930s until dispersed by the victory of Nazism in Austria. For the Circle, there was an overt political dimension to the struggle between a secular, progressive science and the reactionary theology and metaphysics of the Catholic Church in Austria. Its leader, Moritz Schlick, was assassinated by a student who, although doubtless mad, did also make the political point that Schlick's teachings were undermining traditional certainties.

The end of World War I ushered in the second science wars, where the "academic left" initially made its presence felt. The war exposed the technological weaknesses of the British Empire and led to direct government intervention in the management of science. The monopoly of universities as research institutions was broken as new research institutions were established with public and private funding. To many intellectuals and scholars, particularly of Marxist persuasion, a relationship between science and economics became plainly evident. It led to the formation, in 1918, of the National Union of Scientific Workers (later the Association of Scientific Workers) with a categorically socialist agenda for science. Increased expenditure on science, along with centralized planning, it was argued, would release the liberating potentials of science.

The connection between science and ideology was made explicit in 1931 when a conference on the history of science in London played host to a delegation from the Soviet Union. The key event at the conference was a paper by Boris Hessen on "The social and economic roots of Newton's *Principia*".[3] Hessen argued that Newton's major work was not so much a product of scientific genius or a result of the internal logic of science, but rather a consequence of social and economic forces in seventeenth-century Britain. It fulfilled the needs of the British bourgeoisie. The young British left-wing scientists and historians of science attending the conference took a few years to grasp the full import of Hessen's arguments. But with the publication of J. D. Bernal's *The Social Function of Science* in 1939, the radical science movement had truly arrived. Bernal saw science as a natural ally of socialism: its function was to serve the people and liberate them from capitalism. Bernal combined his Marxist humanitarianism with technocratic and reductionist motives. Despite all its problems, Bernal held on to his faith in science as an objective, neutral mode of inquiry that could produce peace and plenty for all were it not for the corruption of science under capitalism.

The idea of a "socialist science," first suggested in the Soviet Union, also gained currency in Britain. But its realization in the Soviet Union came to be seen as a crude and opportunistic exercise. The Lysenko affair of the 1940s and 1950s, which involved the Soviet geneticists in arguing that heredity can be transformed by means of environmental manipulation and grafting, did great harm to the idea of a socialist science. Later, the avowedly radical British Society for Social Responsibility in Science did manage to organize a conference on the question "Is There a Socialist Science?," but the outcome remained definitely inconclusive.

In the popular perception of science, World War II completed what World War I had started. This time, science was seen to be running the show in the battlefield, as well as moving into government. Scientists were responsible not just for developing new and deadlier forms of chemical and biological weapons but for conceiving, producing, and finally unleashing "the Bomb." The mushroom clouds of the atomic weapons dropped on Hiroshima and Nagasaki declared the end of the era of scientific innocence. Now the connection between science and war was all too evident, the complicit relationship between science and politics had come to the fore, and all notions of scientific autonomy had evaporated. The public, which had hitherto concerned itself largely with the benefits of science, suddenly became concerned with its devastating downside.

The protest against militarized science, starting with the launching of the dissident journal *Bulletin of the Atomic Scientists* by nuclear physicists totally disenchanted by the Manhattan Project in the US, was consolidated by the emergence of CND (Campaign for Nuclear Disarmament) in the later 1950s. Many scientists were concerned that the Bomb should not be seen as an inescapable consequence of physics. This would discourage bright young scientists with ethical concerns about the Bomb from a career in physics. The ploy was to claim that science is neutral: it is neither good nor bad; it is society that puts it to good or bad use. The neutrality argument became a dominant defense of science during the 1950s and the 1960s, and it enabled many scientists to work in atomic physics, even accepting grants from defense establishments, while professing to be politically radical.

The neutrality argument also played a very important part in the evolution of development theory. When development first became a catchword in international politics, in the early 1960s, most of the newly independent countries of the Third World were seen as "underdeveloped."[4] Some, however, were viewed as "developing" along a model similar to the industrial development in Europe. At the foundation of this ethnocentric view of the world—a manifestation of the social Darwinist ideas of the Victorian era, which produced such notions as "White man's burden" and "manifest destiny"—was the belief that science and technology could transform the developed and developing countries into carbon copies of European industrialized states. Science was seen as something that had to be acquired from the West, and technology had to be "transferred." Many Third World scientists totally embraced the ideology of neutrality of science, and spent their entire careers on problems that were conceived in the West and had no relation to their society in the hope that their efforts would bring economic benefits to their countries.

While the radical science movement questioned the neutrality of science, debated its social function, and campaigned against the Bomb, it still saw science very much as a Western concern. Thus while radical historians of science were eager to show how social forces shaped the development of science, they remained largely silent on the role non-Western cultures played in shaping science. So Bernal, for example, explains his reasons for writing *Science in History* as follows:

> In the last thirty years, largely owing to the impact of Marxist thought, the idea has grown that not only the means used by natural scientists in their researches but also the very guiding ideas of their theoretical approach are conditioned by the events and pressures of society. This idea has been violently opposed and as energetically supported; but in the controversy the earlier view of the direct impact of science on society has become overshadowed. It is my purpose to emphasize once more to what extent the advance of natural science has helped to determine that of society itself; not only in the economic changes brought about by the

application of scientific discoveries, but also by the effect on the general frame of thought of the impact of new scientific discoveries.

(Bernal 1954: i: 1)

But Bernal perceived "society" largely as an autonomous Western society, and civilization (always in the singular) for him is essentially Western civilization which starts with the Greeks and progresses linearly to "our time." In a four-volume study, he devoted less than ten pages to Islamic science. China and India do not even get a mention.

However, the historiography of science was about to change quite radically. The foundation for this change had been established by two truly monumental studies. The first was George Sarton's *Introduction to the History of Science*, published between 1927 and 1948. What is surprising about Sarton's study is that the first three volumes of the four-volume chronological study are largely devoted to science in Islam. Sarton not only made it clear that Western science is inconceivable without Islam, but suggested that the sheer scientific contribution of Islam, both in terms of quantity and quality, should concern those who see science purely as a Western enterprise. Perhaps the reason for Sarton's influence was that his work was little more than a list of names and references with hardly any synthesis. The second study, Joseph Needham's massive multi-volume *Science and Civilisation in China*, published from 1954 onwards, performed the same function for China, and even more effectively.

Both Sarton and Needham showed that science was not limited to Western societies; non-Western societies also had highly developed and sophisticated cultures of science. But for them this did not mean that there could be different sciences, or indeed different definitions of science. Indeed, Needham was able to isolate the "problematic" areas of Chinese science, such as acupuncture, and label them "non-science." Science may be tainted with politics, and embroiled with the military, but it was still largely seen as a neutral, objective, and universal pursuit of truth.

Thus the history of science still presented science as a linear pursuit of progress, where the sciences of other civilizations were so many tributaries—in some cases, as Islam and China, rather large tributaries but tributaries nevertheless—which merged into the great universal river of Western science. The philosophy of science, as well as the broader public image of science, also promoted the assumption that science gives truth and is the only way to truth, and that the truth accumulates as a single, universal perspective of Western civilization. This was imbibed, most strongly of all, by students of science itself.

In this picture, science had been almost universally seen in heroic terms. The lone scientists struggled against all odds for the sake of truth. Science was a pure, autonomous activity, separate from technology and industry and above society. The purity of scientific research was particularly enshrined in universities where research was pursued for the sake of knowledge and where future generations of scientists were trained. The scientist was someone engaged in a unique social role who required protection and had autonomous existence from the rest of society. The scientists, particularly great scientists, were the object of inquiry for historians and philosophers of science. Thus the emphasis of the history of science was on discoveries by great scientists and the justification of these discoveries in the unique objectivity, impartiality, and universality of science.

But there was a contradiction lurking in this beautiful picture. If science is always true, and also always progressive, how do we account for the changes in theories and explanations? One way is to deny that the changes are real, and to see progress as the simple discovery of new things. But that does not hold; thus even Newton espoused a theory which in the nineteenth century was considered incorrect, namely that light travels as particles rather than as waves. So the history books fell back on another explanation: when new truths were discovered, or errors exposed, it was the good scientists who went along with progress. Those who opposed what we now know to be true were somehow bad scientists, were not following scientific method. The historians then had their work defined: to show that science is always true, and when it is not, that the good scientists were right.

The unravelling of the triumphalist, dogmatic ideology of science is associated with the exposure of the contradiction between infallible truth and permanent progress. The first move was made by Karl Popper. While Popper was loosely associated with the Vienna Circle in the 1920s, he was not a member of it, being highly critical of some aspects of its philosophical position. The Circle asserted that metaphysics and theology were meaningless, for they consisted of propositions that could not be verified. By contrast, Popper hit upon "falsification" or "falsifiability" as the real demarcation criterion between scientific knowledge and knowledge of other sorts (which he did not altogether dismiss). He argued that there is no final truth in science, and that scientific progress is achieved by "conjectures and refutations."[5] By positing the self-critical spirit as the essence of science, Popper shifted the defense of science from its achieving the truth of objective knowledge to its embodying the good of the values of a liberal society. He can be seen as the last of the defenders of the traditional ideology of science. But he had already given away too much. The arrival of Thomas Kuhn, who was the true philosophical revolutionary, however reluctant and inconsistent he was in his attitudes to what he had wrought, spelled the beginning of the end of science as we have known it.

Kuhn reduced scientists from bold adventurers discovering new truths to simple puzzle-solvers within an established world view. Instead of world view, Kuhn used the term "paradigm." By using the term paradigm, he writes,

I mean to suggest some accepted examples of actual scientific practice— examples which include law, theory, application, and instrumentation together—provide models from which spring particular coherent traditions of scientific research. These are traditions which history describes under such rubrics as "Ptolemaic Astronomy" (or "Copernican"), "Aristotelian dynamics" (or "Newtonian"), "corpuscular optics" (or "wave optics") and so on.

(Kuhn 1962: 10)

In Kuhn's scheme, the term paradigm is closely related to "normal science": those who work within a dogmatic, shared paradigm use its resources to refine theories, explain puzzling data, establish increasingly precise measures of standards, and do other necessary work to expand the boundaries of normal science. This dogmatic stability is punctuated by occasional revolutions. Kuhn describes the onset of revolutionary science in vivid terms. "Normal science," he suggests, "often suppresses fundamental novelties because they are necessarily subversive of its basic commitments . . . [but] when the profession can no longer evade anomalies that subvert the existing tradition of scientific practice" (Kuhn 1962: 5–6), then extraordinary investigations begin. A point is reached when the crisis can only be solved by revolution in which the old paradigm gives way to the formulation of a new paradigm. Thus "revolutionary science" takes over; but what was once revolutionary itself settles down to become the new orthodoxy, the new normal science. So science progresses, argues Kuhn, through cycles: normal science, which is the science we find in the textbooks, is followed by revolution which is followed again by normal science and then again by revolution. Each paradigm may produce a particular work that defines and shapes the paradigm: Aristotle's *Physica*, Newton's *Principia* and *Optiks*, and Lyell's *Principles of Geology* are examples of works that defined the paradigms of a particular branch of science at particular times.

In the publication of *The Structure of Scientific Revolutions* and the debate that followed we find the genesis of the third—and current—science wars. The right-wing Kuhn was a radical departure from the left-wing radical critique of science which was concerned more with tinkering with the periphery rather than changing the center. The post-war academic left still held on to a belief in a science that gradually progressed to cumulative acquisition of knowledge—all that was necessary was to purge it of its bourgeois influence and bring it into the service of the working classes. In sharp contrast, Kuhn presented normal science as a dogmatic enterprise. If we regard outmoded scientific theories such as Aristotelian dynamics, phlogistic chemistry, or caloric thermodynamics as myths, he argued, then we can just as logically consider the current theories to be irrational and dogmatic. After Kuhn, the understanding of science could never be the same again.

The developments that followed after Kuhn—the debate between Paul Feyerabend and Imre Lakatos,[6] the emergence of sociology of knowledge, the evolution of the feminist critique of science, right down to the Sokal hoax[7]—have been documented, debated, and discussed quite thoroughly elsewhere. But what has been happening over the past three decades, besides the science war—away from the center where defenders of the purity of science and its critics among the "academic left" and the feminist—is far more interesting. The last three decades have seen the emergence of what we can describe as postcolonial science studies. The rubric "postcolonial" does not mean "after colonialism." Rather it signifies how the colonizing nature of contemporary science continues to shape the relationship between Western and non-Western science, how the dominating tendencies of Western science are resisted, and what is being done to replace the grand narrative of Western science and give voice to non-Western discourses of science and learning. The postcolonial enterprise of science will probably have far greater impact on the future of science than the current phase of the science wars.

Kuhn's analysis shows how science works in one civilization: the Western civilization. His insights are hardly news for postcolonial writers on science: the very premise of all non-Western sciences is that science operates and progresses within a world view. Kuhn does, however, provide (Western) legitimacy for the existence of science in other, non-Western, paradigms. Other civilizations, such as Islam, China, and India, and other cultures, such as those of the Pacific Islanders, Sub-Saharan Africans, and Native Americans, can now be recognized as having different practices and different kinds of sciences based on their own paradigms. One of the primary goals of postcolonial science studies is to show that this in fact is the case. What makes Western science distinctively Western is its metaphysical assumptions about nature, universe, time, and logic. The idea that nature is there only for the benefit of man (*sic*) and, as Bacon put it, has to be "tortured" to reveal its secrets, is totally alien to most non-Western cultures. Islam and China, for example, do not look at nature as an object. In Islam, nature is a sacred trust that has to be nurtured and studied with due respect and appreciation. In Chinese tradition, nature is seen as a self-governing web of relationships with a weaver, with which humans interfered at their own peril. Similarly, Western ideas of universe and time are culturally based. The Western idea of universe as a great empire, ruled by a divine logos, owes more to centralized royal authority in Europe than to any universal notion—it is totally incomprehensible to the Chinese and Indians. Similarly, while Western science sees time as linear, other cultures view it as cyclic as in Hinduism or as a tapestry weaving the present with eternal time in the hereafter as in Islam. While modern science operates on the basis of either/or Aristotelian logic (X is either A or non-A), in Hinduism logic can be fourfold or even sevenfold. The fourfold Hindu logic (with these extra forms: X is neither A nor non-A, nor both A and non-A, nor neither A nor non-A) is both a symbolic logic as well as a logic of cognition. It can achieve a precise and unambiguous formulation of universal statements without using the "for all" formula. Thus the metaphysical assumptions underpinning modern science make it specifically Western in its main characteristics. A science that is based on different notions of nature, universe, time, and logic would therefore be a totally different enterprise from Western science.[8]

The conventional (Western) history of science, however, does not recognize different types of civilizational or cultural sciences. It has represented Western science as the apex of science, and maintained its monopoly in four basic ways. First, it denied the achievements of non-Western cultures and civilizations as real science, dismissing them as superstition, myth, and folklore. This dismissal is carried out by using a tautological argument whereby Western culture is defined as superior to all other cultures; by analogy the science, technologies and medicines of inferior cultures are, well, inferior. William Henry III provides the most recent example of this kind of shameful thinking in his book *In Defense of Elitism*. Henry defines superior cultures in terms of certain basic criteria. "A superior culture," he writes, "preserves the liberty of its citizens," "provides a comfortable life, relatively free from want," and "expands, by trade or cultural imperialism or conquest." Now, since non-Western cultures are seen as authoritarian, unable to fulfill the basic needs of their people and were colonized by the West, they are by definition inferior. So, Henry has no problem in reaching his conclusion that a "superior culture promotes modern science (and) Western medicine" (Henry 1994: 29–31). It was this kind of analysis that led to ruthless suppression, during colonialism, of Islamic and Indian medicine. In India, for example, these systems were dismissed as mere mumbo jumbo and their practice banned. In Tunisia the French actually instituted a death penalty and killed numerous practitioners of Islamic medicine. Only recently have these systems been recognized by the World Health Organization as legitimate medical systems on a par with Western medicine—after their use by and benefits to rural populations were amply demonstrated.

Second, the histories of non-Western sciences were largely written out of the general history of science. So wide is this practice that it has become an integral part of Western consciousness. For example, in Floyd Bloom's (2000: 229–231) timeline of discovery, published "to help readers negotiate *Science* magazine's year-long series, *Pathways to Discovery*," nothing exists between 131 and 200 (when Galen wrote his textbook on anatomy) and between 1285 and 1349 (when William of Ockham produced his razor, the logical implement he wielded to trim absurdities out of arguments). This despite the fact that Galen was rewritten by Ibn Sina, whose Canon of Medicine was a standard medical text in Europe for over six hundred years, and the fact that William of Ockham learned all his logic from Muslim philosophers. As Don Ihde points out (2000: 803) in his comments on *Science*'s "timeline," this is a "traditional and parochial display of Eurocentrism regarding the history of science and technology." We know, at least, that Su Sung's heavenly clockwork, a mechanical clockwork, was operating in China by 1090. Gutenberg may have developed the moveable type in 1454, but metal (copper) moveable type was invented in Korea two centuries earlier. However, the point here is not who did what first, but a mindset that sees the period between Greek sciences and the emergence of European science as a dark era where nothing worthy ever happened.

Third, Europe rewrote the history of the origins of European civilization to make it self-generating. Many notable scientists, Newton in the late seventeenth century and Kelvin in the late nineteenth century among them, were involved in creating and disseminating the revisionist history of the origins of modern European civilization and the creation of the Aryan model. This model introduced the idea that Greek culture was predominantly European, and that Africans and Semites had nothing to do with the creation of the classical Greek civilization. But the identification of Greek culture as European is questionable on several grounds. For one thing, the idea of "Europe," and the social relations such an idea made possible, came centuries later— some would date it to Charlemagne's achievements, others to the fifteenth century. (Greece and Rome were civilizations of the Mediterranean.) Moreover, it was Islam that introduced Greece to Europe, and due to the spread of Islam the diverse cultures of Africa and Asia can also claim Greek culture as their legacy.

Fourth, through conquest and colonization, Europe appropriated the sciences of other civilizations, suppressed the knowledge of their origins, and recycled them as Western. We know that many scientific traditions were appropriated and fully integrated into Western sciences without acknowledgment. Thus the pre-Columbian agriculture that provided potatoes and many other food crops was absorbed into European agricultural practice and science. Mathematical achievements from Arabic and Indian cultures provide another example. Francis Bacon's three great inventions that made modern Europe—printing, gunpowder, and the magnetic compass—are now admitted to have all come from China. Knowledge of local geographies, geologies, botany, zoology, classification schemes, medicines, pharmacologies, agriculture, and navigational techniques were provided by the knowledge traditions of non-Europeans.

The emergence of postcolonial science studies is an attempt to expose this Eurocentrism, reclaim the history of non-Western sciences, and rediscover the modes and styles of doing non-Western sciences today. Postcolonial science studies began with empirical work in the history of Islamic, Indian, and Chinese sciences. For example, Fuat Sezgin's monumental work on Islamic science, *Geschichte des Arabischen Schrifttums* (1967–), and the work of scholars in France working with Roshdi Rashed[9] reveal how truly awesome, both in depth and breadth, were the scientific achievements of Muslim civilization. Ekmeleddin Ihsanoglu's work (1999)[10] on Ottoman science has revealed it to be far from as "insignificant" as it is often projected. Similarly, D. M. Bose, S. N. Sen, P. V. Sharma, and numerous other historians have shown that Indian science cannot be easily dismissed.[11]

While the Western camp has been forced to acknowledge the new historical reality, its counterattack has been based on the argument that great scientists of Islam, for example, were all secularists. Thus their achievements owe little to Islam but everything to secularism and they can be represented as a part of the great history of Western science.[12] This is a patently absurd suggestion. We are talking about highly religious men before the age of secularism; the separation of the sacred and the profane was beyond their wildest imagination. They were all, even the most unorthodox, Muslim first and anything else second. For them, science without values was profane. Many of them were indeed also humanists; but their humanism was derived from their own world view and was a product of their Islamic commitment. Everything they did had an Islamic subscript; this is why they spent so much time establishing the direction of the Makkah from every point on the globe (qibla), developing a mathematics for the Islamic laws of inheritance, studying the heavens, establishing hospitals, developing medicine, and generally pursuing learning.

But postcolonial scholarship of science goes much further than an empirical historical undertaking. It also seeks to establish the connection between colonialism, including neo-colonialism, and the progress of Western science. For example, in his several books, Deepak Kumar,[13] the Indian historian and philosopher of science, has sought to demonstrate that British colonialism in India played a major part in how European science developed. The British needed better navigation, so they built observatories, funded astronomers, and kept systematic records of their voyages. The first European sciences to be established in India were, not surprisingly, geography and botany. Throughout the Raj, British science progressed primarily because of the military, economic, and political demands of the British, and not because of the purported greater rationality of science or the alleged commitment of scientists to the pursuit of disinterested truths. Moreover, postcolonial science critics seek to develop a specific position on Western science as demonstrated by the work of Indian scholars Ashis Nandy (1980; 1988) and Claude Alvares (1991; 1992) and a string of young Muslim scholars, including my own output (Sardar 1982; 1988). Finally, postcolonial scholarship of science seeks to reestablish the practice of Islamic, Indian, or Chinese science in contemporary times. There is, for example, a whole discourse of contemporary Islamic science devoted to exploring how a science based on the Islamic notions of nature, unity of knowledge and values, public interest, and so on could be shaped.[14] A similar discourse on Indian science has also emerged in the last decade.[15]

The main parties to the science wars have ignored much of the postcolonial scholarship. The same fate has befallen Jerome Ravetz's seminal work *Scientific Knowledge and Its Social Problems* (1971) which has played a key, though underlying, role in shaping a great deal of postcolonial science criticism. Ravetz's identification of the social problems of science could be easily witnessed by postcolonial writers in their own societies. His four problematic categories of science—shoddy science, entrepreneurial science (where securing grants is the name of the game), reckless science, and dirty science—may have been somewhat shrouded in the West but they were all too visible in countries like India, Pakistan, Egypt, and Malaysia. Moreover, Ravetz's contention that we need to abandon the idea that "science discovers facts," or that it is "true or false"—presented long before sociology of knowledge became a fashion—in favor of a broad interpretation of science as a craft takes us back, or rather forward, to a common notion of science in non-Western societies. If science is seen as craft, then "truth" is replaced by the idea of "quality" in the evaluation of scientific output. Quality firmly places both the social and ethical aspects of science, as well as scientific uncertainty, on the agenda. All this was evident at a famous conference on "The Crisis in Modern Science," organized by the Consumer Association of Penang and held during November 21–26, 1986 in Penang, Malaysia.[16] The Penang conference, which produced a famous declaration on science and technology, was a key event in the development of postcolonial science discourse: it was here that the possibility of contemporary non-Western discourses of sciences was first established.

With the emergence of postcolonial science, defenders of scientific purity encounter a contradiction all of their own. Should they refuse to engage in dialogue with these new enemies of (Western) reason, declaring them, as Popper had declared Kuhn a few decades earlier, to be the enemies of civilization? If so, then they would be exposed as not belonging to the polity where all different opinions, short of those engaging in violence, should be debated. But engagement brings its own risks. For no one can deny that Western civilization has operated a totally closed system where the only true knowledge is Western knowledge and the only true science is Western science, thus marginalizing, suppressing, and rendering invisible sciences of all other civilizations. But now that this science is exposed as a social activity, where choices have to be made and errors in scientific judgment and social behavior occur, the clearly identifiable difference between Western and non-Western science evaporates. The superiority of Western science cannot be defended any more.

To a large extent, postcolonial science studies make "science wars" quite irrelevant. Moreover, the rapid change in circumstances will also gradually deflate the science wars. One is an ironic twist in the relations of science and religion, which may well overturn the whole ideology laid down by Galileo and Descartes. For while science still claims exclusive possession of truth about nature, in the matter of ethical judgments about the consequences of scientific advance, no one can claim that science has all the answers. The recent decision by Craig Venter, to consult with clergymen before going ahead to construct a virus from its parts, puts a completely different perspective on the traditional debate. But this is only a particularly salient point in the general transformation of the social and ethical situation of science. Science is simply not what the new realists and old idealists claim it to be. Its ideological and value-laden character has been exposed beyond doubt. But it is not simply a question of how political realities of power, sources of funding, the choice of problems, the criteria through which problems are chosen, as well as prejudice and value systems, influence even the "purest" science. Or that the burden of proof, in terms of statistical inference, can be found at the heart of scientific method. Or that most of the metaphysical assumptions of science are those of the European civilization. It is more an issue of how science is now associated with uncertainties and risks. A great deal of the most important contemporary science is no longer normal science in Kuhnian terms. As can be seen from a string of recent controversies from the BSE (Mad Cow Disease) affair in Britain to the issues of genetically modified foods, science cannot deliver hard and fast answers to a host of contemporary issues. The old paradigm of science which provided certainty and assurance is no longer valid.

The paradox mentioned above, that Western "neutral science" can affect social and economic affairs in the developing countries, has returned in a new form and with a vengeance; it is precisely that same reductionist, abstracted science which shapes the new intensive technologies like genetically modified organisms. And these are now fully identified with neo-colonialism through such products as "terminator" crops. Moreover, the close link of such technologies with biopiracy is beyond doubt. It is Kuhnian "normal scientists" who go out to sample the biological heritage of the non-Western world, so that their multinational bosses can then steal it by patenting it as their own.

Many working scientists could regard this triumphalist view of Western science as somewhat exaggerated. The initial reaction could be that this view of Western science has a lot more to do with Western historians and philosophers of science, particularly those with imperialist agendas, rather than the scientists themselves. Well, dogmatism in science has certainly existed in past epochs; one only has to read the first few paragraphs of Kuhn to see what the history of science has been. While the historians and philosophers perpetuated an imperialist view of science, the scientists themselves participated in shaping it. For example, it was scientists at the forefront of medical research in the colonies who sought and participated in the ruthless suppression of non-Western medical systems. A more considered view could be that science may have been dogmatic in the past but Western science just is not like that any more. Now most Western scientists regard science as a tool. But if that had been the attitude just fifty years ago, we would not have had Kuhn. And had this attitude existed only a decade ago, we would not have had science wars. It was only a few years ago that distinguished American scientists confidently looked forward to discovering the genes for violence and homelessness. There are still some prominent scientists who believe and proclaim that genetic engineering is a precise technique, giving us just the properties we want and no others. The recent Darwin versus Creationism controversy also illustrates how much dogmatism still persists in science. As Steve Fuller notes (see this volume), the American science establishment considers the treatment of Darwinian evolution and Creation science as mutually exclusive options in the American public school curriculum. Although two thirds of Americans who believe in evolution also believe that it reflects divine intelligence, such compatibility has yet to be seen as a philosophically respectable option, and consequently has no legal import. But what exactly would be wrong with teachers trying to render findings compatible with the Creationist commitments of most of their students? One common answer is that the presupposition of a divine intelligence or teleology has retarded biological inquiry in the past and has not contributed to evolutionary theory since the time of Darwin's original formulation. Yet the contrary presuppositions of mechanistic reduction and random genetic variation have equally led to error (Fuller 2000: 110).

Science teaching remains as dogmatic as ever. But this does not mean that many working scientists do not realize that scientific knowledge is always contingent and that the next experiment or observation may cast doubt on what has gone before. However, this increasing common sense among working scientists is very recent, partial, and differentiated. It is a product of the radical transformation in science itself, which has ceased to be science as we know it. Now it has become what Funtowicz and Ravetz (1993: 735–755; text slightly modified—private communication) call "post-normal science":

> We are now witnessing a growing awareness among all those concerned with global issues that no single cultural tradition, no matter how successful in the past, can supply all the answers for the problems of the planet. Closely connected with the emergence of these changed attitudes is a new methodology that reflects and helps us guide the development of a new scientific approach to problem solving for global environment issues. In this, uncertainty is not banished but is managed, and values are not presupposed but are made explicit. The model for scientific argument is changing from a formalized deduction to an interactive dialogue. The paradigmatic science is no longer one whose explanations are unrelated to space, time, and process: the historical dimension, including human reflection on past and future change, is now becoming an integral part of a scientific characterization of nature and our place in it.

In other words, science is returning to its non-Western roots in Islam, India, and China. Funtowicz and Ravetz's studies, over the last decade, of the emergence of post-normal science, lead them to believe that the scientific community would no longer be limited simply to scientists. In situations where "facts are uncertain, values in dispute, stakes high, and decisions urgent" (Funtowicz and Ravetz 1992: 251–273, 254),[17] the questions of quality in science, along with issues of policy, will become paramount. They would lead to an "extended peer community" which would use "extended facts" which would include even anecdotal evidence and statistics gathered by a community. Lay persons, journalists, campaigners, housewives, and theologians will join scientists in making decisions of science policy and shaping and directing scientific research. Science would thus be democratized and values of multiculturalism would play an increasing role in shaping its character. So out goes the supremacy of Western culture and in come the very ethics and values that bring terror to the hearts of alleged neutral objectivists. This is the essence of the moral panic in a large segment of the scientific community—a panic that produced the science wars. This manifestation of the uncertainties inherent in science is a mark of nostalgia for a secure and simple world that will never return.

Notes

1 For a concise survey of Islamic science, see Donald R. Hill (1993).
2 See also George Makdisi's *The Rise of Colleges: Institutions of Learning in Islam and the West* (1981), which shows how Europe appropriated the idea of the university, complete with "professorial chairs," from Muslim civilization.
3 Hessen's paper can be found in N. Bukharin *et al.* (1971).
4 For a discussion of the concept of "development," see Sardar (1999a: 44–62).
5 See Karl R. Popper (1963), see also Karl R. Popper (1959).
6 Represented by Paul Feyerabend (1975) and Imre Lakatos (1976); see also Imre Lakatos and Alan Musgrave (1970).
7 In the interest of constructivist objectivity, I should mention that Sokal cites this humble author in his bibliography!
8 For a detailed discussion of non-Western ideas on nature, time, and logic see Goonatilake (1998).
9 Summarized in Roshdi Rashed (1996).
10 There are also sister volumes on astronomy, chemistry, geography, and other disciplines.
11 D. M. Bose *et al.* (1971), P. V. Sharma (1992), and Debiprasad Chattopadhyaya (1992).
12 The strongest proponent of this position, and a good stereotype of the colonial view of history of science, is Toby Huff. See his *The Rise of Early Modern Science: Islam, China and the West* (1993). See also my review of this book in *Nature*, 368, 376–378 (March 24, 1994).
13 See Deepak Kumar (1995) and (1991). See also Satpal Sangwan (1991), Susantha Goonatilake (1984), R. K. Kochar (1992–1993), and George Sheverghese Joseph (1995).
14 On the Islamic science debate see Ziauddin Sardar (1989); the special issue on "Islamic Science," edited by Ahmad Bouzid, of *Social Epistemology*, 10(3–4), July–December 1996; and numerous articles in the *Journal of Islamic Science* (Aligarh, India).
15 On contemporary rediscovery of Indian science, see the proceedings of the Indian Congress on Traditional Sciences and Technologies of India, November 28– December 3, 1993, Indian Institute of Technology, Bombay, Conference Programme: 101–102.
16 Sardar, *The Revenge of Athena* (1988), is based on the conference and contains the Penang Declaration on Science and Technology.
17 For further discussion on post-normal science see Jerome Ravetz (editor) "Post-Normal Science," Special Issue *Futures* 31(7), September 1999.

Bibliography

Alvares, Claude (1991) *Decolonising History: Technology and Culture in India, China and the West, 1492 to the Present Day*, Goa: Other India Press.
Alvares, Claude (1992) *Science, Development and Violence*, New Delhi: Oxford University Press.

Berkeley, George, Bishop of Cloyne (1951) *A Defence of Freethinking in Mathematics*, published in *The Works of George Berkeley, Bishop of Cloyne*, ed. A. A. Luce and T. E. Jessop, Vol. 4, Edinburgh and London: Nelson.

Bernal, J. D. (1954) *Science in History*, London: Pelican.

Bloom, Floyd E. (2000) "The endless pathways of discovery," *Science* 287: 229–231 (14 January).

Bose, D. M., Sen, S. N., and Subbarappa, B. V. (eds) (1971) *A Concise History of Science in India*, New Delhi: National Commission for the Compilation of History of Sciences in India.

Bouzid, Ahmad (1996) *Social Epistemology*, special issue on "Islamic Science," 10(3–4) (July–December).

Bukharin, N., *et al.* (1971) *Science at the Crossroads*, London: Frank Cass.

Chattopadhyaya, Debiprasad (ed.) (1992) *Studies in the History of Science in India*, New Delhi: Asha Jyoti.

Chejne, A. G. (1982) *Ibn Hazm*, Chicago: Kazi Publications.

Descartes, R. (1960) *Discourse on Method* (1638), tr. A. Wollaston, London: Penguin Books.

Feyerabend, Paul (1975) *Against Method: Outline of an Anarchistic Theory of Knowledge*, London: New Left Books.

Fuller, Steve (2000) *The Governance of Science*, Buckingham: Open University Press.

Funtowicz, S. O. and Ravetz, J. R. (1992) "Three types of risk assessment and the emergence of post-normal science," in Krimsky, S. and Golding, D. (eds) *Social Theories of Risk*, Westport CN: Praeger.

Funtowicz, S. O. and Ravetz, J. R. (1993) "Science for the post-normal age," *Futures* 25(7) (September): 735–755.

Galilei, Galileo (1953) *Dialogue on the Great World Systems* (1633), ed. G. de Santillana, Chicago: University of Chicago Press.

Goonatilake, Susantha (1984) *Aborted Discovery: Science and Creativity in the Third World*, London: Zed.

Goonatilake, Susantha (1998) *Towards Global Science: Mining Civilizational Knowledge*, Bloomington: Indiana University Press.

Henry, William A., III (1994) *In Defense of Elitism*, New York: Doubleday.

Hill, Donald R. (1993) *Islamic Science and Engineering*, Edinburgh: Edinburgh University Press.

Huff, Toby (1993) *The Rise of Early Modern Science: Islam, China and the West*, Cambridge: Cambridge University Press.

Ihde, Don (2000) "Timeline travails," *Science* 287 (February): 803.

Ihsanoglu, Ekmeleddin (ed.) (1999) *History of Mathematical Literature During the Ottoman Period*, 2 vols, Istanbul: Organisation of Islamic Conference's Research Centre for Islamic History, Art and Culture.

Indian Congress on Traditional Sciences and Technologies of India, November 28–December 3, 1993, Indian Institute of Technology, Bombay, Proceedings, Conference Programme: 101–102.

Joseph, George Sheverghese (1995) "Cognitive encounters in India during the age of imperialism," *Race and Class* 36(3): 39–56.

Kochar, R. K. (1992–1993) "Science in British India" *Current Science* 63(11) (December): 689–694 and 64(1) (January): 55–62.

Kuhn, Thomas S. (1962) *The Structure of Scientific Revolutions*, Chicago: University of Chicago Press.

Kumar, Deepak (1995) *Science and the Raj*, New Delhi: Oxford University Press.

Kumar, Deepak (ed.) (1991) *Science and Empire*, New Delhi: Anamika Prakashan.

Lakatos, Imre (1976) *Proofs and Refutations*. Cambridge: Cambridge University Press.

Lakatos, Imre and Musgrave, Alan (eds) *Criticism and the Growth of Knowledge*, Cambridge: Cambridge University Press, 1970.

Makdisi, George (1981) *The Rise of Colleges: Institutions of Learning in Islam and the West*, Edinburgh: Edinburgh University Press.

Makdisi, George (1990) *The Rise of Humanism in Classical Islam and the Christian West.* Edinburgh: Edinburgh University Press.

Nandy, Ashis (1980) *Alternative Sciences: Creativity and Authenticity in Two Indian Scientists*, New Delhi: Oxford University Press.

Nandy, Ashis (ed.) (1988) *Science, Hegemony and Violence*, New Delhi: Oxford University Press.

Popper, Karl R. (1959) *The Logic of Scientific Discovery*, London: Hutchinson.

Popper, Karl R. (1963) *Conjectures and Refutations: The Growth of Scientific Knowledge*, London: Routledge and Kegan Paul.

Rashed, Roshdi (ed.) (1996) *Encyclopaedia of the History of Arabic Science*, 3 vols London: Routledge.

Ravetz, Jerome (1971) *Scientific Knowledge and Its Social Problems* Oxford: Oxford University Press (2nd edn, New Brunswick: Transaction Publishers, 1996).

Ravetz, Jerome (ed.) (1999) "Post-normal science," *Futures*, Special Issue 31(7) (September).

Sangwan, Satpal (1991) *Science, Technology and Colonisation: The Indian Experience 1757–1857*, New Delhi: Anamika Prakashan.

Sardar, Ziauddin (1988) *The Revenge of Athena: Science, Exploitation and the Third World*, London: Mansell.

Sardar, Ziauddin (1989) *Explorations in Islamic Science*, London: Mansell.

Sardar, Ziauddin (1999a) "Development and the location of eurocentrism," in Munck, Ronaldo and O'Hearn, Denis (eds) *Critical Development Theory*, London: Zed.

Sardar, Ziauddin (1999b) *Orientalism*, Philadelphia: Open University Press.

Sardar, Ziauddin (ed.) (1982) *The Touch of Midas: Science, Values and the Environment in Islam and the West*, Manchester: Manchester University Press.

Sezgin, Fuat (1967–) *Geschichte des Arabischen Schrifttums*. Leiden: Brill.

Sharma, P. V. (1992) *History of Medicine in India*, New Delhi: Indian National Science Academy.

Sokal, Alan (1996) "Transgressing the boundaries: towards a transformative hermeneutics of quantum gravity," *Social Text* 46–47: 217–252.

9 Voodoo medicine in a scientific world[1]

Robert L. Park

The most common of all follies is to believe passionately in the palpably untrue.

(H. L. Mencken)

Introduction

In 1993 *Ageless Body, Timeless Mind: The Quantum Alternative to Growing Old* by Deepak Chopra MD (1993) was at the top of the *New York Times* bestseller list week after week, even while *Quantum Healing* (1989), also by Chopra, was still in the top ten from two years earlier. The promise of both books was that illness and even the aging process can be banished by the power of the mind. If anyone should doubt it, Dr. Chopra explains that it is all firmly grounded in quantum theory. Commenting on the occasional spontaneous remission of cancer, for example, Chopra explains that "such patients apparently jump to a new level of consciousness that prohibits the existence of cancer . . . this is a quantum jump from one level of functioning to a higher level." Lest you imagine that he was using "quantum" in some metaphorical sense, he informs the reader that "once known only to physicists, a quantum is the indivisible unit in which waves may be emitted or absorbed."

Physicists wince at Chopra's use of "quantum" in the context of curing cancer. Much of the sort of New Age quackery that is so popular these days is peddled for vague chronic symptoms such as headaches, fatigue, back pain, or digestive disorders. Treatments such as magnet therapy, homeopathy or reflexology, which have only a placebo effect, may actually benefit the not-very-sick-to-begin-with if they replace unneeded antibiotics or antidepressants. But if something like Chopra's spiritual healing is substituted for genuine medical intervention in the treatment of cancer, it may deny patients any prospect of a cure, while adding a sense of guilt to their suffering. Reality, when at last it sets in, is all the more cruel.

Society, however, holds it to be a virtue to hold certain beliefs in spite of any evidence to the contrary. Belief in that which reason denies is associated with steadfastness and courage, while skepticism is more often identified with cynicism and weak character. The more persuasive the evidence against a belief, the more virtuous it is deemed to persist in it.

But something does not add up. According to a Gallup poll,[2] nearly half of all Americans believe in a literal interpretation of the Biblical account of creation—a world less than ten thousand years old in which humans were created in essentially their present form. This percentage has remained almost constant for fifteen years, unaffected by new fossil discoveries, DNA evidence, modern cosmology, or Supreme Court decisions blocking the teaching of Creationism.

It has remained unaffected as well by the 1993 all-time blockbuster film *Jurassic Park*. The theme of *Jurassic Park*, I should note, was profoundly anti-science: having discovered the secret of life itself, scientists use their awesome power not to eradicate disease and hunger, but to create an amusement park. Nevertheless, the movie depicts, more or less accurately, aspects of a world that existed sixty-five to a hundred million years ago.

It is difficult to find anyone who did not see the movie. Millions of schoolchildren, and even pre-schoolers, can identify a half-dozen dinosaurs by name. People flock to museum exhibits of prehistoric life, seeming to have an insatiable appetite for anything having to do not only with dinosaurs, but also with our hominid ancestors. Can it really be that something like half the population believes the world is less than ten thousand years old? How can people have this fascination with our prehistoric past and yet accept the Biblical account of creation?

People, it seems, have a way of compartmentalizing their beliefs. Which set of beliefs the pollster taps into depends on the context of the question. The question concerning Biblical creation, for example, challenged the respondents to demonstrate their faith.

Society honors faith. Faith can be a positive force, enabling people to persevere in the face of daunting odds, but the line between perseverance and fanaticism is perilously thin. Carried to extremes, faith becomes destructive—the Heaven's Gate cult, for example. The faith of the cult members was tested and unfortunately they passed the test. By contrast, defending a belief in the Biblical account of creation to a pollster carries no risk whatever. Unlike mass suicide, such a poll does not measure depth of conviction.

It is, for example, easy to read too much significance into polls showing widespread public belief in UFOs and alien visits to Earth. Carl Sagan saw in the space-alien myth the modern equivalent of the demons that haunted medieval society (Sagan 1996), and for a susceptible few they are no doubt a frightening reality. But for most people, beliefs involving UFOs and space aliens do not seem to be deeply held. They are a way to add a touch of excitement and mystery to uneventful lives. Besides, polls are anonymous: they offer a safe way for people to thumb their noses at authority.

Scientists, of course, also hold beliefs that go beyond the scientific evidence. To what extent, it is fair to ask, are the interpretations given to scientific evidence shaped by the world view of the scientist? A good place to examine this question is the current controversy over global warming. It is the sort of dispute that is seized upon by postmodern critics of science as proof that science is merely a reflection of cultural bias, not a means of reaching objective truth. They portray scientific consensus as scientists "voting on the truth."

The great global warming debate

André Gide, the great French moralist, wrote in his journal a half-century ago that "man's responsibility increases, as that of the gods decreases." Every step taken by science claims territory once occupied by the supernatural. Where once we accepted storms and drought as divine will, there is now overwhelming scientific evidence that we ourselves are influencing Earth's climate. Scientists have the responsibility of telling the world whether our planet is headed for some climatic catastrophe of our own making and, if so, what steps can be taken to avoid it.

The evidence comes from a revolution in climate research over the past decade, brought about by new observational techniques including satellites, and a prodigious increase in computational and data-storage capabilities made possible by microelectronics. It now seems undeniable that surface temperatures are warmer than they were a hundred years ago. There is also no doubt that the burning of fossil fuels since the beginning of the industrial revolution has resulted in a significant increase in atmospheric carbon dioxide.

What is in dispute are the long-term consequences if these trends continue. The presence of CO_2 and other greenhouse gases in the atmosphere helps to keep our planet warm. CO_2 is also the raw material for plant growth. Using the energy of sunlight, plants draw CO_2 from the air to make hydrocarbons, releasing oxygen into the atmosphere as a by-product. When the plant dies and decays, or is burned, or is eaten by an animal, the carbon is recombined with oxygen and returned to the atmosphere as carbon dioxide, completing the cycle.

Before the industrial revolution, the concentration of atmospheric carbon dioxide represented a natural balance, but in a little more than a century, humans have disrupted that balance by burning fossil fuels that were built up in underground deposits over a period of hundreds of millions of years. If this release of carbon dioxide into the atmosphere continues, climatologists warn, there could be disastrous consequences in the next century: many of the world's great cities will be submerged by rising sea levels as the polar ice caps melt, and drastic changes in rainfall patterns could wreak havoc on food production. The nations of the world, many scientists argue, should take immediate steps to control the burning of fossil fuels, at least until we can better predict the consequences. We have no right, they declare, to place future generations in jeopardy.

Not all scientists agree. A number of prominent scientists point out that there were periods of global warming long before man began burning fossil fuels, and CO_2 is a relatively minor greenhouse constituent in the atmosphere.

They contend that any rise in global temperature since 1850 may simply be the result of natural solar variations. Moreover, the increase in atmospheric CO_2 has stimulated plant growth, making this a lusher, more productive world, capable of sustaining a much larger population. Besides, if there is some greenhouse effect it may be just what Earth needs to stave off another ice age. The more industrial growth we have, including increased burning of fossil fuels, they argue, the better off we will be. They stop just short of telling people they have a moral obligation to burn more hydrocarbons.

If scientists all claim to believe in the scientific method, and if they all have access to the same data, how can there be such deep disagreements among them? What separates the two sides in the climate controversy, however, is not so much an argument over the scientific facts, scientific laws or even the scientific method. If the climate debate was just about the laws of physics, there would be little disagreement. But the climate is the most complicated system scientists have ever dared to tackle. There are huge gaps in the data for the distant past which, combined with uncertainties in the computer models, means that even small changes in the assumptions result in very different projections far down the road. Neither side disagrees with that. Both sides also agree that CO_2 levels in the atmosphere are increasing. What separates them are profoundly different political and religious world views. In short, they want different things for the world.

The great global warming debate then, is more an argument about values than it is about science. It sounds like science, with numbers and equations and projections tossed back and forth, and many of the antagonists believe sincerely that they are engaged in a purely scientific debate. Most scientists, however, were exposed to political and religious world views long before they were exposed in a serious way to science. They may since have adopted a firm scientific world view, but earlier world views "learned at their mother's knee" tend to occupy any gaps in their scientific understanding, and there are gaps aplenty in the climate debate.

The special responsibility of scientists is to inform the world of its choices. But it may be years before anthropogenic effects on climate are well enough understood to make those choices clear. On one side, there are scientists who warn that we cannot afford to wait. These Malthusian pessimists argue for the "precautionary principle." Changing human behavior takes time, they contend, and if we do not start now it may be too late to prevent a catastrophe.

On the other side are the technological optimists, who insist that to make policy before we understand the problem, if indeed a problem exists, is to invite failure. To have followed such a policy in the past, they argue, would have denied the world the unquestioned benefits of industrialization. They insist that science will always find solutions to the problems generated by population growth and industrialization.

That scientists are influenced by their beliefs is undeniable. But so long as both sides adhere to the scientific process, the ideological passion of Malthusian pessimists at one extreme and technological optimists at the other may actually serve as a powerful motivation for better science. Each side in the climate debate knows that every flaw in their data, or oversight in their analysis, will be seized upon by their opponents. Both sides strive to produce better data and better analysis in the conviction (faith if you wish) that the truth will vindicate their prejudice. The numbers, when science finally learns them, will ultimately decide the winner. In the end, the result will be a better understanding of global climate. To the frustration of its postmodern critics, science works.

Science works precisely because its results are always tentative. When better information becomes available—better measurements or a more comprehensive theory—science textbooks are rewritten with hardly a backward glance. Many people are uneasy standing on such loose soil; they seek a certainty that science cannot offer. For these people the unchanging dictates of ancient religious beliefs or the absolute assurances of zealots and quacks have a more powerful appeal. Paradoxically, however, their yearning for certainty is often mixed with a grudging respect for science. They long to be told that modern science validates the teachings of some ancient scripture or New Age guru.

The purveyors of quack cures have been particularly successful at exploiting this ambivalence, often repackaging ancient medical practices in the language and symbols of modern science. It is perhaps in this area of "alternative medicine" that the dangers of the anti-science movement are most immediately apparent.

Strange attraction

The current revival of magnet therapy is a good example. It seems to have started on the golf course, which was also the epicenter of the copper bracelet fad twenty years ago. At first, golf pro shops were about the only places you could buy therapy magnets. Now they are sold in department stores and pharmacies everywhere. Worldwide, this has quickly grown into a billion-dollar business.

Those who market therapy magnets point out that magnetic cures were used by the Chinese thousands of years ago. That is true, but the Chinese were also using powdered rhinoceros horn to restore virility. Unfortunately, they still do, with the result that the world is running out of rhinos. Rhinoceros horn and magnet treatments date back centuries before the discovery of the circulation of blood, or the germ theory of disease—indeed, to a time when almost nothing was known of human physiology or disease. By contrast, the great medical advances that are extending and improving our lives today emerge from a detailed scientific understanding of how the body works. Viagra, for example, may yet save the rhino from extinction.

In the early sixteenth century the famed alchemist and physician Paracelsus began using powdered lodestone in salves to promote healing. A naturally occurring magnetic mineral, the mysterious power of lodestone to move iron without even touching it suggested great power. However, William Gilbert, physician to Elizabeth I and the father of the scientific study of magnetism, pointed out that the process of grinding the lodestone into powder destroyed the magnetism (Livingston 1997). Nevertheless, magnetic cures were introduced into England a century later by Robert Fludd, who declared it to be a remedy for all disease—if properly applied. "Properly applied" included placing the patient in the "boreal position," with the head north and the feet south, while being treated.

By far the most famous of the "magnetizers" was Franz Mesmer, who carried the technique from Vienna to Paris in 1778 and soon became the rage of Parisian society (Mackay 1841). Dressed in colorful robes, he would seat patients in a circle around a vat of "magnetized water." Iron rods protruding from the vat were held by the patients, while Mesmer waved magnetic wands over them. Eventually, however, Mesmer discovered that it was just as effective if he left the magnets out and merely waved his hand. He called this "animal magnetism." Benjamin Franklin, who was in Paris on a diplomatic assignment, suspected that Mesmer's patients did indeed benefit from the strange ritual, because it kept them away from the bloodletting and purges of other Parisian physicians

These physicians bitterly resented Mesmer, an outsider who was attracting their most affluent patients. At the urging of the medical establishment, Louis XVI appointed a royal commission to investigate. This remarkable group included Franklin, who was the world's foremost authority on electricity, Antoine Lavoisier, the founder of modern chemistry, and Dr. Joseph Guillotin, whose famous invention would one day sever the head of his friend Lavoisier.

The commissioners designed a series of ingenious tests in which some subjects were deceived into thinking they were receiving Mesmer's treatment when they were not, while others received the treatment, but were led to believe they had not. The results established beyond any doubt that the effects of Mesmer's treatment were due solely to the placebo effect. The commission report, drafted by M. Bailly, an illustrious historian of astronomy, has never been surpassed for clarity or reason. It destroyed Mesmer's reputation in France and he retired to Austria.

Nevertheless, magnetic therapy eventually crossed the Atlantic. Its most famous practitioner in the United States was Daniel Palmer, who opened Palmer's School of Magnetic Cure in Davenport, Iowa in 1890. Like Mesmer, Palmer soon discovered that his patients recovered just as quickly if he omitted the magnets and merely "laid on hands." Thus was founded "chiropractic therapy," and his school became Palmer's College of Chiropractic.

The history of medicine is littered with the bones of medical practices that millions of people once swore by and are now known to be worthless or even harmful. In *The Fragile Species*, Lewis Thomas points out that treatments such as purges and leeches were finally abandoned only when they were objectively compared to simply allowing the illness to take its course. How remarkable as we enter a new millennium, with all that science has learned about both magnetism and physiology, that magnetizers should once again attract a great following. Alas, there is no government commission of Franklins and Lavoisiers to challenge their claims.

Modern research into the effect of magnetic fields on the human body has been driven not by magnetic therapy, but by safety considerations associated with the phenomenal growth in the use of magnetic resonance imaging (MRI) for medical diagnoses and research. MRI subjects the entire body to a magnetic field about a hundred times stronger than the localized field of a therapy magnet. Happily, no ill effects have been found from exposure to MRI fields. Indeed, there are almost no effects at all—just a few faint sensory responses, such as a slight metallic taste and visual sensations of flashing lights if patients move their eyes too rapidly. The fact is that the stuff we are made of just is not very magnetic.

Scientists might be more inclined to take reports of the efficacy of magnets more seriously if there were some plausible explanation of how the magnets work. One claim is that blood, because it contains iron, is attracted by the magnets. The iron in hemoglobin, however, is in a chemical state that is not ferromagnetic—that is, it is not attracted to a magnet.

It's easily tested. An excess of blood shows up as a flushing or reddening of the skin. That is why the skin turns red when you use a hot water bottle: blood is being diverted to the heated area to serve as a coolant. But you will discover that placing a magnet of any strength against your skin produces no reddening at all. In fact, blood is weakly diamagnetic, which is to say that at sufficiently high fields it would be repelled by a magnet.

It has also been suggested that a magnetic field causes water molecules in the blood to align, somehow improving circulation. But in fact no alignment of water molecules is observed even at the field strength of MRI magnets. At the temperature of blood, water molecules are jostling each other so violently that their orientation is randomized. To align them, a magnetic field would have to be strong enough to overcome this thermal energy. Dr. John Schenck, at General Electric's Research and Development Laboratory, the leading authority on the effect of MRI fields on the body, calculates that fields thousands of times stronger than any that have ever been generated on Earth would be needed to align a significant fraction of the water molecules. Indeed, at the field strength of therapy magnets it is hard to imagine any mechanism that would overcome thermal effects.[3]

How strong are the fields of therapy magnets? They are typically rated at a few hundred gauss. The strongest and most expensive I could find were gold-plated neodymium alloy magnets rated at 800 gauss, measured at the surface. That is not much compared to the 30,000–40,000-gauss electromagnets used in MRI, but it is a lot for a small permanent magnet. Fifty years ago, permanent magnets had to be long to prevent the demagnetization effect, and were usually made in the shape of a horseshoe. The development of thin, powerful permanent magnets using rare-earth compounds and ferrites is one of the unsung triumphs of modern materials science, making possible everything from miniature Walkman headphones to laptop computers. It also triggered the new magnet therapy fad—no one was going to show up on the golf course wearing horseshoe magnets.

The makers of therapy magnets warn against using them "around credit cards or during pregnancy." The instructions on one therapy kit, however, show a magnet being worn on the wrist. Your wrist normally passes within an inch or so of your hip pocket when you walk. That is where most men keep their credit cards—and 800 gauss is certainly enough to wipe out the magnetically coded information on the cards. Why do the magnets not erase people's credit cards?

They make therapy magnets the same way they make refrigerator magnets. Since refrigerator magnets are only meant to hold phone messages and Dilbert cartoons, they are designed to have a very short range field. This is done by making them in the form of narrow strips of alternating north and south poles. Right at its surface, such a magnet may be quite strong, but a very short distance away, depending on the width of the strips, the north and south poles will effectively cancel.

How quickly the field of a therapy magnet drops off is easily estimated by using it the way you would use a refrigerator magnet—attach slips of paper to a refrigerator or file cabinet with one of the magnets. Even the strongest, you will find, will hold no more than about ten slips of paper. Ten thicknesses of paper is about one millimeter.

The field of these magnets would hardly reach through the skin, much less into muscles and joints. Not only does the magnetic field have no power to heal, it does not even reach the injury. The only power of the magnet is the power of the placebo.

Given time, we recover from most of the things that afflict us without any sort of intervention. Evolution has equipped our bodies with an elaborate array of natural defenses for dealing with injury or disease: bones knit, blood clots, antibodies seek out invading organisms, and so on. However, if we have been given herbal tea, or sugar pills, or someone who is reputed to be a healer utters an incantation or shakes a rattle over us, we are easily persuaded that the healing, when it comes, is the work of the healer. Depending on the culture, the healer will use props, such as a witch doctor's mask, or a stethoscope hung around the neck, to make the association more vivid. Our brain credits the treatment with any improvement that follows.

There is another part to the story, however. Once we are convinced of the healing power of a doctor or a treatment, something very remarkable happens: a sham treatment induces real biological improvement. This is the "placebo effect." Healers have relied on the placebo effect for thousands of years, but until recently it was usually referred to as the "mysterious" placebo effect. Scientists, however, are beginning to understand the complex interaction of the brain and the endocrine system that gives rise to the placebo effect.

People seek out a doctor when they experience discomfort, or when they believe that something about their body is not right. That is, they suffer pain and anxiety. The response of the brain to pain and fear, however, is not to mobilize the body's healing mechanisms, but to prepare it to meet some external threat. It is an evolutionary adaptation that assigns the highest priority to preventing additional injury. Stress hormones are released into the blood stream to increase respiration, blood pressure and heart rate. The brain is preparing the body for action—recovery must wait.

The first objective of a good physician, therefore, is to relieve stress. That usually involves assuring patients that there is an effective treatment for their condition, and that the prospects for recovery are excellent—if they will just follow the doctor's instructions. Since we recover from most of the things that afflict us, the brain learns to associate recovery with visits to the doctor. Most of us start to feel better before we even leave the doctor's office.

Even in the first half of the twentieth century, most medicine was based on the placebo effect. Before 1940, about the only medicines doctors had in their bags were laxatives, aspirin and sugar pills. Studies have shown, in fact, that if the patient believes the sugar pills will relieve pain, they will be about 50 percent as effective as the aspirin. The mechanism, however, is presumably quite different. Pain is a signal to the brain that there is a problem and something needs to be done about it. It is induced by prostaglandins released by white blood cells at the site of inflammation. Aspirin blocks the production of prostaglandins.

The placebo, on the other hand, works by fooling the brain into thinking the problem is being taken care of. Once the brain is persuaded that things are under control, it may turn the signal level down by releasing endorphins, opiate proteins found naturally in the brain. Rather than blocking the production of prostaglandins, the endorphins block their effect. As powerful as the placebo effect can be, it is extremely doubtful that placebos can cause hair to grow on bald heads or shrink tumors, as some have claimed, but there is no doubt that placebos can influence the perception of pain.

Whether a person responds to a placebo depends almost entirely on how well the doctor plays his part. All the medical props, from the stethoscope to the framed medical school diploma, and all the soothing assurances given to the patient, can be wiped out by an unguarded frown or a slightly raised eyebrow as the doctor goes over the patient's lab report. A placebo is most likely to work, therefore, if the doctor genuinely believes it to be a cure and communicates that conviction to the patient. Not surprisingly, then, those who imagine they possess miraculous healing powers, or truly believe they have discovered some wondrous cure that everyone else has overlooked, tend to be particularly good at evoking the placebo response.

As medical scams go, magnet therapy may not seem like a big deal. Magnets generally cost less than a visit to the doctor and they certainly do no harm. But magnet therapy can be dangerous if it leads people to forego needed medical treatment. Even for the not-very-sick-to-begin-with, magnet therapy tends to reinforce a sort of upside-down view of how the world works, leaving people vulnerable to predatory quacks if they become seriously ill.

What is science?

Scientists generally believe the cure for pseudoscience is to raise science literacy. We must ask, however, what is it we would like a scientifically literate society to know? There are a few basic concepts—Darwinian evolution, conservation of energy, the periodic table of the elements—that every educated person should know something about, but the explosive growth of scientific knowledge has left scientists themselves struggling to keep up in their own specialties. It is not so much knowledge of specific science that the public needs as a scientific world view: an understanding that we live in a universe governed by physical laws that cannot be circumvented.

A scientific world view is not "natural." Our brains are constantly processing information coming in from our senses and forming new beliefs about the world around us, using a very simple algorithm: If we observe that B follows A, then the next time A occurs, the brain is primed to expect B to follow. With repetition the belief is solidified. This sort of belief generation was going on long before our ancestors began to resemble humans, but with the advent of language we are exposed to vicarious beliefs—beliefs conveyed to us by others. This is clearly useful, but that which allows us to learn from others also exposes us to manipulation by them.

But we are not condemned to suffer the tyranny of this primitive "belief engine" (Alcock 1995). Although it is still in place, evolution provided us with an antidote in the form of the marvelous pattern recognition ability residing in the higher centers of the human brain. Indeed, we are driven to seek patterns in everything our senses respond to. So intent are we on finding patterns that we often insist on seeing them even when they are not there, like familiar shapes constructed from Rorschach blots.

Once we recognize how easily we can be fooled by the belief-generating machinery of the brain, we can use the higher centers of the brain to construct a more refined strategy that combines our aptitude for recognizing patterns with the accumulation of observations about nature made possible by language. Such a strategy is called "science."

E. O. Wilson defined it this way: "Science is the systematic enterprise of gathering knowledge about the world and organizing and condensing that knowledge into testable laws and principles" (Wilson 1998). It boils down to two questions: is it possible to devise an experimental test?, and does it make the world more predictable? If the answer to either question is "no," it is not science.

The success and credibility of science are anchored in the willingness of scientists to expose their ideas and results to the scrutiny of other scientists, and to modify or abandon accepted facts and theories in the light of more complete or reliable experimental evidence. Adherence to these rules provides a mechanism for self-correction that sets science apart from other ways of knowing.

There are those who are not content with the world revealed by the scientific process. They long for a world in which things are some other way than the way they are. Some cannot accept that we are prisoners of the Sun. They look wistfully at the stars that fill the night and imagine that there must be some way to overcome the limitations of space and time. Others refuse to believe that the dreams and emotions that stir within us can be reduced to the laws of physics. They seek in science some evidence of a cosmos that cares about them. All that scientists can do is to explain what we have learned.

For a million years, our species was confronted with a world we could not hope to understand. Now, almost within the span of a single human lifetime, the book of nature has been opened wide. On its pages we are finding, if not a simple world, then at least an orderly world in which everything from the birth of stars to falling in love is governed by the same natural laws. Those laws cannot be circumvented by any amount of piety or cleverness, but they can be understood. Uncovering them should be the highest goal of a civilized society. Not, as we have seen, because scientists have any claim to greater intellect or virtue, but because the scientific method transcends the flaws of individual scientists. Science is the only way we have of separating the truth from ideology, fraud, or mere foolishness.

Notes

1 Adapted from Robert L. Park (2000) *Voodoo Science: The Road from Foolishness to Fraud.* New York: Oxford University Press.
2 The Gallup poll results were cited in Kenneth Chang, ABCNEWS.COM, 17 August, 1999.
3 John Schenck, private communication, 18 August, 1999.

Bibliography

Alcock, J. E. (1995) "The belief engine," *Skeptical Enquirer*, May–June: 14.
Chopra, D. (1989) *Quantum Healing*, New York: Bantam.
Chopra, D. (1993) *Ageless Body, Timeless Mind: The Quantum Alternative to Growing Old*, New York: Random House.
Livingston, J. D. (1997) *Driving Force: The Natural Magic of Magnets*, Boston: Harvard.
Mackay, C. (1841) *Extraordinary Popular Delusions and the Madness of Crowds*, London: Bentley.
Sagan, C. (1996) *The Demon-Haunted World: Science as a Candle in the Dark*, New York: Random House.
Thomas, L. (1997) *The Fragile Species*, 2nd edn, New York: Simon and Schuster.
Wilson, E. O. (1998) *Consilience: The Unity of Knowledge*, New York: Knopf.

10 The stigma of reason

Irrationalism as a problem for social theory

David Norman Smith

Introduction

Irrationality is ancient, but protests against reason are specifically modern. Self-conscious "irrationalism," indeed, initially crystallized as the mirror image of the rationalism of the early modern era. In this century, irrationalism has risen to unprecedented heights, and it has often taken an anti-scientific form. The aim of this chapter is to explore in a preliminary fashion how and why this happened, with particular attention to several prominent currents of contemporary irrationalism. Such currents of thought repudiate reason in the name of "higher" principles: spirit and heart, life and blood, body and soul; wilderness, nature, the earth; experience and will, fate and fantasy, authenticity and existential resolve. Reason, irrationalists say, suppresses life rather than serving it.

Historically, the leading forms of irrationalism have flown the colors of romanticism (in the eighteenth and nineteenth centuries) and neo-romanticism (in the twentieth century). These, I would argue, are cultural currents that share, as their core tendency, a spirit of resistance to many of the decisive features of modern capitalism, including science.[1] Capitalism is viewed by romantics as a dehumanizing force that reduces the local to the universal, the personal to the impersonal, and the concrete to the abstract. Money displaces the sacred, calculation infiltrates the imagination, and even nature is subjugated. The romantic response, in other words, is oppositional. But here a contradiction arises. Some romantics defy capitalism in the name of reason —a rehumanized reason which, they say, is needed to overcome the purely formal, dehumanizing "logic" of the balance sheet. For romantics of this type—of whom Marx is the paradigm case—the profit motive is malignant precisely to the degree that it is humanly irrational, placing the acquisitive needs of capital above the qualitative needs of people. Other romantics, however, defy reason altogether, calling for a return to the enchantment of faith and myth. This impulse—which is plainly irrationalist—was the central tendency of the original "Romanticism" that flourished in the wake of the French Revolution of 1789.

The early Romantics were defenders of everything that grew, blindly and "organically," from the tangled roots of the past. Hence when the leaders of the French Revolution tried to cloak their Enlightened rationalism in mythic form—offering a "Cult of Reason" in lieu of traditional religion—the Romantics were not deceived. They saw that, beneath this cultic form, there lurked a powerful wish to remake the world by reason alone. Many leading Romantics rejected this wish as hubris, and scorned Kant's new critical rationalism as lifeless pedantry. This led Hegel, as an uncompromising defender of philosophic reason, to assail the "self-styled" Romantic philosophizing that declares "the cognition of truth to be a futile endeavor." It is appalling, he declared, "that *reason*, and again *reason*, and in endless repetition *reason* is arraigned, belittled, and condemned" (Hegel [1821] 1991: 18–19). In particular, Hegel opposed Schleiermacher's popular romantic theology, which rested on the irrationalist claim that religious truth can be found only in "feeling." This assertion, Hegel believed, betrays "contempt for, and hatred of, thinking—the misology of which Plato spoke long ago."[2]

For Hegel, such misology is utterly naive. Since "feelings" can affirm absolutely anything, they prove nothing: "Feeling," he warned, "is the absolute indeterminacy which acknowledges itself as a standard"; it is "the arbitrary will . . . to do whatever it pleases and to make itself into an oracle of what has worth" (Hegel [1822] 1987: 261). For Hegel, irrationalist "feeling" doctrines are both arbitrary and relativist, since they salute whatever springs from the subterranean depths of emotion. What is "felt" today will differ from what is felt tomorrow. What is felt in one culture will be unknown or even unknowable elsewhere. Thus in this worldview anything can be deemed "true," given the right circumstances.

For Hegel, on the contrary, there is only one truth—the truth of reason. Claims are either true or false, objectively.

The gift of uncertainty

Hegel's defense of reason was highly influential, but irrationalism remained attractive as well. Indeed, many people in the later nineteenth century were so disturbed by the culturally dissonant implications of rationalist critique that they clung to irrationalism with renewed fervor. This was true, for example, of the deeply religious Danish philosopher Sören Kierkegaard. While Hegel had insisted that the truth of Christianity is objectively knowable, Kierkegaard could find no rational reply to the objection that particular individuals can never truly "know" universal truths. It is paradox, Kierkegaard felt, to say that eternal truth is knowable by transient selves—to believe that finite minds can encompass infinite wisdom. There is a fatal contradiction, Kierkegaard concluded, between mortal mind and immortal truth. Still, he refused to say that finitude alone is real. On the contrary, Kierkegaard remained steadfast in his Christian resolve. The Infinite truth, he maintained, has nothing to do with objectivity, reason, or cognition. Only the spirit is capable of truth, and Truth, indeed, is spiritual, not rational. It is, ultimately, subjective, a "passion" for the unknowably Infinite.

For Kierkegaard, that is, the contradiction between human finitude and Infinite Truth can be resolved only by a leap of faith. Can he "know" that this faith is valid? By no means. But Kierkegaard scorns the quest for metaphysical "certainty" as a parlor game. The object is not to "know" the Unknowable, but rather to trust the Almighty. Indeed, objective "certainty" about the truths of the Trinity would make faith superfluous for the believer, who would "know" with dry complacency what now requires a surrender of prideful reason. Hence truth, for Kierkegaard, is precisely the spiritual embrace of the Infinite in all its infinite uncertainty.

Uncertainty may be a trial for the believer, but it is also a gift—for without uncertainty, without paradox, there can be no true faith. Faith leaps, Kierkegaard reminds us, only where reason hesitates: "If I wish to preserve myself in faith I must constantly be intent upon holding fast the objective uncertainty, so as to remain out upon the deep, over seventy thousand fathoms of water, still preserving my faith" (Kierkegaard [1846] 1941: 182).[3]

Anyone, even a pagan, can will the infinite, Kierkegaard says. "But Christianity also requires that the individual risk his thought, venturing to believe *against the understanding . . .*" Without this final step, "the whole affair becomes mere prattle and old wives' bawling," worthy only of "Jews and women" (Kierkegaard [1846] 1941: 182). Nor, he adds, can "anyone who has not been demoralized with the aid of science" doubt that truth lies in the infinite passion of faith. Uncertainty, not certainty, is the ground of truth. It tempts the believer with the apple of doubt, which only faith can resist.[4]

Blinded by the light

The sacrifice of reason, then, is among Kierkegaard's highest ideals. Implicitly, he gives reason a central role in his system, since only reason can gauge the uncertainty that faith must accept. But there is a new vehemence in Kierkegaard's anti-rational animus, which gives his indictment of objectivity a wrathful quality. Reason is now arraigned, belittled, and condemned with scorn. This polemical tone, together with Kierkegaard's exaltation of existential passion and decision, recurs often in the various neo-romantic irrationalisms which have captivated wider audiences in the twentieth century. So, too, does his habit of referring, however casually, to Jews and "science" as bearers of heartless objectivity. Indeed, in the hands of other writers, this argument would soon leave the shadows to eclipse all others as a rationale for anti-rationalist thought. Jews and Reason came to be regarded as almost synonymous—and both were reviled.

Ernest Renan, in 1859, was among the first to draw this connection. Positing race as the "secret" of history, and calling Semites and Indo-Europeans the two racially opposed "poles of the movement of humanity," Renan traced the "essential inferiority" of Jews to their allegedly austere and abstract mentality. The "Semitic intelligence," he said, is indifferent to life, change, and imagination.[5] Obsessed by a dogma of the One True God, Jews are dead to the world of myth and multiplicity. Their worldview is "immutable," their language "metallic," their wit and creativity nil. Jews have "a minimum of religion," and they lack all appreciation for the mythopoetic depth of the Aryan mind. Aryans, by contrast, are free spirits. Where Jews can grasp only abstraction, Aryans delight in myths and allegories that leave "the boundaries of God, humanity, and the universe floating in an indeterminate haze."[6]

For Renan, that is, Jews personify small-minded, inflexible Reason, restricted by racial destiny to demythologizing clarity and consistency. Jews embrace a sterile and dogmatic certainty that leaves no room for spiritual fertility. Blinded by the light of divine revelation, Jews can see nothing else. Aryans, in contrast, embody all the contrary virtues of Romantic poetry—imagination, subjectivity, creativity.[7]

This way of thinking had a powerful impact. In the 1880s and 1890s antisemitism grew to massive proportions in France, Germany, Austria, and Russia, and many leading antisemites (Barrès, Maurras, Soury, Drumont, Picard, and others) faithfully reproduced Renan's portrait of the Semitic mind (Wilson 1982: 471). Barrès, for example, held that Jewish thinking is "too clear, impersonal, like a bank account" (Wilson 1982: 611). Many others portrayed Jews as intellectual rather than intuitive, calculating rather than creative. In these ways the allegedly "deracinated" Jews were said to differ wholly from Indo-Europeans, whose spirit was characterized as germinal and prolific, like the earth itself.[8]

Race and reason

Jews, then, had become idols of reason for the antisemite. Sculpted by fertile "Aryan" fancy into mythic figures, Jews became visible signs of abstract reason. But antisemitism in this phase was not yet anti-scientific. For many antisemites, science was a productive enterprise, remote from dogmatic rationalism. Scientists were praised for their openness to experience, their willingness to suspend judgment and countenance uncertainty, their creativity and Puritan ethic. Thus, at this stage, Romantic objections to reason did not necessarily apply to empirical research. Indeed, antisemitism itself struck a pseudo-scientific pose in this period, often blending indictments of abstract reason with "scientific" accounts of race, language, and prehistory.

Antisemitic pseudo-science has remained formidable, but at the turn of the century a new, more consistent anti-rationalism won an audience as well. Houston Stewart Chamberlain, for example, drew many disciples—including Kaiser Wilhelm and the future Nazi ideologue Alfred Rosenberg—with a radicalized version of Renan's antithesis between Jews and Aryans.[9] Like Renan, Chamberlain held that, while Aryans are poets and dreamers, Jews are "born rationalists . . . The creative element, the real inner life, is almost totally wanting in them."[10] But Chamberlain went beyond Renan in two crucial ways. On the one hand, he deployed a rhetoric of race. This had fateful consequences—"the great popularity of the racial doctrine," Franz

Neumann says, "dates from the publication" of Chamberlain's book (Neumann 1944: 107).[11] His second innovation was to place a heightened emphasis on Aryan subjectivity. Even racism was now grounded in intuition: "The possession of 'race' in our *own consciousness* carries immediate conviction as nothing else does. Any member of a decidedly pure race will sense the fact all the time." For Chamberlain, that is, science is unnecessary even for the zoological notion of race: "Without troubling myself about a definition, I have demonstrated what race is in my own breast."[12]

Reason, which is credited to the Semitic race, is now discredited by Aryan intuition. The anti-scientific implication was perfectly plain, and Chamberlain was sternly rebuked by purportedly "scientific" racists. "Wilser censures me," he mused unapologetically, "because I never formulate a clear concept, but leave the reader to infer . . . what I mean by race; the characteristics of a race 'hover vaguely' before my eyes; I go so far, and am so 'hopelessly unscientific,' as to evolve them out of my 'consciousness'." Chamberlain proudly accepts this characterization, adding disdainfully that "Wilser himself is one of the dogmatists of race," seeking the chimera of assured knowledge on matters "which neither he nor I nor anyone else can really 'know'."[13]

This, plainly, is just a step away from a general repudiation of science.[14] That step would soon be taken.

The neo-romantic turn

Many streams of self-conscious irrationalism—*Lebensphilosophie*, intuitionism, vitalism and others—bubbled to the surface in the early twentieth century. The popularity of these currents made possible the successful emergence of "a demagogic populism," Zeev Sternhell tells us, "that decried intelligence and the use of words and glorified action, energy, and force" (Sternhell 1986: 36). This demagogy grew more strident as the war approached, and flourished as never before in its aftermath.

Max Weber, lecturing on "Science as a Vocation" in 1918, called attention to the breadth and depth of the anti-scientific mood then sweeping Germany. For youth in particular, Weber stressed that "the intellectual constructions of science constitute an unreal realm of artificial abstractions which with their bony hands seek to grasp the blood-and-the-sap of true life without ever catching up with it" (Weber [1918] 1946: 140–141). The shock of defeat, the failure of Prussian martial and industrial prowess to assure victory, left many Germans cynical about science, technology, business, and politics. "They believe they have experienced the agony and collapse of the militarist world and universal democracy, the decay of capitalism and socialism. They thirst for a unified *Weltanschauung*." So wrote Weber's friend Troeltsch ([1921] 1989: 59). This questing mentality, Weber added, leads its votaries into "the service of idols whose cult today occupies a broad place on all street corners and in all periodicals"—idols of irrational "personality" and "experience," proffered as vehicles of "redemption from the intellectualism of science in order to return to one's own nature and therewith to nature in general" (Weber [1918] 1946: 137, 142). Genius, inspiration, and intuition were now deemed the sole paths to existentially valid insight. On all sides, "impresarios" of inspiration boasted of their gifts of grace and insight. "Today," Weber concludes, "such conduct is a crowd phenomenon" (Weber [1918] 1946: 137).[15]

The key intellectual representatives of this new anti-scientism—Scheler, Bergson, Klages, Spengler, and George—hearkened back to early Romanticism. All, besides valuing intuition over intellect, went a decisive step further as well, mounting a challenge not only to reason but also to the most basic tenets of the rational-scientific outlook—that is, the notions of objective causality and reality. To this we now turn.

The pathos of the biocentric

Intimations of the anti-scientific mood of the new romanticism were widely apparent on the eve of World War I. Max Scheler, for example, voiced a characteristic sentiment when he called, in 1913, for a *Lebensphilosophie* inspired by a "new attitude"—"a *surrender* of self to the intuitional content of things, . . . a movement of profound trust in the unshakableness of all that is simply *given*." This, he says, requires a break with scientific norms: "This is not the squinting, critical gaze" of Descartes, which starts with "universal doubt," but rather a "wide-eyed gaze of wonder." Kant's critique, which, "in its dominating fashion . . . penetrates the world of things," threatens what Scheler values most—surrender, not mastery; trust, not doubt.[16] "Bergson rightly says," Scheler later remarked, "that 'confidence' is the philosopher's basic attitude towards the world, 'defiance' that of science."[17] Hence the new worldview that Scheler defends is "the extreme opposite of any philosophy born out of the spirit of technical civilization" (Scheler 1913, cited in Staude 1967: 21).

In this anti-technical spirit, Scheler goes so far as to affirm that genius, like sanctity, is "*not* subject to causal explanations by science" (Scheler [1919] 1987: 17). Genius defies explanation, just as (more broadly) transcendence defies science. But Scheler did not elaborate this anti-causal premise. For this we must turn to Ludwig Klages and Oswald Spengler.

Klages, the founder of an occult pseudo-psychology, was in some ways a conventional neo-romantic. Positing a decisive "antagonism between 'heart' and 'head,' . . . instinct and reason," Klages sided, unsurprisingly, with Heart and Instinct against "the authority of reason."[18] He railed against Enlightenment and democracy, protested the "incarnate skepticism" of the Jews, and attributed the rise of humanitarian morality to race-mixing and (quite literally) "bad blood."[19] But in principle and in detail Klages was unprecedentedly extreme. Affirming "Biocentrism" against "Logocentrism"—Blood versus Mind, Body versus Ego—Klages was so deeply anti-rational that he regarded even feeling with suspicion, since "feelings are nearly always conscious" (Green 1974). On similar grounds, he was wary of will and imagination, since will tends to subject nature to an "empire" of its own design—a design that springs from intellect and imagination.[20] Klages was also an iconoclast with respect to the "personality," which he abhorred as a vessel of purpose and planning.[21]

In short, Klages embraces the usual premise—that intellect is "the killing of life."[22] He does so with such extremism, however, that he winds up rejecting anything even remotely linked to mind. Imagination, feeling, will, personality—these, ordinarily, are the highest ideals of neo-romanticism. But Klages is so inflamed by romantic irrationalism that he goes to new extremes. Now, even subjectivity is suspect, since the "subject," too, is often willful and objective.[23] Pulsing blood and the pounding heart are his new ideals. "Never before," as Lukács observes, "had reason been challenged so openly and radically" (Lukács [1962] 1980: 524).

This ultra-romantic stance, in the ensuing years of fury and extremism, made Klages "perhaps . . . the most radical and most admired of the neo-German 'Dionysian' philosophers of 'Life'" (Kolnai 1938: 68).

He was, in addition, one of the most radical and admired German opponents of science. The crux of his objection to science was both ontological and epistemological. What we see in the immediacy of Life, he says, is a world of seamlessly flowing images—not, in fact, a world of clearly bounded "things." Our primal experience of this "Image World" (*Ausdruckswelt*) is unfiltered and unprocessed, and thus, for Klages, authentic. But when this raw experience is seized and processed by the productive mind, "Life" becomes Data; rhyme gives way to reason, and a manufactured "Object World" (*Dingwelt*) fills the imagination. The unbroken flow of experience is dissolved by analysis; the stream of images, scientifically reified, becomes a world of stereotyped "objects" and artificially definite "boundaries."

All this, for Klages, is alienation and perversity. Only in unmastered experience, in pure receptivity, can life and truth be found. Sleep, not wakefulness, is the ideal state; and images, not "facts," are the stuff of dreams. Myths, meanwhile, are valid because, like dreams, they spring from the spontaneous entwining of images. But science demystifies—and thus kills. Driven not only by Reason but by Will, science deprives phenomena of all experiential qualities, making them into "colorless and lifeless centers of causal relations that interest man in his practical activity" (Leander 1937: 21).

In immediate reality, in Life, images have "no solidity, no separate identity." But mind, Klages says, disrupts our "vitally magnetic connection with the images of the world." "Whatever is touched by the ray of the Mind is instantly changed into a mere thing, into an enumerable object for our thought that afterwards is only mechanically connected with other objects."[24] As science develops, society declines and the soul is deranged: "ancient peoples had no desire to pry into nature through experiments, to enslave her in machines"; indeed, Klages adds, the rationalist forgets that the "suggestive phantasms" of early peoples—including fairy tales, totemic myths, and even the magic arts—"were passing blossoms on the tree of an immanent Life possessing a deeper knowledge than all his science."[25]

Science, for Klages, is quite literally mistaken about everything—causality, objectivity, even "objects" (Leander 1937: 22ff). And myths are not just icons of free subjectivity, but rather Truths of the deepest kind.[26]

Soon, thanks to Spengler, this extremism became a new form of irrationalist conventional wisdom.

The irrational at zenith

Oswald Spengler's *Decline of the West* (1918) is unquestionably a classic of modern irrationalism. Few books have been equally popular. Embarking, as he immodestly announced, on the "venture of predetermining history" (Spengler 1926: 3), Spengler had predicted that *Decline* would have the impact of "an avalanche in a shallow lake."[27] He was not disappointed. *Decline* was a sensation, selling over a hundred thousand copies in countless editions and winning international acclaim. In 1922, Manfred Schröter published a study of the "struggle over Spengler,"[28] citing four hundred sources. Simmel, Wittgenstein, Freyer, and other major intellectuals were electrified by Spengler's vision, and the novelist Thomas Mann called *Decline* "the most important book" of the age.[29] Even Max Weber, a stalwart critic, treated Spengler with respectful courtesy.[30]

Spengler's appeal was so broad that he was equally popular among industrialists and rebel youth.[31] This "powerful and strange man," as Golo Mann called him, was the brightest star of the "conservative revolution" in thought and a trusted ally of right-wing politicians.[32] Overall, Ernest Manheim writes (1948: 365), "Spengler's effect on German postwar nationalism can hardly be overestimated."

The peculiarity of this enthusiastic reception lies in the fact that Spengler's treatise was far from "popular" in any ordinary sense. *Decline* is vast, cerebral, eccentric, and augustly Olympian in tone, with a relentless focus on history and the philosophy of science. It is, indeed, Spengler's stress on science that makes *Decline* so unique. Other writers matched Spengler's hostility to reason; but his tireless attention to science was unrivalled.[33] This is why, for Troeltsch, Spengler's worldview is essentially "a high and mighty sectarianism (*hochmütiges Sektentum*) which believes itself superior to all science."[34]

At times, Spengler sounds just like Klages: "Scientific worlds are superficial worlds, practical, soulless . . . Life is no longer to be lived as something self-evident—hardly a matter of consciousness, let alone choice—or to be accepted as God-willed destiny, but is to be treated as a problem, presented as the intellect sees it, judged by 'utilitarian' or 'rational' criteria" (Spengler 1926: 353). Elsewhere, in patented neo-romantic style, Spengler affirms (1926: 117) "life-experience and not scientific experience, the power of seeing and not that of calculating, depth and not intellect."[35] Also like Klages, but with even greater emphasis, Spengler abjures causality (1926: 118): "Causality is the reasonable, the law bound, the describable, the badge of our waking and reasoning existence"; it is also, he says, deadly. Unlike blind, pre-determined

Destiny, which we are told to humbly and gladly accept, the notion of cause "requires us to *distinguish* and, in distinguishing, to dissect and destroy"; thus, "destiny is related to life and causality to death." The solution? "The stiff mask of causality is lifted by *mere ceasing to think*" (Spengler 1926: 18–19).[36]

Spengler argues similarly with respect to science and reason in general (1926: 388): "The words Time and Destiny, for anyone who uses them instinctively, touch Life itself in its deepest depths—Life as a whole, which is not to be separated from lived-experience. Physics, on the other hand—that is, the observing Reason—*must* separate them." Life is instinct, thought is death—and so on.

All this is familiar by now. Spengler is unique, however, not merely because he pleads his case with rare clarity and detail,[37] but also because he adds a new claim to legitimate it. Under the rubric of "comparative morphology," Spengler gives his irrationalism a new justification: cultural relativism.

The death of truth

Spengler believed that irrationalist prophecy could have world-saving effects, and that he alone knew the saving secret—research: "Before my eyes there seems to emerge, as a vision, a hitherto unimagined mode of superlative historical research" (Spengler 1926: 159). This new form of research, which Spengler calls "comparative morphology," rests on a single premise—that every truth-claim, no matter how self-evident it may seem, is in fact "valid" only for the culture that creates it. Nothing whatever is really "true" in a deeper sense. Indeed, even mathematics is always and entirely culture-bound: "*There is not, and cannot be, number as such.* There are several number worlds, as there are several cultures"—and each is "fundamentally peculiar and unique, an expression of a specific world-feeling" (Spengler 1926: 59).[38]

From this starting point, Spengler advances to a universal proposition: "Every Culture possesses a wholly individual way of seeing and comprehending the world-as-Nature; or—what comes to the same thing—it *has* its own peculiar 'Nature' which no other type of man can possess in exactly the same form" (Spengler 1926: 131).[39] Spengler means this quite literally. Nature is not simply interpreted differently, it actually differs from culture to culture. Reality is "determinate," that is, only for the beholder; what is "true" today will be false tomorrow.

Part of the appeal of this argument is that it rests on a kernel of truth. Spengler has learned, from Kant, that there is no such thing as immaculate perception: "Every fact, even the simplest, contains *ab initio* a theory" (Spengler 1926: 379). Like every critic of positivism, Spengler grasps that perception is filtered through cultural presuppositions: "Even if an investigator puts aside every hypothesis that he knows as such, as soon as he sets his thought to work on the supposedly clear task, he is not controlling but being controlled . . . for in living activity he is always a man of his Culture, of his age, of his school and of his tradition" (Spengler 1926: 379).[40] Similarly, like every critic of Eurocentrism, Spengler stresses that even cognitive categories are never wholly culture-blind: "The modern physicist is too ready to forget that even words like quantity, position, process, change of state and body represent specifically Western images" (Spengler 1926: 379). From these premises Spengler deduces that the observer is always present in the observation: "Nature-knowledge is a subtle kind of self-knowledge—Nature understood as picture, as mirror of man . . ." (Spengler 1926: 389).

If Spengler had limited himself to these fairly modest claims, he might be remembered as an early sociologist of knowledge. Scheler, who claimed precisely this mantle, praised Spengler as a source of "profound insights" in this field (Scheler [1926] 1980: 200 n. 11). But Spengler was unwilling to say merely that knowledge is culturally conditioned. His object, rather, was to deny the possibility of objective knowledge in general. This is a kind of epistemological nihilism, in which knowledge is treated in a reductionist fashion as an artifact of the culture in which it arises—and nothing more. The possibility that insight specific to a culture may also be substantially accurate is simply denied. Thus Spengler adds (1926: 387), in Delphic tones, "Every atomic theory is a myth"; indeed, every "cognized structure" is merely "a projection of the cognizing being." So, too, every scientific concept—force, work, tension, heat, energy, and so on—"contains a veritable scientific myth of its own" (1926: 382). Spengler adds (1926: 382), in a closing gesture, that "Numbers, formulae, laws *mean* nothing and *are* nothing."

In contemporary terms, this epistemological nihilism is the exact counterpart of a view that remains popular under many names—including, for example, "strict social constructionism." I have addressed this point more fully elsewhere,[41] but briefly: many people now recognize, with varying degrees of clarity, that truth-claims are always culturally conditioned—that is, "socially constructed," formed in society and under the influence of inherited cultural assumptions. This realization has been one of the most productive spurs to research in recent years. But the claim that all knowledge is culturally conditioned does not entail the corollary that all truth-claims are false or mere rhetoric. Among "social constructionists" only so-called "strict constructionists" take this further step, thereby joining the ranks of epistemological nihilists. "Contextual" constructionists take a radically opposed position, namely that many truth-claims in every culture are substantially valid, comprising genuine knowledge, however partial or culturally coded.

Between these two positions there is an unbridgeable gulf, despite the apparent similarity of language. Culturalist nihilism, reborn under whatever name, seeks to sabotage knowledge of the very realities that contextualists and other social realists affirm. Simulating a tender concern for *Kultur*, Spenglerian nihilism renders actual cultures entirely opaque. Spengler's morphology dissolves every signification into the empty formality of cultural difference, posited abstractly. Where only difference matters, what cultures share—what they can learn from each other—is utterly negated.

Epistemological nihilists, briefly, want to roll back what intellect has accomplished. This, clearly, was Spengler's intent. "The re-treatment of theoretical physics, of chemistry, of mathematics as a sum of [culturally determined] symbols—this will be the definitive conquest of the mechanical worldview by an intuitive, once-more religious world outlook" (Spengler 1926: 425).[42] By means of "research," ironically enough, Spengler wants to undo reason and science altogether. This, indeed, is what he believes his new morphological method will achieve: "In this very century, I prophesy, the century of scientific-critical Alexandrianism, of the great harvests, of the final formulations, a new element of inwardness will arise to overthrow the will-to-victory of science. Exact science must presently fall upon its own keen sword" (Spengler 1926: 425).[43]

Beware, the death of truth is nigh.

Either/or

"Suppose," Kierkegaard once mused,

> that someone wished to communicate the following conviction: Truth is inwardness; there is no objective truth, but the truth consists in personal appropriation. Suppose him to display great zeal and enthusiasm for the propagation of this truth, since if people could only be made to listen to it they would of course be saved.
>
> (Kierkegaard [1846] 1941: 71)

With luck, this prophet of subjectivity would find disciples to carry his message forward. The result, Kierkegaard reflected, would be the emergence of a strange new breed, "town criers of inwardness"—and this, he adds dryly, would be not only a remarkable event but "quite a remarkable animal" as well (Kierkegaard [1846] 1941: 71–72).[44]

In Spengler's day remarkable animals of this kind could be found on every street corner, spreading the gospel of inwardness to all who would listen. Many did—and Spengler's voice carried furthest. Unlike Kierkegaard, whose apologia for uncertainty was posed as open paradox—or even Renan, whose delicacies of vision were wreathed in an "indeterminate haze" of myth— Spengler posed as a prophetic sage, broadcasting a message that Destiny had disclosed to him alone: Reason and science are dead. Indeed, they had never lived; they were rather, from the start, mere illusions of certainty reflecting the "autumnal" decadence of the Western spirit. But autumn is nearly over, rebirth approaches, and Spengler's cultural morphology will bring salvation.[45]

This prophecy was not greeted with universal acclaim. "Science," Weber countered ([1918] 1946: 152),[46] "is a 'vocation' organized in special disciplines in the service of self-clarification and knowledge of interrelated facts. It is not the gift of grace of seers and prophets dispensing sacred values and revelations."

Troeltsch agreed, adding flatly, "On this point I confess my utter allegiance to the old science, because, apart from it, there is no science" (Troeltsch [1921] 1989: 63). But Weber and Troeltsch were relatively isolated in this period.

Paul Forman, in a seminal 1971 monograph, showed that even many of the leading scientists and mathematicians in Weimar Germany (1918–1933) were fervent Spenglerians. Focusing on what he calls the "doctrinal touchstone of Spenglerism"—Spengler's reductionist assertion that science, like every cultural artifact, "is simply and solely an expression of the soul of that particular culture and as such is neither 'valid' nor even 'comprehensible' outside that culture" (Forman 1971: 31, 57)—Forman offers abundant evidence to show that many scientists either warmly agreed with Spengler[47] or hesitated to criticize him. Schröter, in his 1922 study of Spengler's reception, judged that the "cornerstones of the book, the first and sixth chapters, mathematics and physics, have remained almost unanswered."[48] Fearing that this would remain true, Troeltsch called for a professional exposé of Spengler's sins against science. But unhappily, as he later recalled, "when I asked one of our most eminent mathematicians and physicists to give his opinion of the book . . . he refused."[49] Adorno, writing in 1954, still professed amazement at "how completely the German mind [had] collapsed when confronted with an opponent" of this caliber and outlook (Adorno [1954] 1994: 54).

This collapse is what Forman seeks to explain. Why, he asks, did so many Weimar scientists embrace Spengler's rejection of causality, truth, and knowledge? More recently, similar questions have been prompted by Alan Sokal's parody of "postmodern" discourse on science. Sokal, like Forman, seeks to expose and oppose epistemological nihilism.[50] Yet oddly enough, Forman too is among the targets of Sokal's parody.

This raises an interesting question. If Forman, like Sokal, confronts anti-scientific dogma, where and why do they differ? The answer, I believe, exposes a deep ambiguity in Sokal's notion of irrationalism—and an ever-present danger for critics of irrationalism. Irrationalism, briefly, is easy to identify but difficult to understand. Sokal's ambiguities, I believe, are enlightening in this respect.

The social reality of irrationalism

How can we explain irrationalism? This question has seldom been raised more contentiously—or fuzzily—than in the "Sokal affair." I should say, to begin with, that I completely sympathize with Sokal's objective. He is right, I believe, to scourge today's neo-romantics for their epistemological nihilism.[51] He is right to object when academics dismiss the objective knowability of empirical reality. But Sokal's approach to irrationalism is deeply flawed nonetheless. This is not just because he overlooks history and culture—a point he freely concedes—but rather because he confuses irrationalism with the historical and cultural theory needed to explain it.

Sokal frequently writes as if anti-rational claims spring simply from error or intellectual slovenliness.[52] I contend, on the contrary, that irrationalism has deep roots in society, culture, and psychology. In making this claim, my object is not to reduce the content of an idea to its context. Rather, I want to understand why, in any given social context, certain ideas take wing while others remain obscure. Why is totemic religion nearly universal in clan cultures, but almost completely absent in class societies? Why is ancestor worship common among peasants, but not in urban settings? Why, with the memory of the Holocaust still vivid, is the phoenix of antisemitic extremism rising from the ashes once again?[53] What explains the power of racism?

Questions of this kind require social, historical, and contextual answers. Simply saying, as Sokal does, that epistemological nihilism is wrong—that objective reality does in fact exist—is true but trite. The deeper problem is that irrationalism itself is an "objective reality"—a specifically social reality. To oppose irrationalism, we need an adequate grasp of why it flourishes, not just a technically accurate counter-argument. The irrational, by definition, appeals to people for whom reason is uncongenial. It is thus naive to rely on objective rational argument to persuade mystics that mysticism is not rational. They know this perfectly well. That, in fact, is precisely why they embrace mysticism—the better to resist rationality. Nor does it help to ridicule irrationalists to amuse their opponents. Unless our goal is to preach to the converted, we must reach out to the unconverted—that is, to the undecided, the ambivalent, those who remain uncertain about uncertainty. And that, in turn, takes insight—social, historical, cultural, and psychological.

Who can we reach? According to many studies, most people are neither confirmed rationalists nor consistent irrationalists.[54] They cluster, rather, around the middle of the rationality spectrum, showing a degree of genuine ambivalence about reason, skepticism, and certainty. This intermediate group, I contend, is our natural constituency. But how exactly are we to understand ambivalence? What, culturally and personally, is the origin of uncertainty? What steps can we take to move people away from obscurantism? And how will our answers to these questions vary from culture to culture?

Irrationalism in context

Much of the best thinking on these questions has been "social constructionist" in nature, in fact if not in name.[55] This, in turn, should not be surprising, since every worldview—racism, romanticism, irrationalism, and so on—is a "social construction" in the simplest sense. Unlike the momenta of physics or chemistry, worldviews exist in societies and minds alone. Irrationalism, like genocidal prejudice, arises in definite cultural milieus, under the influence of specific conditions and presuppositions. It is thus ironic that Sokal, who is presumably serious about opposing irrationalism, aims many of his sharpest barbs at precisely this premise.

One problem is that Sokal's parody is ambiguous, despite his professed wish to spur "intellectual rigor" and "a willingness to think *slowly* and *clearly*."[56] In fact, the implications of his parody proved so elusive that Sokal felt obliged to add a revealing warning in his recent book, *Fashionable*

Nonsense, co-authored by Jean Bricmont. Readers "are cautioned," he writes, "not to infer my views on any subject" from the parody alone; indeed, even, "the fact that I have parodied an extreme or ambiguously stated version of an idea does not exclude that I may agree with a more nuanced or precisely stated version of the same idea" Sokal (1998b: 268 n. 1).

This sweeping caveat leaves Sokal free to clarify and modify his views in many respects. Yet even now he continues to make the criticism of social constructionism a pillar of his perspective.

Sokal's hoax had three primary targets: "subjectivists" who deny the reality of space, time, and the "pre-linguistic world of material objects"; intellectuals who frivolously misuse scientific concepts; and social constructionists who argue that scientific interpretations of the world are often influenced, to a degree, by the cultural milieus in which they arise (Sokal 1996b: 218, 222–224, 228).

Sokal returns often to the latter thesis, lavishing mock praise on the social constructionist perspective. Later, in a sequel to the parody, he says that his main goal is "to combat a currently fashionable postmodernist/post-structuralist/social-constructivist discourse . . ." (Sokal 1998a: 269).[57] Perhaps most revealing, concretely, is his casually dismissive attitude towards Stanley Aronowitz's modest constructionist account of the cultural correlates and antecedents of Copenhagen indeterminism.

Sokal opens his parody with sustained tongue-in-cheek praise for the well-known claim that the anti-objectivist spirit of the Copenhagen interpretation of quantum mechanics reflected the influence of the mid-1920s milieu in which Niels Bohr and Werner Heisenberg lived. At the heart of his exposition, Sokal quotes strong statements from Bohr and Heisenberg on the irrelevance of themes of objective reality in the quantum domain, which he follows with this remark: "Aronowitz (1988b: 251–256) has convincingly traced this worldview to the crisis of liberal hegemony in Central Europe in the years prior to and subsequent to World War 1" (Sokal 1996b: 219).

Sokal's argument is not a model of clarity, either here or elsewhere. Thus it remains possible that he does not mean to impugn social constructionism or Aronowitz as flatly as he implies. But it is problematic, to put it mildly, that he makes this theme one of the pivots of his parody. For here we trespass into the realm of Forman's analysis of the neo-Spenglerian irrationalism championed by many leading Weimar-era scientists. This, and this alone, is what Aronowitz discusses in the passage that Sokal underscores. And it is this kind of critical inquiry into the recesses of irrationalism that Sokal evidently fails to appreciate.

Forman tries to understand. Sokal, in contrast, merely castigates—and indeed, he understands the ulterior problem so poorly that he questions even the relevance of Forman's research. In one of the sequelae to his parody, for example, Sokal concedes—with direct reference to Forman—that questions about social influence on quantum theory merit careful study. But he stoutly denies that the answers to these questions have any bearing whatever on the "underlying" issue—that is, "the ontological question" of how atoms behave (Sokal 1998a: 273).

This shows, with utmost clarity, the failure of Sokal's critical imagination in this realm. For critics of irrationalism, the immediate problem is not ontology but, rather, what people think about ontology. The established atomic facts are reasonably clear, for anyone who accepts the results and methods of scientific inquiry[58]—as Sokal and Aronowitz both plainly do.[59] But irrationalists tend to reject science—and that, in turn, is the problem we face. To oppose mysticism, we must understand mystics.

Atoms, plainly, are unaffected by argument—but minds can be changed. Minds, not atoms, are the bearers of fashionable nonsense. Hence, for anyone who seriously wishes to oppose irrationalism—to be more than a town crier of facts—the first and paramount mission is to grasp why, at times, people resist facts. Repeating the obvious to the oblivious is a recipe for failure; for facts are "self-evident" only to certain kinds of selves.[60]

The truth of this point is plainest, I believe, in the literature on personality. But it is also clear in the study of intellectual history.[61]

Objectionable nonsense

We have seen, above, that anti-scientism arose alongside science. What began as neo-romantic vision and Kierkegaardian soliloquy became, in the age of Spengler, widespread opposition to reason. Evidently, the success of science does not preclude the rise of epistemological nihilism. Indeed, in some situations, the rejection of certainty can be so tempting that even leading scientists unresistingly embrace it. This, briefly, is what Paul Forman shows.

Einstein, in 1932, replied sharply to an interviewer who had said that "it is now the fashion in physical science to attribute something like free will even to the routine processes of inorganic nature." "That nonsense," Einstein said, "is not merely nonsense. It is objectionable nonsense."[62]

Why, then, did so few Weimar scientists object to objectionable claims of this kind? Why was "nonsense" fashionable, even among scientists?[63] Forman echoes Einstein's interviewer, Murphy, who warned Einstein that, in defending the principle of causality,

> you'll be going out of fashion . . . Scientists live in the world just like other people. They cannot escape the influence of the milieu in which they live. And that milieu at the present time is characterized largely by a struggle to get rid of the causal chain in which the world has entangled itself.
>
> (Forman 1971: 108–109)

Pursuing this theme further, Forman finds "overwhelming evidence" that early Weimar scientists were, in fact, deeply influenced by the anti-objectivism of public opinion. Although later developments in quantum theory gave physicists an apparent scientific justification for anti-causal sentiments, Forman found rich data showing "that in the years after the end of the First World War but before the development of an acausal quantum mechanics . . . large numbers of German physicists, for reasons only incidentally related to developments in their own discipline, distanced themselves from, or explicitly repudiated, causality in physics" (Forman 1971: 3).

As many historians have shown, public opinion in early Weimar Germany was deeply dissonant, at once disillusioned and millenarian. Heisenberg, who in 1925 and 1926 spearheaded the formalization of quantum mechanics, later recalled the public mood in 1920, when he first entered the University of Munich: "Our defeat in the First World War had produced a deep mistrust of all the ideals which had been used during the war and which had lost us the war."[64] Everything was open to question and anything could be believed. Max Planck, the elder statesman of quantum physics, lamented in 1923 that "precisely in our age, which plumes itself so highly on its progressiveness, the belief in miracles in the most various forms—occultism, spiritualism, theosophy, and all the numerous shadings . . . penetrates wide circles of the public, uneducated and educated, more mischievously than ever."[65]

Of particular concern to Planck was what he described as a "violent dispute over the significance of the law of causality."[66] This dispute extended far beyond circles influenced by Spengler. Indeed, in 1937 an exiled German scholar defined anti-causalism as perhaps the central motif in Weimar thought: "War cancelled causality," he wrote. "It seemed to do so, at least, to the German people" (Mendelssohn-Bartholdy 1937: 20).[67] As Forman shows, many top scientists agreed. Franz Exner, who had revealed anti-causalist tendencies even before the war,[68] was perhaps the first leading scientist to reject causality altogether. But he was soon joined by many others, including Hermann Weyl, who voiced a typical sentiment in quasi-Kierkegaardian terms. In the sphere of ultimate Being and Becoming, Weyl wrote, "natural causality relaxes, and there remains . . . room for autonomous decisions, causally absolutely independent of one another, whose locus I consider to be the elementary quanta of matter. These decisions," Weyl added, "are what is *actually real* in the world."[69]

Forman shows (1971: 40) that, in 1921 in particular, "quasi-religious conversions to acausality" became common.[70] Schrödinger, Reichenbach, von Mises, and Wien—who, with Planck, was then "the most prominent spokesman for physics in Germany"—were key converts in this period. And there were many others. The most important, of course, was Niels Bohr, who had long been under the spell of Kierkegaardian doubt.[71] Bohr, whom Heisenberg said "was primarily a philosopher, not a physicist,"[72] had been deeply influenced at an early age by the anti-causalism of the Danish philosopher Harald Høffding. But it was not until the 1920s that Bohr began to make his acausalism plain and public. At times he struck a self-deprecating pose on this subject—saying, for example, with respect to Kierkegaard's metaphorical pledge to remain suspended over seventy thousand fathoms of water, "holding fast to objective uncertainty" to preserve his faith—that with us "it is much worse—we are suspended over a bottomless pit—caught in our own words."[73] But Bohr was not joking about "holding fast to objective uncertainty." In a series of major essays on the quantum revolution, Bohr argued that the ideas of objectivity, certainty, and causality must be renounced. The very notion of an objective reality independent of an observer, he wrote (1934d: 54), "can neither be ascribed to the phenomena nor to the agencies of observation." Such a notion is, on the contrary, an artifact of subjective illusion. Nor is the idea of causality defensible on objective grounds—"causality," Bohr says (1934a: 116–117), is rather "a mode of perception by which we reduce our sense impressions to order." Even the hope that natural phenomena will prove "visualizable" in objective, certain, or causal terms must be renounced (1934a: 108–114). And all this, Bohr argues, is true not only at the quantum level, but *vis-à-vis* life and mind as well. Life, he writes, is inherently indeterminate—an arena of free choice which is absolutely irreducible to causality. So, too, is the life of the mind (1934c: 92–101). Further—decisively—Bohr argues that the vocabulary of free will is apropos for the description of quantum as well as intentional phenomena: "In the case of atoms," he writes, "we come upon a particularly glaring failure of the causal mode of description"—so much so, in fact, "that in this case we can scarcely avoid speaking of a choice between various possibilities on the part of the atom" (Bohr 1934b: 13).[74]

This affirmation of "free choice" in the inorganic realm is, of course, precisely what Einstein rejected as "objectionable nonsense." And Bohr, quite without evidence, does not hesitate to transfer his intuitions about the failure of causal reasoning from the quantum level to the human level. Indeed, for Bohr, this equation of the quantum and the human levels is the beginning of wisdom. In both realms, he believed, there is "the necessity of a final renunciation of the classical idea of causality and a radical revision of our attitude towards the problem of physical reality."[75]

"Sudden and annihilating doubt"

If Bohr, Weyl, and the others had restricted their causal skepticism to the quantum realm, their conjectures would be far less provocative—since quantum interactions are plainly complex in ways that require open-mindedness about the nature and efficacy of causal principles at the subatomic level. But it is far riskier to argue that "unvisualizable" quantum events discredit the principle of causality at the macroscopic level of everyday life, or to deny that reason can discern causal patterns in nature or society. This, however, is precisely the logical leap that was taken by so many Weimar-era scientists, both before and after the formalization of quantum mechanics and Bohr's subsequent "Copenhagen" popularization of quantum phenomena. "Out of this skepsis," the German mathematician Max Dehn wrote in 1928, "there develops a certain resignation, a kind of mistrust for the power of the human mind in general."[76]

It is important to recall the extremism of the views professed in this period. While some scientists voiced reasoned objections to specific scientific deductions, many others were anti-rational in far more sweeping ways. They rejected mind, abstraction, logic, and the wish to rationally redesign society in all the familiar accents of neo-romanticism.[77] As Theodor Litt wrote in 1927, *Lebensphilosophie* had triumphed; on all sides there was implacable opposition to "the mechanism and determinism of a causal explanation which calculates everything in advance, makes everything comparable, dissolves everything into elements," and which relies, in turn, on "the rationalism and formalism of a logical system which deduces everything, classifies everything, subjects everything to concepts" (Litt 1927: 32–33).[78]

Spengler was thus right, in the revised edition of his renowned book (1923), to stress the wider significance of "the sudden and annihilating doubt that has arisen about things that even yesterday were the unchallenged foundation of physical theory . . . This doubt," he added, "is no longer the fruitful doubt . . . which brought the knower and the object of his knowledge together; it is a doubt affecting the very possibility of a Nature-science" (Spengler 1926: 418).

On the specifics of this "annihilating doubt," Spengler proved remarkably prescient. Writing several years before the formalization of quantum mechanics, Spengler maintained that thermodynamics and, indeed, the entire "dynamic" worldview of earlier physics had been "destroyed" by "the Quantum theory of Planck and the conclusions of Niels Bohr therefrom as to the fine structure of atoms." In addition, Spengler anticipated concepts later associated with Heisenberg's "uncertainty principle" with rare intuition: "Every physics . . . must break down over the motion-problem, in which the living person of the knower methodically intrudes into the inorganic form-world of the known" (Spengler 1926: 418–419).[79]

The key fact here is not Spengler's prescience, however, but rather his belief that science itself was undermined by quantum theory. In countless idioms he praised "the Incomprehensible, the Almighty that is too mighty for the intellect." He extolled the Uncanny, the Unapproachable, the Unforeseen—everything, that is, which proves "inaccessible to thought" (Spengler 1926: 123, 140, 145).[80] Knowledge is not just power over nature, he wrote, but rather power against nature. "What is named, comprehended, measured is *ipso facto* overpowered, made inert and taboo" (Spengler 1926: 123). In a similar way, the physicist's wish to name and define natural forces ("'atom,' 'energy,' 'gravitation,' 'cause,' 'evolution'")—is mere life-killing superstition, "not essentially different from the fetishism of Neanderthal Man." Thus Spengler looked forward to the day when the vain intellectualism of science would give way to "the causation-free, living Grace which can only be experienced as an inward certainty" (Spengler 1926: 141, 397, 397 n. 1).

It is Forman's singular merit to have shown just how widely these sentiments were shared by Weimar scientists. Many posited "a failure of the human intellect," while others "went even further, expressing an existentialist revulsion against intellectuality" (Forman 1971: 112). "We Germans," Heisenberg later reminisced, "tend to look upon logic and the facts of nature . . . as a sort of straitjacket."[81] Many German scientists, indeed, were openly anti-causal and even Spenglerian in this period.[82] Causality, objectivity, and intellect were widely disdained—not merely by youth, but by leading virtuosos of *Wissenschaft*.

This, Forman concludes, is powerful testimony to the force of popular opinion. When the public is seized by an irrationalist mood, even the convictions of scientists are vulnerable to annihilating doubt.

Irrationalism as a problem

Irrationalist anti-scientism, in other words, has deep social roots. So, too, does the affirmation of reason and science. To what extent, then, can we rely on social explanation to better understand these socially constructed worldviews?

Spengler, of course, reduced every science to culture alone. Every scientific fact, he believed, is an utterly cultural artifact, and every cultural artifact is equally false from a comparative standpoint. Only what lies behind culture, obscured and choked by the overgrowth of thought and knowledge, is truly living and valid for Spengler. The rhythm of blood and life, the humility of inward surrender to the Unknown and Unknowable—these, he says, are the only sources of a Truth beyond the cultural moment.

For Forman, this pure culturalism is irrationalism. Much of what science professes is simply and transculturally valid—hydrogen is the simplest element, hydrogen combines with oxygen to form water, water is necessary for life—and hence is not simply reducible to the fleeting idiosyncrasies of cultures. Why, therefore, would major Weimar scientists accept Spengler's viewpoint?[83]

Forman believes, briefly, that many Weimar-era scientists were so demoralized by World War I that they found solace in a rejection of everything "Western," "enlightened," and "modern." This, of course, is not the whole explanation; as Forman freely concedes, "the 'sociological' model employed in this paper cannot be the whole truth." There is so much unexplained variability in the spectrum of scientists' attitudes that recourse must also be made to "factors which are excluded from the model," most notably personality and intellectual biography. But Forman does think that his sociological model offers "a general framework, and seems to work especially well in certain extreme cases" (Forman 1971: 114).[84] It is relevant, above all, for an understanding of how scientists interpret what they learn. Hence Forman focuses mainly on meta-empirical statements of scientific philosophy, rather than on the *differentia specifica* of scientific discovery—and here, in the Weimar era, he finds more irrationalism than insight (Forman 1984: 344).[85]

Most notably, Weimar-era scientists rushed to conclude that quantum discoveries justified the rejection of causal reason in every realm, not merely in subatomic interactions. Why did they make this logical leap? For psychological reasons, Forman suggests, driven by forces and factors specific to the immediate postwar period. Aronowitz extends and modifies this explanation by saying that other factors played a role as well—specifically modern factors that transcend the particularities of the German experience. Irrationalism, Aronowitz observes, has proven attractive to significant strata of the intelligentsia in many cultures in this century. The Weimar example has echoed and re-echoed in many contexts. Most recently, Aronowitz says, this has been plain in the popularity of poststructuralist philosophy, which "abandons positing 'things' in favor of discourses which have no fixed referent of 'external' reality." Further, Aronowitz says, many currents of poststructuralism defend an "antifoundationalist" rejection of the knowability of extra-discursive reality which amounts to a new epistemological nihilism. And the widespread popularity of this new nihilism—the very "fashionability" of the views that Sokal and Bricmont oppose—reveals, Aronowitz believes, "that the milieu surrounding modern physics is part of an episteme that transcends particular cultural contexts" (Aronowitz 1988: 255–256).[86]

Weimar acausalism, in other words, was not utterly unique, an aberration in a century of science. It was, rather, the clearest and most consequential form of an anti-scientific irrationalism that has roots in the depths of modern society itself. Irrationalism recurs in so many contexts, Aronowitz argues, because the deep and abiding irrationalities of our formally "rational, calculating" society make reason and science suspect. Thus while Weimar-era acausalism may have been unique in many of its specific features, it was not, in this century, an abnormal or solitary cultural phenomenon. On the contrary, irrationalism tends to arise again and again, in one guise or another.

Irrationalism redivivus

What Sokal documents, viewed in this light, is precisely such a rebirth. The names change, the rhetoric evolves, but the outlook remains the same. Take, for example, Lyotard's argument about science in the famous text which gave the word "postmodern" its trademarked cachet. Sokal notes that Lyotard relies indiscriminately on the usual litany of pseudo-scientific rationales for an anti-scientific worldview, incongruously and incompetently blending Gödel's undecidability theorem, Heisenberg's uncertainty principle, Mandelbrot's fractal geometry, and several other prestigious scientific and mathematical principles that New Age thinkers find attractively ambiguous in their implications. Sokal complains that Lyotard "has here thrown together at least six distinct branches of science," without grasping them or even genuinely arguing to defend his views. This is certainly true. But what Sokal does not see is precisely what Aronowitz stresses—that Lyotard's commitment to anti-causalism is a form of irrationalist conventional wisdom in the century of Spengler and Klages. What Lyotard trumpets as "postmodern" was once simply anti-modern.

The basic philosophic premise of Lyotard's affirmation of "postmodern science" as "the search for instabilities" is the claim that the world is inherently uncertain, and that, therefore, "perfect control" over any system, whether natural or social, is a quixotic fantasy (Lyotard 1984: 53, 55). "Quantum theory and microphysics require a far more radical revision of the idea of a continuous and predictable path" from the present to the future than previously imagined. Nor, Lyotard adds, can we hope to reduce this uncertainty by ever more precise scientific understanding. On the contrary, the "quest for precision" is limited "by the very nature of matter. It is," further, "not true that uncertainty (lack of control) decreases as accuracy goes up: it goes up as well" (Lyotard 1984: 56). Lyotard pauses to illustrate this claim with a brief reference to air density,[87] and then leaps from the physical level to society, suggesting that uncertainty is inherent not only in matter but in culture: "It will be argued that these problems concern microphysics," Lyotard warns,

> and that they do not prevent the establishment of continuous functions exact enough to form the basis of probabilistic predictions for the evolution of a given system . . .[88] There is, however, a current in contemporary mathematics that questions the very possibility of precise measurement and thus the prediction of the behavior of objects even on the human scale.
>
> (Lyotard 1984: 57–58)

At this point, after a page of fuzzy allusions to the fractal geometry of irregular curves and a nod to the mathematics of catastrophe theory, Lyotard concludes that society, too, is discontinuous and beyond rational control. His ensuing illustration of this point—virtually his only argument on this subject—is worth quoting in full:

> Take aggressiveness as a state variable of a dog: it increases in direct proportion to the dog's anger, a control variable. Supposing the dog's anger is measurable, when it reaches a certain threshold it is expressed in the form of an attack. Fear, the second control variable, has the opposite effect, when it reaches its threshold it is expressed as flight. In the absence of anger or fear, the dog's behavior is stable (the top of Gauss's curve). But if the two control variables increase together, the two thresholds will be approached simultaneously. the dog's behavior becomes unpredictable and can switch abruptly from attack to flight, and vice versa. The system is said to be unstable: the control variables are continuous, but the state variables are discontinuous.
>
> (Lyotard 1984: 59)

In other words: a fearful dog flees, an angry dog attacks, and a dog that feels both fear and anger may fight or flee. This, Lyotard feels, is a paradigmatic case of outcomes which cannot be predicted—and which can only be represented by equations derived from catastrophe theory (or, he adds helpfully, by a three-dimensional graph which demonstrates that there are "2 + 1" state and control variables). On the basis of this singular claim—and this alone

—Lyotard draws a grand conclusion: "This provides us with an answer in the debate between stable and unstable systems, determinism and non-determinism." In "the majority" of cases, he announces, "circumstances will prevent the production of a stable form. This happens because the circumstances are usually in conflict." While "islands" of stability occasionally appear, "catastrophic antagonism is literally the rule" (Lyotard 1984: 59).

For society, this means that prediction, certainty, and "perfect control" are unattainable—and indeed, Lyotard adds, "the idea (or ideology) of perfect control over a system . . . in fact lowers the performance level it claims to raise. This," he adds, "explains the weakness of state and socio-economic bureaucracies: they stifle the systems or subsystems they control and asphyxiate themselves in the process (negative feedback)" (Lyotard 1984: 55–56).

Society is unmasterable, in other words, because causal reason is powerless in the face of indeterminacy; and "objects on the human scale" are indeterminate in most cases. We know this, Lyotard says, by mathematical inference from the alleged ambivalence of a dog faced with a fight-or-flight decision.

The flight from reason

The implication of this curious argument is that self-determining collective action is futile, or worse. The Unexpected, in short, is Destiny. And any effort to disprove this contention in practice will actually reduce our power to control our fate.

Lyotard's defense of this proposition could hardly be weaker. It is a truism, at best, to say that people are indecisive when they have mixed feelings. To claim on this basis that people (and societies) are hopelessly unpredictable is to disregard everything that psychologists and sociologists have learned. Even ambivalence is well understood in many respects, and aggressiveness has been very productively studied.[89] Lyotard may prefer paradox, but social science offers data.

Politically, meanwhile, Lyotard's broadside against planning could hardly be more conventional. It closely parallels the *laissez-faire* defense of unregulated markets which, in the age of Reagan, Thatcher, the IMF and the World Bank, has become the most pious of orthodoxies. "It is essential for the growth of reason," the pro-market ideologue Hayek argued, "that as individuals we should bow to forces and obey principles which we cannot hope fully to understand" (Hayek 1955: 92)—that is, market forces and principles. State interventionism can only "asphyxiate" the social grassroots, Lyotard says—and it would be folly to imagine that rational planning could do better.

In both respects, politically as well as logically, Lyotard's position is highly reminiscent of the stance taken by Regis Debray in a work effectively criticized by Sokal and Bricmont. Invoking and "extending" Gödel's undecidability theorem—"an inexhaustible source of intellectual abuses," Sokal and Bricmont say—Debray affirms as "a logical law" that *"there can be no organized system without closure and no system can be closed by elements internal to that system alone*" (Debray 1983: 170).[90] On this ground, he concludes, portentously, that in a sense "the incompleteness axiom plays into the hands of every ruling class," since it compels us to recognize that popular sovereignty is a vain hope: "Just as it would be a biological contradiction for an individual to give birth to himself . . . the government of a collective by itself—*verbi gratia* 'of the people by the people'—is a logically contradictory operation ('generalized workers' control' as political aporia). Self-regulation by the many is a *flatus vocis*—at best an ideal regulator of Political Reason derived from a logic of appearance, but more probably a concept without intuition which no historical experience can satisfy" (Debray 1983: 177).

Sokal and Bricmont show just how falsely and illogically Debray interprets Gödel, and they incisively critique his fashionable political pessimism. But they seem unaware that irrational pessimism of this type is, as Max Weber said long ago, a veritable crowd phenomenon. To successfully oppose irrationalism and anti-democratism, we must explore them as such. Why exactly do fashionable irrationalists draw a crowd? Why, time and again, is irrationalism in fashion? To answer questions like these, we have to recognize that hostility to reason has deep, gnarled, and tenacious social roots. For critics of irrationalism, who wish to contribute directly to the understanding and undoing of anti-rational prejudice, I would argue that social constructionism (as illustrated here) has much to offer. The object is to understand people— and people are formed in society.

Notes

1 As Hans Eichner writes, "Romanticism is, perhaps predominantly, a desperate rearguard action against the spirit and implications of modern science—a rearguard action that . . . was bound to fail"; see Eichner (1982: 8).
2 This passage is from Hegel's foreword to a book by Hermann Hinrichs, reprinted in von der Luft (1987: 260, n. 27)
3 On the centrality of this text, and this argument in particular, to Kierkegaard's overall project, see Walter Lowrie (1942: 170–171).
4 Kierkegaard adds that, besides the uncertainty that arises from the essential paradox that truths of eternal Being are sought by transient selves, there is a fateful "absurdity," as well, in the New Testament claim that the Infinite and Eternal was incarnated in flesh in the Becoming of history. It is, indeed, an even greater test for the "infinite decisiveness" of faith to welcome the absurd, Kierkegaard maintains, than it is to believe the uncertain (Kierkegaard [1846] 1941: 183ff). Hence absurdity, like uncertainty, is a temptation to skepsis which only self-blinding piety can overcome. This, plainly, is an elaboration of Tertullian's epigram *credo quia absurdam*.
5 Renan claims to be speaking of "Semites" in general, but in fact he focuses almost exclusively on Jews and Hebrews. His dualism thus resolves itself into the familiar Jew/Aryan dichotomy (where Aryan = Indo-European).
6 All citations are reproduced from Maurice Olender (1992: 52–67). For the broader context in which this argument appeared, see Smith (1997).
7 Olender (1992: 170, n. 30) compares Renan directly to Schleiermacher.
8 The consensus, as Picard explained, is that Jews and Aryans differ "in every order of thought, action, and feeling." See the interview with Picard in Henri Dagan (1899: 1–4), cited in Wilson (1982: 459).

9 See Aurel Kolnai (1938: 274ff) for a subtle account of Chamberlain and Rosenberg.
10 Cited by Léon Poliakov (1974: 317). Chamberlain's debt to Renan was warmly avowed and central to the argument in his famous book, *Foundations of the Nineteenth Century*, Vol. 1, first published in 1899.
11 Chamberlain's book had sold more than a hundred thousand copies by 1915. See Friedländer (1997: 90). Hans Kohn (1965: 268 n.) remarks that "even the English translation . . . went through five large printings" between 1910 and June 1914; he adds that Chamberlain's success prefigured the even greater success, after the war, of Spengler's *Decline of the West*. About Spengler, see below.
12 Indeed, "life itself . . . shows everywhere that race is a fact of importance to all organic existence . . . , life does not wait for scholars . . . to get to the bottom of it." Chamberlain, *Foundations of the Nineteenth Century*, cited by Lukács in *The Destruction of Reason* ([1962] 1980).
13 This passage is from the preface to the fourth German edition of Chamberlain's bestseller, as quoted by Magnus Hirschfeld (1938: 48–49).
14 Chamberlain's anti-scientific tendency was implicit in his deprecation of "materialism" as the epitome of Semitic philosophy.
15 Troeltsch adds ([1921] 1989: 67): "I personally believe . . . that all these phenomena run deep and should be taken very seriously."
16 Scheler (1913) cited in Staude (1967: 21). "Significantly," Staude notes, this passage occurs in Scheler's discussion of Bergson.
17 Max Scheler ([1919] 1987: 187). Further echoing Bergson, Scheler assails the "proud sovereignty of the 'thinking reed'," calling, instead, for a humble and "courageous letting-oneself-go in intuition." Here and elsewhere Scheler cites the seminal lecture given by Bergson in 1911 at the Bologna Congress of Philosophy. This lecture, "L'intuition philosophique," is available in Bergson ([1934] 1990: 135–162).
18 Klages (1929: 86, 88), cited in Leander (1937: 26).
19 For Klages, in other words, some people are literally "born slaves," to use Aristotle's idiom. See Green (1974: 351, 373).
20 This hostility even to will and feeling led Klages to what was, for a German neoromantic, an unusually ambivalent embrace of Nietzsche. "In his ingenious aversion to will and spirit," Karl Löwith explains, "Klages divides Nietzsche and declares him to be an 'orgiastic' philosopher of the 'body' and 'soul,' retaining the Nietzsche of Dionysian philosophy at the expense of the will to power and to nothingness." See Löwith ([1941] 1967: 190).
21 See Kolnai (1938: 68ff), citing a comparatively early paper; and cf. Green (1974: 77), citing a later work. "Personality," Kolnai (1938: 69) quotes Klages, "and Universal Nature are hostile antipodes: one must eliminate the former to realize the latter."
22 Cited in Lukács ([1962] 1980: 524), from Klages (1937: 51).
23 Klages appears to have been driven to this extremism by an astute but one-sided critique of Puritanism, which he evidently interpreted as the archetype of the inevitably moralizing will. As Max Weber once remarked ([1916–17] 1951: 244, 297), Klages's writings contain many "very good remarks" on "the peculiar confinement and repression of natural impulse which was . . . ingrained in the Puritan."
24 The phrase "no solidity, no separate identity" is a paraphrase by Leander (1937: 21). The other two passages are reproduced by Leander (1937: 24) from *Mensch und Erde* (1929: 157). Also, note that where Leander renders *Geist* as "Spirit," I write "Mind." This is, I think, closer to the spirit (so to speak) of Klagesian philosophy, since his main enemy is willful and analytic reason, not "Spirit" in the vaguely occult sense this term usually conveys. And Klages praises "soul," which converges with "spirit" in popular usage.
25 Klages (1929: 167), cited in Leander (1937: 25).

26 With an idiosyncratic consistency that is wonderful to behold, Klages quite literally accepts the occult truth-claims of fairy tales and magic lore. And he takes comfort in the fact that, in totemic cultures, people "believe that they are themselves in reality jaguars or red parrots" (Leander's paraphrase, 1937: 21). Nothing that is believed so spontaneously for so long, he says, can be untrue; the ancients, uncorrupted by science, were still open to experience.

27 Cited in Herman (1997: 244).

28 *Der Streit um Spengler: Kritik seiner Kritiker* (1922), reprinted in expanded form as *Metaphysik des Untergangs: Eine kulturkritische Studie über Oswald Spengler* (1949).

29 On Simmel, see Troeltsch ([1923] 1961: 595, n. 318). On Wittgenstein, see Monk (1990: 315–317). On Mann, see the comments in his *Diaries 1918–1939* (1983: 61–64), as cited by Herman (1997: 244). On Freyer, see Muller (1987: 120–121).

30 In December 1919 Weber invited Spengler to a session of his University of Munich seminar. There, Marianne Weber recalls ([1926] 1975: 674), he "attacked very cautiously and with the most chivalrous of weapons. His respect for the other man's dissimilar intellect made his critique bearable. Others proceeded more ruthlessly. Spengler maintained his gentlemanly self-control as his intellectual structure was gradually demolished." Spengler's disciples tried to turn the tables. Otto Köllreuter, later a leading Nazi jurist, published an article in 1925 contrasting Spengler, as a paragon of romantic realpolitik, with Weber, as an archetype of Enlightenment and "abstraction" (Köllreuter 1925: 481–500).

31 Walter Struve, in *Elites against Democracy* (1973), gives rich detail on Spengler's active role as a key adviser to industrial magnates and rightist politicians and agitators. Joan Campbell, in *Joy in Work, German Work* (1989), shows that Spengler was the prime inspiration for DINTA, the association of industrialists which led the struggle in the Weimar republic to win the workers to a concept of "factory community" (*Werksgemeinschaft*) rather than class struggle.

32 See Golo Mann (1968: 375). Mann offers a good overview of Spengler's general political tendency, with special emphasis on his appeal to the youth movement and the "conservative revolution" in German thinking.

33 *Decline* begins with a chapter on "the meaning of numbers"; Chapter 3 takes causality as its theme; and the final chapter probes physics and other "knowledge of nature."

34 Spengler disdains science, Troeltsch notes, "yet everywhere works with its acquisitions and categories" (Troeltsch [1923] 1961: 649). Adorno ([1954] 1994: 63) agrees, implying that Spengler is impaled on the horns of a transparent contradiction: "By denouncing itself the mind makes itself capable of providing anti-ideological ideologies." Actually, though, Spengler had "answered" this objection in advance in *Decline*: When I favor Destiny over Causality, Spengler says (1926: 308 n. 1), this "must not be supposed to be the result of reasoned proofs. It is," rather, "the outcome of (quite unconscious) tendencies of life-feeling." This, I would say, is difficult to dispute.

35 "The brain rules," he intones (1926: 353), "because the soul abdicates."

36 Compare Spengler's paradoxical remark (1926: 126) that the notion of Life, as a "counter-conception," "arises only in opposition to thought."

37 Spengler offers a massive superstructure of supporting argumentation, revolving around his systematic distinction between "types" of cultures—Faustian, Magian and so on. Like a busy magpie he ransacks all of history, especially art history, to spangle his argument with baubles of suggestive detail; indicts every alternative way of looking at the world (for example, Marxian and sociological); pours scorn on the humanitarian ideals of "enlightenment," "humanity," "progress," and "world peace"; argues that the love of reason is driven, psychologically, by hatred of life; equates the rational quest for "penetration" of the world with sexual intercourse;

affirms the "eternal hatred of the sexes"; and waxes eloquent about the greatness of those, like Napoleon, who personify Destiny in the most literal sense and thus can dispense even with metaphysical insight, "since between himself as a fact and other facts there is a harmony of metaphysical rhythm which gives his decisions their dreamlike certainty." See Spengler (1926: 120, 123, 127–128, 138, 142–149, 155, 308, 352, 355, 367, 423, and passim).

38 For Spengler, quite literally, $2 + 2 = 4$ only under specific cultural circumstances. This clearly gibes with the spirit of Klagesian thinking as well, since the apparent simplicity of arithmetic of this kind requires the prior assumption that distinct "objects" are enumerable in discrete fashion; presumbably, a culture of pure flowing Life and Intuition might not even have "numbers" in the Logocentric sense.

39 Translation amended.

40 "There is no science that is without unconscious presuppositions of this kind, over which the researcher has no control" (Spengler 1926: 380).

41 See Smith (1996).

42 Translation slightly amended.

43 Translation slightly amended.

44 Kierkegaard felt that his own ministry to the truth of objective uncertainty evaded this snare by practicing "the elusiveness and the art of a double reflection" ([1846] 1941: 70); the object, he said, is not to remain among the Deadly Earnest who wish to propagate a new truth with all the blithe certainty of the old, but rather to stand up for paradox by means of a new form of communication. Whether he succeeded in this remains . . . uncertain.

45 In fairness to Spengler it should be noted that his comparative morphology was relatively free of overt racism—and hence differed from proto-Nazi ideologies in this and several related respects. It was for this reason, in fact, that the leading Nazi philosopher Rosenberg, who was in many ways deeply influenced by Spengler, "chides Spengler for his environmental instead of 'racial-organic' explanations of culture." See Peter Viereck ([1941] 1961: 235).

46 Whether Weber had Spengler in mind when he gave this speech is unclear—he didn't meet with Spengler until weeks afterward—but it clearly applies to Spengler as a virtually ideal-typical spokesman for the prophetic anti-scientism of the period.

47 See below.

48 Cited in Forman (1971: 56), from Schröter (1922: 56–57, 70).

49 Cited in Forman (1971: 56), from Troeltsch's *Gesammelte Schriften*, Band 4, 682.

50 Forman was concerned about recent as well as bygone trends, "especially the neo-Spenglerianism" that he believed was gaining influence in the contemporary scientific community (Forman 1971: 5 n. 4).

51 Sokal's parody offers a good sampler of many of the characteristic epistemological follies that have flourished in some academic circles in recent decades.

52 Repeatedly, Sokal indicts anti-objectivism and epistemological nihilism for its "silliness," "sloppiness," lack of "rigor," and so on. Indeed, on the central question of the objectivity of reality, he questions the very sanity of his opponents. They are not, it seems, just irrational, but rather, literally, crazy: "There *is* a real world; its properties are *not* merely social constructions; facts and evidence do matter. What sane person would contend otherwise?" This rhetorical question appears in Sokal's original revelation of his hoax (1996: 63).

53 See Smith (1996) for an extensive treatment of this subject. See also the related argument in Smith (1998b).

54 For an exceptionally subtle meditation on this subject see Adorno ([1954] 1994). For rich data on the current psychological distribution of tendencies to think irrationally, ethnocentrically, dogmatically, and in blind conformity with authority, see Altemeyer (1996), passim.

55 I would argue, for example, that Marx, Weber, and Durkheim were "social constructionists" *avant la lettre*. On Weber's constructionism, see Smith (1998a).

56 "Intellectual rigor": see Sokal (1996: 62 and passim). "Slowly and clearly": see Sokal (1998: 276 n. 14).

57 This paper was originally submitted to *Social Text* as a sequel to Sokal's hoax, and later appeared in *Dissent* (Fall, 1996). Later, in a reply to Aronowitz—who denied any sympathy for the anti-objectivist tendencies that he believed Sokal had linked to deconstructionism—Sokal says that the actual object of his critique was "the sloppy thinking loosely associated with 'social constructivism,' not with deconstruction" (1997: 110). Here, as elsewhere, Sokal apparently feels comfortable with sloppy generalities about currents of thought of which he knows little. Elsewhere, when Sokal says (1998a: 259) that he satirized an "extraordinarily radical version of social constructivism," he makes no effort to establish whether other, more balanced versions may have something genuinely instructive to offer.

58 Even this seemingly innocent claim is, of course, controversial. Partisans of the "Strong Programme" in science studies often argue, in archetypally postmodern fashion, that experimental results are just as inherently uncertain as popular prejudices. Indeed, Trevor Pinch goes so far as to say that "What is being claimed is that many pictures [of the natural world] can be painted, and furthermore, that the sociologist of science cannot say that any picture is a better representation of Nature than any other." See Pinch (1986: 8). This is tantamount to the claim that we cannot distinguish on scientific grounds between Salk's polio vaccine and, say, a "crystal healing mantra" advertised in a New Age journal. It is, of course, true that scientific findings can be contaminated by unreliable methods, extra-scientific prejudices, and personal ambitions—but it is no less true that existing scientific methods produce a great many wholly reliable findings. For further insight into this subject, see the essays by William McKinney and Allan Franklin in Noretta Koertge (ed.) (2000) *A House Built on Sand* (133–150 and 151–165).

59 Aronowitz's bemusement over Sokal's choice of *Social Text* as the target of his parody is hence understandable: "For the fact is," he wrote, "that *Social Text*, of which I am a founder and in whose editorial collective I served until 1996, has never been in the [epistemologically nihilist] camp; nor do its editors or the preponderance of its contributors doubt the existence of the material world" (Aronowitz 1997: 107).

60 In this connection, it is perhaps relevant to mention that Sokal's recent work has moved farther from the critique of irrationalism, rather than vice versa. In his parody, he focused above all on the avant garde academic denial of the objective existence and knowability of reality, with a secondary emphasis on abuses of scientific terms and concepts by latter-day prophets of uncertainty and undecidability. In his recent book, however, this emphasis is reversed. Now, Sokal and his co-author give primary attention to misuses of science by the literati, leaving the deeper issue of anti-objectivism largely in the background.

61 For a recent overview of pertinent personality issues, see *Sociological Thought and Research* 21 (1/2), 1998 (a special issue on authoritarianism). For examples of the relevance of intellectual history, see Wilson (1982) and Kolnai (1938).

62 Einstein, in "Epilogue: a Socratic dialogue. Planck–Einstein–Murphy," in Planck (1932: 201f), cited in Forman (1971: 108). The interviewer, who also translated the book, was James Gardner Murphy.

63 Forman found that there were only a few major "unregenerates" who went "against the tide" in the crucial period from 1922 to 1923, when conversions to anti-causalism and anti-objectivism were common among scientists (Forman 1971: 91ff). Max Planck, sounding very much like Max Weber, was one of the few to object to what he called "a lively but unfruitful dilettantism," which seeks, romantically,

anti-causalist insight from "the rich tree of life, in contrast to the so-called school or guild science, which only in hard, protracted, specialized studies is able to gather one tiny grain after another into its barn. Today it cannot be foreseen when and where these colorfully iridescing foam bubbles will finally burst." This is excerpted from a lecture Planck gave on June 29, 1922, cited in Forman (1971: 92).

64 Cited in Feuer (1969: 159).

65 Cited in Forman (1971: 12).

66 Cited in Forman (1971: 65), from the same speech, "Causal law and free will" (delivered by Planck on February 17, 1923, to the Prussian Academy of Science).

67 Cited in Forman (1971: 63).

68 See Forman (1971: 67 n. 11), reporting Exner's 1908 rectoral address at the University of Vienna, in which he affirmed that, if enough were known about submolecular phenomena, "we would perceive nothing but a chaos of chance events, in which we would seek in vain for any regularity."

69 Weyl's essay was published in English as early as 1923, in the collective work *The Principle of Relativity*. See Forman (1971: 78). On Exner, see Forman (1971: 74ff).

70 Forman (1971: 82) calls particular attention to what may have been the first explicitly anti-causal "manifesto" by a quantum theorist—Walter Schottky's "Problem of causality in the quantum theory as a basic question for natural science," June 1921 (in German).

71 In 1933 Bohr told J. Rud Neilson that Kierkegaard "made a powerful impression upon me when I wrote my dissertation in a parsonage in Funen, and I read his works night and day." Cited in Feuer (1969: 132). For further insight into the voluminous evidence on this subject, see the writings of Jan Faye.

72 Heisenberg ([1967] 1985: 95); cited in Feuer (1969: 130).

73 See Rozental ([1967] 1985: 328), cited by Feuer (1969: 144).

74 For Bohr's general perspective on the appropriateness of the concept of free will for the description of quantum phenomena, see Bohr (1934b: 19–20; cf. 21–24, 115–117).

75 This conclusion is offered by Bohr in a commentary on Einstein's life and work, which appears in Schilpp (1949: 233), cited in Feuer (1969: 139). Compare also the many further citations which Feuer presents here.

76 Cited in Forman (1971: 54).

77 Forman offers myriad examples of this kind of irrationalism, far too numerous to summarize here. See also important later studies by M. Norton Wise, Gerald Holton, and Jan Faye, among others.

78 Cited in Forman (1971: 18).

79 Spengler also intuited that the turn to probabilistic reason—which is also central to Bohr's reading of quantum mechanics—itself reflects uncertainty: "what a depth of unconscious Skepsis there is in the rapidly increasing use of enumerative and statistical methods, which aim only at *probability* of results and forgo in advance the absolute scientific exactitude that was a creed to the hopeful earlier generations" (Spengler 1926: 418). On atomic physics, Spengler cited 1920 books by Planck and Born.

80 Spengler writes: "Everything living, we can only repeat, has "life," direction, impulse, will, a movement-quality (*Bewegtheit*) that is most intimately allied to yearning and has the smallest element in common with the motion (*Bewegung*) of the physicists. The living is indivisible and irreversible, once and uniquely occurring, and its course is entirely indeterminable by mechanics. For all such qualities belong to the essence of Destiny" (1926: 122).

81 Cited by Feuer (1969: 174).

82 In connection with Spengler's culturalist nihilism and "morphological" claims in particular, Forman discusses what he calls the "capitulation to Spenglerism" of such figures as Courant, Mie, von Mises, Schrödinger, and Madelung.

83 "By means of language," the physicist Madelung explained, "a communal world image is created as a convention"; this convention, not objective reality, is the raw material of science. Hence, he continued, "I have not the least interest in the world, but only in the image that I possess of it." See Forman (1971: 57 n. 133); and compare the even more detailed and orthodox Spenglerian remarks of the mathematics professor at Berlin, Richard von Mises (cited by Forman 1971: 48ff).

84 Here again I would stress the special relevance of the personality variables explored in Altemeyer (1996).

85 Quantum mechanical equations, for example, have clearly demonstrated great power; but that does not automatically mean that Bohr and Heisenberg were correct about their ultimate ontological or epistemological implications.

86 It is difficult to see, on the strength of this passage, how Sokal can dismiss Aronowitz's argument here with this single sentence: "Quantum mechanics is not primarily the product of a 'cultural fabric'." Yet this is, in fact, what he does; see Sokal (1998: 260–261). And note that Sokal's criticism pivots around precisely this section of Aronowitz's book.

87 To "prove" that uncertainty increases even as scientific accuracy increases, Lyotard offers all of two paragraphs on Perrin's account of the density of air—which is, evidently, the "matter" that proves "by its very nature" that reality is inherently and increasingly unknowable. "Knowledge about the density of air," he intones, "thus resolves into a multiplicity of absolutely incompatible statements" (Lyotard 1984: 57).

88 "This," he adds, "is the reasoning systems theorists—who are also the theorists of legitimation by performance [that is, successful intentional action in the world]— use to try to regain their rights."

89 Pavlov, as it happens, understood even canine aggression quite well.

90 Italics in the original; see also Sokal and Bricmont (1998: 176). Interestingly, although Sokal and Bricmont refrain from criticizing Derrida in their recent book— allegedly on the ground that he is guilty of few overt sins against science—it is, in fact, the case that Derrida has grounded many deconstructionist claims about meaning and culture in oblique references to Gödel's undecidability theorem. He embarked on this path in his very first publication (Derrida [1962] 1989); on this, see John Honner (1994). Subsequently "undecidability," like Logocentrism, became one of his most familiar categories (see, e.g., Derrida [1970] 1992: 172–173).

Bibliography

Adorno, Theodor W. ([1954] 1994) "The stars down to earth," in Crook, S. (ed.) *The Stars Down to Earth and Other Essays on the Irrational in Culture*, London and New York: Routledge, 34–127.

Altemeyer, Bob (1996) *The Authoritarian Specter*, Cambridge and London: Harvard University Press.

Aronowitz, Stanley (1988) *Science as Power*, Minneapolis: University of Minnesota Press.

Aronowitz, Stanley (1997) "Alan Sokal's 'transgression'," *Dissent* (Winter): 107–110.

Bergson, Henri ([1934] 1990) *La Penseé et le mouvant, essais et conférences*, Paris: Presses universitaires de France.

Bohr, Niels (1934a) "The atomic theory and the fundamental principles underlying the description of nature" (1929), in *Atomic Theory and the Description of Nature*, Cambridge: Cambridge University Press.

Bohr, Niels (1934b) "Introductory survey" (1929), in *Atomic Theory and the Description of Nature*, Cambridge: Cambridge University Press.

Bohr, Niels (1934c) "The quantum of action and the description of nature" (1929), in *Atomic Theory and the Description of Nature*, Cambridge: Cambridge University Press.

Bohr, Niels (1934d) "The quantum postulate and the recent development of atomic theory" (1927), in *Atomic Theory and the Description of Nature*, Cambridge: Cambridge University Press.

Campbell, Joan (1989) *Joy in Work, German Work*, Princeton: Princeton University Press.

Dagan, Henri (1899) *Enquête sur l'antisémitisme*, Paris: P.-V. Stock.

Debray, Regis (1983) *Critique of Political Reason*, London: New Left Books.

Derrida, Jacques ([1962] 1989) *Edmund Husserl's Origin of Geometry: An Introduction*, Lincoln: University of Nebraska Press.

Derrida, Jacques ([1970] 1992) "The first session," in *Acts of Literature*, New York: Routledge, 127–180.

Eichner, Hans (1982) "The rise of modern science and the genesis of romanticism," *PMLA* 97(1) (January): 8–30.

Feuer, Lewis (1969) *Einstein and the Generations of Science*, 2nd edn, New Brunswick, NJ: Transaction Books.

Forman, Paul (1971) "Weimar culture, causality, and quantum theory, 1918–1927," in *Historical Studies in the Physical Sciences*, Vol. 3, Philadelphia: University of Pennsylvania Press, 1–115.

Forman, Paul (1984) "*Kausalität, Anschaulichkeit*, and *Individualität*, or how cultural values prescribed the character and the lessons ascribed to quantum mechanics," in Stehr, Nicos and Meja, Volker (eds) *Society and Knowledge*, New Brunswick and London: Transaction.

Franklin, Allan (2000) "Avoiding the experimenter's regress," in Koertge (ed.) (2000: 151–165).

Friedländer, Saul (1997) *Nazi Germany and the Jews*, Vol. 1, New York: Harper.

Green, Martin (1974) *The von Richthofen Sisters*, New York: Basic Books.

Hayek, Friedrich (1948) *The Counter-Revolution of Science: Studies on the Abuse of Reason*, Glencoe and London: The Free Press.

Hegel, G. W. F. ([1821] 1991) *Elements of the Philosophy of Right*, Cambridge and New York: Cambridge University Press.

Hegel, G. W. F. ([1822] 1987) "Foreword" to Hermann Hinrichs "Religion in its internal relation to systematic knowledge," in Erich von der Luft (ed.) *Hegel, Hinrichs, and Schleiermacher on Feeling and Reason in Religion: The Texts of Their 1821–22 Debate*, Lewiston, ME: Edwin Mellen Press.

Heisenberg, Werner ([1967] 1985) "Quantum theory and its interpretation," in Rozental, Stefan (ed.) (1985).

Herman, Arthur (1997) *The Idea of Decline in Western History*, New York: The Free Press.

Hirschfeld, Magnus (1938) *Racism*, London: Victor Gollancz.

Honner, John (1994) "Description and deconstruction: Niels Bohr and modern philosophy," in Faye, Jan and Folse, H. J. (eds) *Niels Bohr and Contemporary Philosophy*, Dordrecht: Kluwer Academic Publishers.

Kierkegaard, Sören ([1846] 1941) *Concluding Unscientific Postscript*, Walter Lowrie (ed.), Princeton: Princeton University Press.

Klages, Ludwig (1929) *Mensch und Erde*, 3rd edn, Munich: Rupprecht-Presse.

Klages, Ludwig (1937) *Der Mensch und das Leben*, Jena: E. Diedrichs.

Koertge, Noretta (ed.) (2000) *A House Built on Sand: Exposing Postmodernist Myths about Science*, 2nd edn, New York and London: Oxford University Press.

Kohn, Hans (1965) *The Mind of Germany*, New York: Harper and Row.

Köllreuter, Otto (1925) "Die staatpolitischen Anschauungen Max Webers und Oswald Spenglers," in *Zeitschrift für Politik* 14: 481–500.

Kolnai, Aurel (1938) *The War Against the West*, London: Victor Gollancz.

Leander, Folke (1937) *Humanism and Naturalism*, Göteborg: Elanders boktryckeri aktiebolag.

Litt, Theodor (1927) *Die Philosophie der Gegenwart und ihr Einfluss auf das Bildungsideal*, 2nd edn, Leipzig: Teubner.

Löwith, Karl ([1941] 1967) *From Hegel to Nietzsche: The Revolution in Nineteenth-Century Thought*, New York: Anchor Books.

Lowrie, Walter (1942) *A Short Life of Kierkegaard*, Princeton: Princeton University Press.

Lukács, György ([1962] 1980) *The Destruction of Reason*, London: Merlin.

Lyotard, Jean-François (1984) *The Postmodern Condition: A Report on Knowledge*, Minneapolis: University of Minnesota Press.

Manheim, Ernest (1948) "The sociological theories of Hans Freyer," in Barnes, Harry Elmer (ed.) *An Introduction to the History of Sociology*, Chicago: University of Chicago Press.

Mann, Golo (1968) *The History of Germany Since 1789*, New York: Praeger.

Mann, Thomas (1983) *Diaries 1918–1939*, London: A. Deutsch.

McKinney, William J. (2000) "When experiments fail: is 'cold fusion' science as normal?" in Koertge (ed.) (2000: 133–150).

Mendelssohn-Bartholdy, Albrecht (1937) *The War and German Society*, New Haven: Yale University Press.

Monk, Raymond (1990) *Ludwig Wittgenstein*, New York: Penguin Books.

Muller, Jerry Z. (1987) *The Other God That Failed*, Princeton: Princeton University Press.

Neumann, Franz (1944) *Behemoth: The Structure and Practice of National Socialism 1933–1944*, 2nd edn, New York: Oxford University Press.

Olender, Maurice (1992) *The Languages of Paradise: Race, Religion, and Philology in the Nineteenth Century*, Cambridge, MA: Harvard University Press.

Pinch, Trevor (1986) *Confronting Nature: The Sociology of Solar-Neutrino Detection*, Dordrecht and Boston: D. Reidel.

Planck, Max (1932) *Where is Science Going?*, New York: W. W. Norton and Co.

Poliakov, Léon (1974) *The Aryan Myth*, New York: Basic Books.

Rozental, Stefan ([1967] 1985) *Niels Bohr: His Life and Works as Seen by His Friends and Colleagues*, Amsterdam and Oxford: North-Holland.

Scheler, Max (1913) "Versuche einer Philosophie des Lebens," *Die Weissen Blätter* 1(3), November: 203–233.

Scheler, Max ([1919] 1987) "Vorbilder und Führer," translated as "Exemplars of persons and leaders" in Max Scheler, *Person and Self-Value*, Manfred Frings (ed.), Dordrecht and Boston: M. Nijhoff.

Scheler, Max ([1926] 1980) *Problems of a Sociology of Knowledge*, London: Routledge and Kegan Paul.

Schilpp, Paul (ed.) (1949) *Albert Einstein: Philosopher-Scientist*, 3rd edn, Evanston: Library of Living Philosophers.

Schröter, Manfred (1922) *Der Streit um Spengler: Kritik seiner Kritiker*, Munich: Beck.

Schröter, Manfred (1949) *Metaphysik des Untergangs: Eine kulturkritische Studie über Oswald Spengler*, Munich: Leibniz Verlag.

Smith, David Norman (1996) "The social construction of enemies: Jews and the representation of evil," *Sociological Theory*, 14(3), November: 203–240.

Smith, David Norman (1997) "Judeophobia, myth, and critique," in Breslauer, S. Daniel (ed.), *The Seductiveness of Jewish Myth*, Albany, NY: Suny Press, 123–154.

Smith, David Norman (1998a) "Faith, reason, and charisma: Rudolf Sohm, Max Weber, and the theology of grace," *Sociological Inquiry*, 68(1), February: 32–60.

Smith, David Norman (1998b) "The psychocultural roots of genocide: legitimacy and crisis in Rwanda," *American Psychologist* 53(7), July: 743–753.

Sokal, Alan (1996a) "A physicist experiments with cultural studies," *Lingua Franca* (May/June 1996): 63.

Sokal, Alan (1996b) "Transgressing the boundaries: towards a transformative hermeneutics of quantum gravity," *Social Text* 46–47: 217–252.

Sokal, Alan (1997) "Alan Sokal replies," *Dissent* (Winter): 110–111.

Sokal, Alan (1998a) "Some comments on the parody," in Sokal, Alan and Bricmont, Jean, *Fashionable Nonsense: Postmodern Intellectuals' Abuse of Science*, New York: Picador.

Sokal, Alan (1998b) "Transgressing the boundaries: an afterword," in Sokal, Alan and Bricmont, Jean, *Fashionable Nonsense: Postmodern Intellectuals' Abuse of Science*, New York: Picador.

Sokal, Alan and Bricmont, Jean (1998) *Fashionable Nonsense: Postmodern Intellectuals' Abuse of Science*, New York: Picador.

Spengler, Oswald (1926) *The Decline of the West, Vol. 1: Form and Actuality*, translated from the revised German edn of 1923 by Charles Francis Atkinson, New York: Alfred A. Knopf.

Staude, John Raphael (1967) *Max Scheler*, New York: The Free Press.

Sternhell, Zeev (1986) *Neither Left Nor Right: Fascist Ideology in France*, Los Angeles and Berkeley: University of California Press.

Struve, Walter (1973) *Elites against Democracy*, Princeton: Princeton University Press.

Troeltsch, Ernst ([1921] 1989) "The revolution in science," in Peter Lassman and Irving Velody (eds) *Max Weber's "Science as a Vocation,"* London and Boston: Unwin Hyman.

Troeltsch, Ernst ([1923] 1961) *Der Historismus und seine Probleme*, *Gesammelte Schriften*, Band 3, edited by Hans Baron, Aalen: Scientia.

Viereck, Peter ([1941] 1961) *Metapolitics: The Roots of the Nazi Mind*, New York: Capricorn Books.

von der Luft, Erich (ed.) (1987) *Hegel, Hinrichs, and Schleiermacher on Feeling and Reason in Religion: The Texts of Their 1821–22 Debate*, Lewiston: Edwin Mellen Press.

Weber, Marianne ([1926] 1975) *Max Weber*, New York: Wiley.

Weber, Max ([1916–17] 1951) *The Religions of China*, Glencoe: The Free Press.

Weber, Max ([1918] 1946) "Science as a vocation," in Gerth, H. H. and Mills, C. Wright (eds) *From Max Weber: Essays in Sociology*, London: Routledge and Kegan Paul.

Weyl, Hermann, Lorentz, H. A., Einstein, Albert and Minkowski, Hermann (1923) *The Principle of Relativity*, London: Methuen.

Wilson, Stephen (1982) *Ideology and Experience: Antisemitism in France at the Time of the Dreyfus Affair*, London and Rutherford, NJ: Fairleigh Dickinson Press and the Associated University Presses.

11 The reenchantment of science

A fit end to the science wars?

Steve Fuller

The science wars as signaling the end of scientific puritanism

Someone who follows the science wars only through hearsay and journalism might reasonably conclude that natural and social scientists align themselves as follows: the natural scientists are keen on reaffirming and perhaps even extending the social authority of their disciplines, whereas the social scientists wish to restrict that influence. However, in reality, the positions are almost reversed. For the most part, the natural scientists have been concerned to protect the integrity of their knowledge claims from extrapolations into realms where they feel that, at best, they have only metaphorical relevance. On the other hand, many humanists and social scientists have taken the various revolutions in twentieth-century science as inspiration for making bold claims about the human condition (Hayles 1998).

To be sure, much of this latter discourse (which travels under the generic label of "postmodernism") aims to "demystify" the natural sciences—but only in a very particular sense. Through a combination of sociological investigation and public controversy, it has become apparent that science does not speak with one voice and consequently the door is open to various constituencies using the theories and findings of science as they see fit. Yet acknowledging this point does not constitute "anti-science" in the usual sense of the word. On the contrary, it reflects a desire to integrate science into larger intellectual currents, institutional practices, and personal lifestyles. This point is worth stressing, as it marks a convergence in the disparate interests that have been demonized as the "Academic Left" in the science wars. For even within the science and technology studies (STS) community, there exist "high" and "low" church constituencies, the former concerned with anti-foundationalism and other recherché epistemological doctrines and the latter with a participatory politics that harkens back to more traditional forms of democratic populism (Fuller 1993). Although hardly natural bedfellows, both STS churches nevertheless refuse to see science as a body of knowledge about which only certified "scientists" can speak authoritatively. The response of professional natural scientists to the combined STS challenge—especially those who feel their own authority under attack—can be summed up as a kind of neo-puritanism that reasserts the value of technical proficiency and the need for self-restraint in its application (Fuller 1999b).

In the British context, the neo-puritan response has been most striking among scientists whose work verges on genetic engineering. The chairman of the Royal Society's Committee on Public Understanding of Science, Lewis Wolpert (1992: Chapter 6), has even claimed that his fellow biologists are not qualified to contribute to discussions on the implications of the Human Genome Project for public policy. Little surprise, then, that I recently found myself on a panel having to tell Graham Bulfield, the director of Edinburgh's Roslin Institute, that he owed the public an account, that went beyond pious condemnations of state-mandated eugenics policies, of how we should think about his laboratory's cloning of Dolly the sheep.

I believe that there is more to scientists' social responsibility than simply demonstrating that they are not monsters, and that being adept at splicing genes does not disqualify one from commenting on the social uses to which the fruits of one's labors may be put (Fuller 2000a: Chapter 8). That Wolpert and Bulfield think otherwise is itself sufficient reason, in my mind, to require natural scientists to take STS courses as part of their professional training. In a more charitable light, Wolpert and Bulfield may be seen as sacrificing their own moral voice to save the epistemic status of science itself. Nevertheless, this point is often masked in larger discussions of science in society, where the emphasis is placed on increasing public involvement, as if this were somehow being usurped by the scientific community. In most cases, it is not.

On the contrary, the neo-puritan retrenchment has sometimes come at the cost of undermining the credibility of distinguished scientific predecessors who uncannily anticipated many of the objectionable appropriations associated with the Academic Left. Here the physicists take center stage. For example, Steven Weinberg (1996) had no qualms asserting that Werner Heisenberg was out of his depth when he pronounced on the subjectivist epistemological implications of the uncertainty principle in quantum mechanics, while the hoax on the editors of *Social Text* perpetrated by Weinberg's student, Alan Sokal (1996), partly relied on cultural studies scholars taking seriously the parallels Niels Bohr himself drew between the complementarity principle and the metaphysics of Taoism and Buddhism.

While it took the science wars to bring these allegedly embarrassing pronouncements into public view, thirty years earlier Thomas Kuhn had already observed similar tendencies in the founders of quantum mechanics, when trying to compile oral histories of their work (Kuhn *et al.* 1967). It would seem that Bohr, Heisenberg, and their contemporaries could not discuss the technical aspects of their research—about which, it turned out, their memories often seemed faulty—outside of the larger philosophical and cultural issues of the 1920s. Like Weinberg and Sokal after him, Kuhn attributed this tendency to mental infirmity (presumably linked to the advanced age of Bohr, Heisenberg, *et al.*). None has considered the possibility that technical and cultural matters were genuinely inseparable, even in quantum mechanics.

Probably the most important rhetorical problem with the science warriors' neo-puritanism is that supporters and opponents of the puritanical conception of science do not neatly correspond to those trained and untrained in the natural sciences. One of the delicious ironies of the science wars is that the sociologists of science who have been most highly esteemed by natural scientists—Robert Merton, Joseph Ben-David, Bernard Barber, Stephen Cole—did not start life as natural scientists; whereas many of the sociologists regarded with most suspicion—Barry Barnes, David Bloor, Andrew Pickering, Steven Shapin, Steve Woolgar—were originally trained in chemistry, experimental psychology, physics, genetics, and engineering, respectively.

Are Merton *et al.* to be congratulated for bolstering disciplines in which they were not trained, and Barnes *et al.* to be condemned for criticizing those in which they were? The epistemology that would encourage affirmative answers to these two questions boggles the mind. Consequently, the "constructivism" or "relativism" that Sokal and others have wanted to present as evidence of incompetence, on closer inspection, has turned out to be based on differences in interpretation or evaluation—not differences in basic competence in science.

It is worth observing that such perverse mixtures of training and judgment are not new to the philosophy of science. To be sure, the original logical positivists were typically trained in mathematics or physics, albeit in the foundational branches most closely aligned with philosophy. Nevertheless, even such influential younger colleagues of the positivists as Karl Popper and Carl Hempel had a more tangential relationship to these sciences: Popper's Ph.D. was in educational psychology, whereas Hempel's dealt with the use of ideal types in the social sciences, such as the ideal rational agent in economics. Moreover, it is fair to say that both Popper's and Hempel's credibility as methodologists rests largely on their popularization of putatively natural science models of inference in social science settings. The same applies with even greater force to the two unreconstructed humanists who imported logical positivism to Oxford and Cambridge, respectively A. J. Ayer and I. A. Richards.

To varying degrees, from the 1930s to the 1950s, all of these thinkers were caught up in the question of demarcating science from pseudo-science in order to enable the production of knowledge to subsist independently of any political commitments to such self-proclaimed "world-historic" movements as Nazism and Communism. As for the actual content of contemporary natural scientific research, Hempel said nothing notable, and whenever Popper did (as in his critiques of evolution by natural selection and the instrumentalist interpretation of quantum mechanics) he was treated only slightly more seriously than today's postmodern thinkers are. The main positive ideological function of their scientific puritanism, then, was to disallow the use of the title "science" from attempts to coerce large numbers of people to do things that, absent any "higher" form of legitimation, they would be disinclined to do, often on conventional moral grounds.

The gap between training and judgment in science among scientific puritans grew once the logical positivists moved to the United States and their intellectual offspring became both the philosophy of science establishment and the philosophy of the science establishment.

From the mid-1950s to the late 1970s most philosophical defenders of what Fred Suppe (1977) has called "the received view" on the nature of scientific confirmation and explanation were primarily trained in mathematical logic, probability theory, and classical epistemology. Their knowledge of science was confined to potted examples from the history of physics—mainly astronomy—between roughly the time of Aristotle and that of Newton. In contrast, the main Anglo-American philosophical critics of the received view during that period were, like today's constructivist sociologists of science, originally trained in the physics of their day (Fuller 2000a: Chapter 6). Among these "historicists" I would include Stephen Toulmin, Thomas Kuhn, Paul Feyerabend, and Larry Laudan.

At the very least, this turn of events shows that the sheer possession of scientific expertise requires neither a puritanical nor even an especially sympathetic attitude towards science. Conversely, some of science's most puritanical gatekeepers have possessed very little technical scientific knowledge. They have acted very much like the guardian class in Plato's *Republic* who do not fully understand the ways of the dialectic but know enough to realize that social order depends on their protecting the Philosopher-Kings from corruption. (Gross *et al.* 1996 contains statements by many who function in just this guardian capacity in the science wars, the most prominent of whom has probably been the philosopher Susan Haack.)

The guardian mentality was first dressed in modern garb by the seventeenth-century British Chancellor of the Exchequer, Francis Bacon, although his own scientific puritanism extended to protecting science from the Church, only to move it closer to the state, with his notional "House of Solomon" functioning as the first government-sponsored laboratory. More influential in the twentieth century has been the image of the "value-neutral" scientist promoted by sociologist Max Weber, which effectively translated the Romantic humanistic ideal of the autonomous inquirer into an academic environment increasingly dominated by positivistic physical science (a good history of this transition is Proctor 1991).

Until the twentieth century, the puritanical conception of science was defensible on at least two grounds. First, the conduct of scientific work did not consume vast public resources; indeed, private funding was the norm. Therefore not much was placed at risk in allowing an activity that might well turn up something of greater significance, but its failure to do so would not incur much social cost. Second, for the most part, science had proven much better at explaining natural phenomena and human invention than at either predicting or producing them. Consequently, a puritanical attitude encouraged a climate of diminished expectations that shielded science from absorbing responsibility for solving the pressing social and intellectual problems of the day.

However, as science has become integral to the workings of the state, industry, and medicine, the puritanical attitude has gradually lost its credibility. A symbol of these times is the critical reception of Collins and Pinch (1993), the first STS work to compete in the science popularization market. The book was expressly written to disarm those who regard STS as antiscientific. Its strategy was to reduce science's social significance to the craft practiced by a group of people working on relatively esoteric topics, usually in a laboratory. Absent from its pages were scares of nuclear war, environmental despoliation, invasive health treatments, and all-round cultural imperialism. The scientific craft was discussed so as to highlight its virtuosity and flexibility, but not its capacity to control the world outside the laboratory. Yet the book turned out to be one of the opening salvos in the science wars. How was that possible?

Perhaps the science wars have caused scientists to rethink their commitment to cultural puritanism and to rediscover their long-discredited roots in scientism, which in its simplest form is the doctrine that science can justify value commitments (Sorell 1991). Thus scientistic thinkers blur the boundaries between "is" and "ought," "fact" and "value," "natural" and "rational"— typically by assimilating the latter term in each binary into the former. For the most part, postmodernists appear to be "anti-science" only because scientists still harbor a puritanical attitude towards science that would drive a sharp wedge between these pairs of terms.

However, seen from a larger historical perspective, many postmodernists, especially those emanating from French philosophical culture, have participated in a revival of scientism that replaces earlier positivistic enthusiasms for the "Newtonian world view" with a fascination with quanta, relativity, and chaos (Fuller 1999b; for a blistering critique, see Bricmont and Sokal 1997). One constructive legacy of the science wars may be a revival of scientism as part of a "reenchantment" of science (see Harrington 1996; Dusek 1999, for provocative precedents). I shall explain the relevant sense of reenchantment in the rest of this chapter.

The secularization of science as a precondition for its reenchantment

Scientism does not normally feature in histories of science. If you doubt the truth of this statement, then consider the role assigned to, say, Auguste Comte, Herbert Spencer, Ernst Haeckel, and Wilhelm Ostwald in histories of nineteenth-century science. These figures are often seen as embarrassments, even among historians who would otherwise go to great pains to contextualize their subjects (see Hakfoort 1995, for a critique of this tendency).

The source of embarrassment is the explicitness with which these scientific thinkers assumed that science could answer the questions of morals and meaning originally posed by religion. To be sure, some, like Comte, mimicked the Catholics in envisaging science as a universal church governed by a distributed hierarchy of priestly experts. Others, like Spencer, resembled the Protestant Reformers in fostering a spirit of scientific amateurism that recalled the founders of the Royal Society, men of independent means and judgment who distrusted the academic establishment of their day.

Be they influenced by Catholicism or Protestantism, these ideologues of scientism presumed a continuity between the goals of science and religion that, in principle, exposed science to the kind of sectarianism that—in light of the Reformation—was to be expected of bodies of knowledge that claimed an ability to settle value disputes. In this spirit, the labels "positivist," "evolutionist," "monist," and "materialist" were all-purpose world views that used scientific trends and findings to justify specific social policies. Thus, in an inversion of the terms of today's science wars, it was common in the early twentieth century to find social scientists like Max Weber complaining about, say, Ostwald's attempt to translate the laws of thermodynamics into the social ethic of "energeticism" (Rabinbach 1990).

Immanuel Kant set the precedent for today's embarrassed silence about scientism. His preference for a cool agnosticism on metaphysical matters over an impassioned scientism reflected life under the "benevolent despotism" of late eighteenth-century Prussia, where free expression was tolerated so long as it did not threaten state religious doctrines. (The conditions under which the King of England was prepared to grant a Charter to the first modern scientific society, the Royal Society of London, bear comparison here: see Proctor 1991.)

Vestiges of Kant's original circumspection were carried into the twentieth century by neo-Kantian philosophers, especially Ernst Cassirer (1950). The result is that many philosophers, intellectual historians and natural scientists have come to think of such nineteenth-century movements as "vitalism" and "reductionism" more as the metaphysical bases of scientific disciplines— "pre-paradigms" in Kuhn's sense—than as they were regarded in their heyday, namely, general cultural sensibilities that operated on several registers which, taken together, blurred the science/politics distinction (Mendelsohn 1964).

The current disrepute of scientism has caused significant parts of the history of science to be discreetly rewritten or forgotten—much like the tendency to write out racist elements from historic defenses of the concept of "culture" (Fuller 2000b). In the end, this is symptomatic of the failure of science's pastoral mission. Scientists would not be so ashamed of their scientistic past, if the natural sciences had developed analogues to religious institutions like the Sacraments and the Sunday school, which were designed to enable the laity to participate in the confirmation, and sometimes even production, of sacred knowledge. The closest that the history of modern science has come to these practices is the public demonstration of experiments, championed by such radical Protestants as Joseph Priestley and Michael Faraday (Knight 1986).

But even this practice betrayed the growing tension of the natural sciences' relationship to the larger society in the nineteenth century. The matter boiled down to whether one wished to stress the "public" or the "demonstration" side of public demonstrations. The "public" side emphasized science's empiricism ("seeing is believing") and its historic roots in amateurism. Knowledge was therefore to be pursued—as the Greeks originally insisted—in the spirit of leisure, not labor. Anyone could participate, if they had the time, money, and, of course, wit. On the other hand, the "demonstration" side moved science towards a more esoteric form of knowledge, an expertise, which can just as easily mystify as illuminate the masses. Science here is not a sophisticated form of play, but hard work—so hard that one needs to be an adept (that is, acquire academic credentials) to engage in it properly.

This tension has deepened over the last 150 years. Observed from the lens of the sociology of religion, it has all the trappings of secularization—only in this case, science is itself the target rather than the agent of secularization (Fuller 1997: Chapter 4; Fuller 1999a: Chapter 6). For purposes of what follows, it is important to recall that the process historically associated with "secularization" is most precisely rendered, in today's terms, as religion's loss of a state-protected market. In other words, secularization does not correspond to a decline in religious belief as such, but to a decline in the view that only one such belief is legitimate. By analogy, then, "science secularized" means that people continue to believe in science, but now also believe that they have a choice as to which science they believe (Feyerabend 1979).

To begin to see what I mean, consider that the average person lives in what Max Weber would regard as an "enchanted" world where both the human and natural realms are fraught with meaning and purpose. From that standpoint, the mark of the modern scientific mind is a disenchanted attitude to the natural realm and an enchanted attitude to the human realm, as epitomized by the belief in "progress." Consequently, nature appears passive or indifferent in relation to organized human activity.

Postmodernists reverse this asymmetry by demystifying the idea of human progress, while reenchanting the natural realm. Here the efficacy of human effort is local, fragmentary, and transient, when compared with the chaotic and complex workings of the non-human, which always just manage to elude scientific strictures. In this respect, Gross and Levitt (1994) are correct in seeing most STS researchers as allied with francophile literary critics, New Age practitioners, creationists, environmentalists, and proponents of identity politics.

In contemporary America, enchanted attitudes towards the human and the natural realms coexist, though characteristically they are upheld by separate groups. Their juxtaposition has produced the climate of cultural unrest that forms the background to the science wars. To appreciate the nature of the current crisis, consider the following two propositions, which encapsulate the state of thinking in the United States (and perhaps elsewhere):

(A) two thirds of scientists who believe that our knowledge of reality has radically changed over time also believe that science is getting closer to "the truth";

(B) two thirds of ordinary citizens (mostly non-scientists) who believe in the evolution of life on Earth also believe God is responsible for the process.

The fact that (A) and (B) pull in opposing directions to an equal extent points to an instance of institutionalized irrationality. In terms of conceptual consistency alone, one should either accept or deny both propositions. In both cases, a contrast is implied between the apparently contingent character of history—be it of science (A) or nature (B)—and an underlying trajectory that supplies meaning to that contingency. One may believe that such attributions of meaning are in general genuine or spurious, but how can one justify an attribution in one case but not the other?

For example, (A) helps explain how it has been possible for scientists to find Shapin and Schaffer (1985) and Latour (1988) "delightful reads" that "enrich" their understanding of how science has made progress. The deflationary picture of history presented in these STS classics would appear to be completely lost on them. But, in principle, this response is no different from religiously motivated students who master evolutionary biology but regard it as the fine-grained detail of the Divine Plan, which in turn leads them to question the explicit prohibition of "intelligent design" arguments from science classrooms.

As for (B), it implies no conflict among science, folk beliefs, and democracy. But if most people find science and religion compatible, where does the conflict come from? There are two main sources: laws that demand a separation of church and state in the US public school system, and academic disciplinary strictures—specifically contemporary evolutionary biology's proscriptions against any appeals to cosmic design. Thus in the right context (like a classroom) the majority of people surveyed could stand accused of illegality and incompetence.

In opposing (A) and (B), respectively, STS researchers and evolutionary biologists would point out that their findings demonstrate that current epistemic and ecological regimes could have been quite other than they are. To speak of "progress" or "design" is unnecessary from the standpoint of Ockham's razor and perhaps even misleading in terms of interpreting the significance of particular cases.

Nevertheless, in the United States, (B) is regarded as a national emergency, whereas (A) passes unremarked and is often seen as quite reasonable. What accounts for this difference? An important part of the answer is that evolutionary biologists have virtually a state-licensed monopoly over instruction on the nature of life, whereas neither STS researchers nor, even, more traditional historians of science enjoy this degree of institutional control over explanations of science's ascendancy. In at least this respect, science remains America's state religion. But is it any more than nominal?

The basis for an affirmative answer may be found in the fact that a state-supported secondary school is still more likely to teach the natural sciences than economics or even business studies. While capitalism allegedly commands the loyalty of most Americans, it is striking that academic subjects explicitly oriented towards wealth creation do not occupy a more central place in the curriculum. Perhaps this can be explained in terms of the US Constitution's provision for patenting as a vehicle for wealth creation, which is attributed to the application of ingenuity to natural process, rather than, say, the pursuit of self-interest wherever it may lead.

Nevertheless, one reason for querying the status of America's devotion to science is the occasional victories that creationists have scored in the state educational system. (As of this writing, August 1999, creationists have managed to persuade politicians in Kansas that evolution need not be taught in state-supported schools.) However, my interest here is not in those who would have either God or Darwin excluded from the classroom, rather it is in the vast majority of Americans who seem willing to have both included. For me, this endorsement of choice is the mark of science's secularization.

To see this process in a broader context, consider Peter Berger's (1967) classic *The Sacred Canopy*, which observed a curious rupture in the semantics of the word "religion" during secularization. On the one hand, "religion" refers to a mindlessly repeated set of sectarian rituals, the paradigm case of unreflectively performed social action that Max Weber called "tradition." Examples include Catholics attending Mass every Sunday and Jews adhering to the dietary strictures of the Torah, but in both cases as detached from the wider cultural contexts that provide a rationale for these practices. On the other hand, "religion" also refers to a general sensibility about the meaning of life, set adrift from any sectarian moorings. In this sense, religion is said to be purely spiritual and even "personal." Here one would be hard pressed to deduce specific courses of action from a belief that, say, Jesus Christ is one's personal savior.

I believe that a similar instability has befallen the meaning of "science." The concentration of support in certain fields like particle physics, and then molecular biology, were originally responsible for the sanctification of "Big Science," but since the end of the Cold War, financial support for scientific research has been increasingly devolved from the nation state and, in that respect, secularized (Fuller 1999a: especially Chapter 6). In terms of larger sociological processes, this devolution has been part of the downsizing of the welfare state, whereby public services are outsourced to private contractors on a competitive basis.

For some, "science" now refers to little more than the subject matter that must be mastered to acquire the credentials needed to succeed in life. There is no deep spiritual commitment to such knowledge, only a pragmatic awareness of its function in the processes of social reproduction: once the exam is over, there is no expectation that the knowledge will ever need to be displayed again. Such people remain agnostic or otherwise disinclined to participate in debates concerning the content of scientific knowledge: they simply adopt whatever happens to be the received view when called upon to do so. Their respect for science extends no further than the yardsticks against which their own competence is measured.

But for others, "science" means a generalized attitude to the world that may include weighting one's beliefs in proportion to the available evidence or adopting a critical or even skeptical approach to taken-for-granted beliefs. These people regard scientific disputes as partisan affairs, and are quite prepared to doubt received scientific opinion if it does not conform to their personal sense of what it means to be scientific. Many adherents to New Age science fall into this category, for example, when they explain the dominance of allopathic over homeopathic medicine as the product of a state-licensed monopoly. These generalized believers in science are especially attracted to the way science popularization blurs the line between the factual and futuristic, concrete and spiritual, and so on.

Distinguishing the enchanted and disenchanted mind: the mark of theodicy

I propose that the most fruitful way to understand the differences between the modernist natural scientists and postmodernist social scientists pitted against each other in the science wars—especially the heat their disagreements have generated throughout the academy—is to reopen a question that Max Weber is normally thought to have closed after Germany's humiliating defeat in World War I. Weber argued persuasively, against the messianic tendencies of both nationalist and communist colleagues in the German academy, that the "scientific attitude" implies a disenchanted view of the world, specifically a recognition that the nature of reality cannot be captured by the strictures of any value system.

There are several ways of stating Weber's thesis. In terms Plato would have understood (and opposed), the true and the good turn out not to converge in the mind of the sincere inquirer; in more theological terms, we have no reason to believe that the ultimate "theory of everything" will reveal the purpose of it all. While we should expect that good things will happen to bad people, and vice versa, we should not expect that there will be a theoretically interesting answer to why things happen that way. There will be only particular answers that relate to the emergent effects of the actions taken by many people in a finite world of which they have finite knowledge. Moreover, because of the number and kind of factors invoked, these answers will not say anything especially revealing about the validity of any specific normative orientation to the world.

Thus, to the Weberian scientist, reality is indifferent to human projects and offers at most hints on whether particular projects conform to its strictures—certainly not the other way around. Those who succeed in their projects may have managed to use these hints more to their advantage, but typically that is because they exploited the opportunities in situations largely not of their own making. Nietzsche, one of Weber's inspirations, was very alive to this complicating factor in any attribution of genius, one which Bernard Williams (1981) has subsequently christened "moral luck." Such luck often depends on the agent's ignorance of the conditions governing his or her situation: a more fully knowledgeable agent might have acted less decisively.

What is generally called the "value-neutrality" of science refers to just this ambivalent attitude toward the unbridgeable gap between what one knows and what one wants. For Weber, it had the methodologically salubrious consequence of enabling the fair test, and especially the falsification, of scientific hypotheses, since no strength of value commitment on the part of the scientist can ultimately gainsay the dictates of reality.

To be sure, Weber's doctrine of value-neutrality has been challenged over the course of the twentieth century, but usually in a rather specific way. Critics generally concede the Kantian metaphysical point that lies behind the doctrine—that reality is indifferent to values—but they question whether scientists can ever distance themselves sufficiently from their value commitments to conduct something that Weber would have recognized as a "fair test." As Freud might have it, whereas Weber saw science's disenchantment of the world as marking the ascendancy of the "reality principle," Weber's critics see it as having opened the door to wishful thinking and related ego defense mechanisms.

However, Weber's doctrine can be challenged at a metaphysically deeper level, namely that it begs the question of the relationship between how things are and ought to be. Just because the relationship is not a straightforward one, such that value categories clearly do not form a one-to-one correspondence with natural categories, it does not follow that there is no relationship whatsoever. The fact that good things do indeed happen to bad people, and vice versa, may be indicative of the need to distinguish between, say, the short- and long-term effects of causes, as well as local and global perspectives on reality. (Elster 1980, remains the most systematic development of this point.)

The postulation of multiple and even cross-cutting cognitive horizons has been essential to theodicy, a now neglected branch of theology, which is literally devoted to fathoming God's sense of justice. At least in the Christian tradition, theodicy has assumed that God acts in ways that may initially appear mysterious but are ultimately comprehensible from a large enough frame of reference, presumably one that approximates the standpoint of a being capable of capturing all of reality in a glance. In the next section, we shall see that theodicy survives in a partly disenchanted form in two rather different scientific "master narratives" that have managed to weather the storms of postmodernism: the invisible hand and evolution by natural selection.

For Weber, an attraction to theodicy is the mark of the "enchanted" mind. The period of Western disenchantment began when Newton's understudy, Samuel Clarke, successfully fended off Leibniz's criticisms that the Newtonian world-picture failed to provide a sufficiently normative ground for the physical universe (Toulmin 1999: Chapter 4). Two generations later, Kant countered latter-day Leibnizians by showing that theodicy was intractable to scientific approaches. At that point, cosmology lost its ties to theology, and soon thereafter theology itself became a properly scientific inquiry (*Wissenschaft*) divorced of specific doctrinal religious commitments. Hegel and his followers on the Left, most notably David Friedrich Strauss, Ludwig Feuerbach and Karl Marx, were among the main legatees of this move. (To be sure, they merely shifted the locus of enchantment from God to "humanity" understood as either a biological species or an organized movement.) Eventually, after the usual period of retrenchment by religious authorities, all academic subjects were disenchanted, as the university came to be a wholly secular institution.

To put it in the most general philosophical terms, the disenchantment of theodicy amounts to the removal of teleology from accounts of nature. Theodicy is relevant to teleology because the clearest way to show that something has a purpose is by observing how it perseveres in the face of resistance from its natural environment. This resistance can be then seen as impeding the automatic realization of the thing's purpose. Examples of this process may include the Divine Plan working its way through imperfect humans or, less grandiosely, a genetically limited organism managing to reproduce itself under adverse conditions. Thus what appear as obstacles to a goal at one level of reality turn out to be vehicles for an even greater achievement at a higher level. (In this respect, Freud's innovation was to internalize this conflict to the individual psyche under the rubric of "sublimation.")

Theodicy's disenchantment has been generally accompanied by the conversion of nature's resistance to a personal deficiency. In other words, nature no longer poses a specifically moral challenge to our will (that is, an opportunity for mind to overcome matter, good to overcome evil, and so on). Instead, nature's resistance is treated diagnostically as a symptom of our cognitive limitations, which, as it happens, turns out to be adaptive when considered from a position that approximates God's standpoint. Although he would be the last to discuss matters this way, Herbert Simon's (1977) concept of bounded rationality fits under such cognitivist appeals to disenchant theodicy (Fuller 1985).

Among the scientific doctrines that would fall under this category are emergentist theories of consciousness, Bohr's version of the complementarity principle in quantum mechanics, the anthropic principle in cosmology and the Gaia hypothesis of Earth as superorganism. Like their more enchanted forebears, the scientific credentials of each of these ideas have been severely challenged, mainly for presuming that the system under study—the human organism, a physics experiment, the physical universe, or the planet Earth—should be treated for scientific purposes as closed under a set of laws. To do so would imply that everything subsumed by the system serves the system's maintenance. A term for this situation that resonates across disciplinary boundaries is "functionalism."

To this, the disenchanted mind immediately counters that the fact that the exact values of many physical parameters seem undermotivated by current physical theory may simply mean that we do not know enough physics, not that the universe has been designed so that we come to realize our place in it. Similarly, the fact that it is very difficult to understand how our neural circuitry produces a sense of consciousness does not imply that the consciousness we have is the optimal output of some resolution of nerve endings. In other words, the disenchanted mind seriously entertains the possibility that, say, there is no humanly interesting reason for the universe's physical parameters being as they are and there is no strictly scientific reason for believing that human consciousness is a sufficiently robust feature of reality to be captured by laws of nature.

In short, the final step from theodicy's disenchantment to its complete dissolution—the moment of Weberian disenchantment—comes when one slips from believing that, say, "the nature of consciousness" or "the meaning of life" is an intractably complex phenomenon to believing that it is a mere pseudo-phenomenon.

To appreciate the difference between an enchanted and disenchanted account of reality, consider two ways of explaining the plight of Job, an ostensibly good man to whom many bad things happen for reasons that remain undisclosed, even at the end of the book of the Old Testament that bears his name:

(A) Enchanted: Either Job (or an ancestor) did something bad in the past for which he is now being punished, or he is being prepared for something much better that will happen to him (or his descendants) in the future.
(B) Disenchanted: Either Job became the victim of natural events beyond his knowledge or control, or he acted on the basis of imperfect information which led him to do things that unwittingly undermined his own interests.

In (A), Job's fate reflects an implicit judgment that either reality or God has passed over something he has done (or perhaps inherited), whereas in (B) no such judgment is reflected. (A) and (B) are based on opposed conceptions of cosmology, which the intellectual historian Alexandre Koyre (1957) called "the closed world" and "the infinite universe," respectively.

In the closed world, reality has a moral center that is manifested by a natural order that tends towards equilibrium. In such a world, all wrongs are eventually made right. Thus, regardless of its complexity (as measured by, say, the inscrutability of God's motives), the world displays the sort of causal closure that enables, on the one hand, guilt and gratitude to be literally about relationships between specific people that project from the present to the past and, on the other, revenge and providence to be about relationships that extend from the present into the future. The first pair of terms marks humanity as passive, the second pair as active. In each pair, the first term captures the negative emotion associated with the relationship, the second the positive emotion.

Weber (1965) identified the two past-oriented attitudes with karma, a common ingredient in the theodicies of the Eastern world religions, and the two future-oriented ones with salvation, a feature shared by the theodicies of the Western world religions. The cognitive character of these two sets of attitudes dropped out as the cosmology of the closed world was replaced by a universe indefinitely open at all points. This change removed a fundamental condition of the moral nexus, namely that at least in principle, the "doer" and "done-to" can recognize each other as such (Pettit 1993: 329–336). After the Koyrean transition, the temporal orientations associated with karma and salvation became "purely psychological" states without clear objective reference.

But this is not to say that the moral nexus has been completely severed. Koyre's closed world remains alive today as a presupposition of courtroom proceedings, especially when the law endeavors to establish the cause of harm for purposes of redressing the damage done (Kelsen 1943). Tellingly, one refers to this presupposition as a "legal fiction." But what would it mean to reinvest such legal fictions with moral import?

For Weber, it would mean the conversion of "science" to "politics." This is because the imposition of ends other than where the free pursuit of truth naturally leads amounts to coercion—the essence of politics for Weber, child of Hobbes. But perhaps we should see the reinvestment of moral import in nature the other way round, namely as putting together two features of our understanding of reality that have been artificially severed. As it turns out, despite the prevalence of Weber's disenchantment rhetoric, theodicy is alive, if not entirely well, in the two most popular master narratives of our times. It is to these that I now turn.

Two disenchanted theodicies: invisible hand and natural selection

Consider the question of theodicy in boldest relief: why is the distribution of good in the world not proportional to the production of goodness? In short, why do good things happen to bad people, and vice versa? Depending on whether one has an optimistic or a pessimistic sense of divine justice, one might think the world displays a surplus or a deficit of goodness; more specifically, the entirety of the human condition is either more or less than the sum or what individual human agents do. The former is epitomized by invisible hand arguments and the latter by selectionist theories of biological evolution.

Invisible hand arguments answer the question of why there is more good than one would expect. The world's surplus good is attributed to the fact that benefiting oneself need not disadvantage others and in fact requires unintentionally benefiting them. When first proposed in the eighteenth century, this argument provided a vivid foil to the zero-sum game of social order presented in Thomas Hobbes's "state of nature," whereby one's win always entails another's loss. In effect, the invisible hand disenchanted the Panglossian view that this is the best of all possible worlds, such that any appearance of evil or imperfection is merely symptomatic of the need for a sufficiently wide or long perspective from which to regard its significance. Indeed, the hand of God may have planted imperfections and other "suboptimalities" specifically to motivate finite beings to become all they can be (Elster 1984).

In spiritual terms, greater knowledge of the whole of Creation is supposed to instill a greater appreciation of the Creator's goodness. But in secular guise, the invisible hand is marked by a dissociation of closure and order. In other words, the order that emerges from an invisible hand process is indefinitely open, leading to interpretations of endless productivity and what John Maynard Keynes originally called "multiplier effects." Thus a classic corollary of the invisible hand is the existence of long-term "trickle down" benefits from wealthy enterprisers to the unemployed poor. Self-interestedness comes to be detached from mere selfishness, as entrepreneurs are compelled to do things that, in the fullness of time, benefit the poor, perhaps more so than the poor could have done for themselves

In that respect, seen in historical perspective, the invisible hand exhibits a karmic dimension, as the unwholesome features of personal motivation are gradually laundered through a system of interactions to produce a net gain for all concerned. The key difference is that the transmission of cause and effect in karma is much clearer than in the invisible hand. This largely reflects the closure of the former and the openness of the latter. Indeed, the workings of the invisible hand are typically so complex (or obscure?) that the recipients of advantage can rarely appreciate how they have benefited from the actions of others; hence the obviation of any sense of gratitude. Indeed, this blockage of mutual recognition conditions easily breeds interpersonal or intergroup resentment.

But, likewise, the bestowers of advantage never know when they have done enough, which saddles them with an ever-present feeling of guilt for possibly not having done enough. This, in turn, creates the compulsive productivity that, according to Weber, enabled the "Protestant ethic" to evolve into the "spirit of capitalism." In this context, the welfare state can be seen as an attempt to socially engineer karmic closure by making the tax system the vehicle by which the poor's debt to the rich is partly commuted by placing the rich in debt to the state *qua* executor of the poor. This practice, in turn, is justified by assuming that exploitation enabled the rich to enjoy their current level of success. Not surprisingly, then, the philosophically deepest objection to the idea of the welfare state challenges the seemingly alchemical ability of distributive justice (specifically, a tax scheme for redistributing income) to satisfy the demands of commutative justice in complex systems (Hayek 1978).

In contrast, natural selection arguments address the question of why there is less good in the world than one would expect. The general form the answer takes is that one's own maintenance and reproduction consume resources, which unintentionally interferes with the capacity of others to maintain and reproduce themselves. Earlier versions of evolutionary theory, such as Lamarck's (and indeed much of contemporary economic development theory), largely accepted the invisible hand assumption that the increase of life on the planet would (perhaps even exponentially) increase the level of collective intelligence, which would in turn continually find new ways to provide the resources needed for sustaining future generations.

Natural selection undermines these progressivist notions of evolution by observing that a world which, on the whole and in the long term, turns out bad—as Keynes famously put it, "in the long run, we are all dead"—is entirely compatible with the presence of delimited times and places in which life very much flourishes. But from a theological standpoint, these moments of beneficence ultimately reflect the wages of sin, or what economists call "time-discounting," whereby people derive pleasure from the present by forfeiting their ability to enjoy still greater pleasures in the future (Ainslie 1992; Price 1993). I have argued that modern conceptions of scientific progress trade on this notion, with the added twist that the goals of science are continually rewritten so that the current state of inquiry always turns out to be a waystation that some suitably trans-generational "we" have been always pursuing (Fuller 1997: Chapter 5).

If the invisible hand disenchants Leibniz's doctrine that this is the best of all possible worlds, natural selection performs a similar move on Augustine's pessimistic reading of the doctrine of original sin, which condemns humanity to ultimate failure. However, as a disenchanted theodicy, natural selection loses the closure of the original Augustinian doctrine. Thus there is no final reckoning, just endless cycles of generation and extinction: Darwin's endless struggle for survival.

Since the struggle never ends, there is no chance for revenge, since a species that is well adapted to its environment will eventually become overadapted and ultimately overcome by other species that are themselves destined to be overcome—unless, of course, the processes of natural selection (specifically, the interventions of humans) alter the fundamental physical conditions of the planet so as to extinguish the propagation of life altogether.

The moral nexus is further attenuated as species become more versatile in altering the selection environment, thereby affecting not only their own fate but also that of other species. It then becomes possible to do harm to others who will not be in a position either to defend themselves or even to recognize the harm-doers as such. This point is most apparent in counterfactual contexts, where it is easy to imagine that self-restraint would have enabled others to flourish. But of course, because these "others" have not been allowed to flourish, the sense of loss is mitigated.

The invisible hand and natural selection first came head to head in debates over the efficacy of free trade in early nineteenth-century Britain. Specifically, how can depressions periodically occur in an economic system that supposedly promotes the free exchange of goods and services? Should free trade not lead to ever-expanding wealth, as Adam Smith taught? In this way, the mismatch between intention and outcome that defines the problem of theodicy was rendered in a perfectly anthropocentric way.

The invisible hand was represented by David Ricardo, the stockbroker who spoke for the emerging bourgeoisie; natural selection by Thomas Malthus (the main source of Darwin's own formulation), the parson whose interests coincided with those of the declining gentry. Together they captured the range of concerns of what is now regarded as "classical political economy" (Fuller 1992; Sowell 1972).

Ricardo argued that depressions pointed to a need to produce more, so that people have the means to acquire the available goods and services in exchange. He assumed that the economic pie can expand indefinitely, mainly because he thought that manufacturing would replace land as the principal source of economic value. Here Ricardo found a role for state intervention in the economy that would be developed in our own century by Keynes. It consists in government assurances of high employment levels so as to enable free trade to issue in an overall increase in wealth production. In this respect, individuals were manipulable in terms of a global utilitarian scheme designed (ironically) to enable the invisible hand to work.

From an ecological standpoint, Ricardo's policy constitutes a rather blatant instance of time-discounting, specifically a mortgaging of the future, as irreplaceable natural resources are absorbed in manufactures. His hope was that human ingenuity—the wellspring of economic innovation—would find substitutes for those resources before they were depleted. From a theological standpoint, Ricardo resonated with the idea that the taint of original sin can be ultimately removed through the commission of good works.

In contrast, Malthus believed that depressions called for a contraction of the economy, since people had already produced more than was sustainable for their collective existence; hence the failure of goods to clear the market. This insight was linked to the traditional idea that land is the ultimate source of value. Accordingly, the value of manufactures is artificial and temporary, which is to say parasitic on the finite natural resources consumed in their production. The notorious Malthusian conclusion was simply to let people fend for themselves in this depraved state, which would eventuate in the extinction of the surplus (aka unemployable poor) population—that is, until the economic system was restored to sustainable levels.

For Malthus, a state-supported welfare scheme would fail to respect individuals as agents complicit in their own fate (say, in their decisions to procreate). As for the Ricardian strategy of time-discounting, it merely highlighted the vanity of humans who think they can either preempt or improve the course of nature. A devotee of the idea that nature heals itself without human intervention, Malthus held that no amount of good works could redeem humanity's overconsumption. Death is the ultimate solution.

Elements of the Ricardian and Malthusian solutions to capitalism's systemic disorders were integrated in Karl Marx's dialectical materialist philosophy of history. As disenchanted theodicies, the invisible hand and natural selection promised an endless stream of effects, be they endless production (Ricardo's beneficent resolution) or endless destruction (Malthus's maleficent resolution). Marx tried to square the circle by arguing that revenge is ultimately wreaked on the capitalists as they are overtaken as a class by people whose collective self-consciousness is an unintended consequence of the capitalists' own rapaciousness.

Contrary to the expectations of both theodicies, what the future holds is not simply a matter of indefinite production or indefinite destruction. Rather, according to Marx, self-interest pursued to the limit eventually turns into bad karma, courtesy of the proletariat, whose increasing numbers are a direct result of capitalism's technical efficiency rendering more of the labor force redundant. At the same time, Marx admitted that communists are in the capitalists' debt for having prepared the way for the revolution by providing the modes of production needed for implementing a just social order—indeed, modes whose levels of efficiency in principle enable everyone a say in how they should be used.

Two features of Marx's theory mark it as a theodicy, albeit a partly disenchanted one. First, key Marxist concepts like "exploitation" do not merely explain how or why something is the case, but more importantly why it is good (or bad) that it be that way. For example, to claim that class-based income disparity is the product of exploitation is to imply that the situation being explained is bad and ought to be changed. Second, normative judgments of what is "good" and "bad" are neither mutually exclusive nor based on criteria external to the theory; rather they are mutually constitutive terms that are grounded in criteria specified by the theory. Thus, for Marx, capitalism is not an unmitigated evil that would have been best avoided in an ideal world that lies beyond the scope of his theory. On the contrary, capitalism's unique strengths and weaknesses are necessary for the realization of communism as Marx himself defined it.

The cost of disenchantment: a failed scientific defense of human freedom

In the preceding section, we saw that, contrary to the expectations of the neo-puritanical scientists who have been most visible in the science wars, the issues raised by theodicy have been disenchanted but by no means eliminated from scientific thought. Considering the postmodern aversion to "master narratives," this alone is quite remarkable. Nevertheless, theodicy's disenchantment has not been trivial in its consequences. Neither the invisible hand nor natural selection promises the sort of closure that would allow for definitive normative judgments.

However, this section presents a complementary problem, namely that of a decidedly non-puritanical scientist who fails to incorporate fully a theodicy orientation into an account of nature that is intended to have normative import. Consequently, his otherwise admirable attempt to specify scientific grounds for human freedom remains insufficiently justified. I have in mind here a recent book by Steven Rose, the founding professor of biology at the Open University and Britain's answer to Richard Lewontin as a leftist critic of the social policy pretensions of his discipline (Rose 1997).

Rose periodically invokes the Marxist motto, "Men [*sic*] make history but in circumstances not of their own choosing," to capture his key concept of lifeline, a non-reductionist, autopoietic version of Richard Dawkins's "extended phenotype" (Dawkins 1982). According to Rose, an organism's genetic and ecological resources constrain the course of its development without fully determining it. The organism's actual trajectory is the result of multivariate interactions at several levels of organization, which together constitute the organism's ongoing struggle to construct a viable future from a fluctuating present.

Despite his grounding in the biochemistry of nervous systems, Rose is obviously sympathetic to the vitalist picture of organisms as actively seeking alternative means in an ever-changing environment to achieve ends that are, in some sense, independent of that environment. In light of this picture, Rose argues that at least some organisms—certainly humans—enjoy a significant measure of freedom. But does Rose's concept of lifeline actually live up to the Marxist motto? More generally, does it constitute an adequate conception of freedom?

The paradoxical character of the theory of history epitomized in the Marxist motto is normally explained in terms of a central tenet of theodicy, one found in Hegel but traceable to Spinoza, Leibniz, and ultimately the Stoics: freedom is the recognition of necessity. Rose (1997: 18) takes this to mean that once we realize the exact extent of our constraints, we can act within our means to construct a world worth inhabiting. However, this is a misleading, or at least incomplete, rendering of what Marx, Hegel, and their predecessors were trying to say. They also believed that you cannot determine the degree of freedom someone enjoys without looking at what follows from that person's actions.

Freedom does not exist in a world where agents pursue many different courses of action that then issue in a much narrower range of outcomes. When the present appears open to alternative futures, agents tend to regard the world solely in terms of the resources it provides to realize their ends. Rose's rhetoric sometimes veers this way. Yet, depending on the pattern of actual outcomes, the situation may be exactly reversed— that our diverse actions are simply means to some other larger end. In that case, anything we do within the available set of options serves the larger end.

Admittedly, this sounds like what Dawkins has called the "gene's-eye view of the world," in which biological diversity has no proper end other than the safe conveyance of genetic information. Yet Marxists have also pointed to the proliferation of consumer choices in advanced capitalism as having this character. Consumers spend an increasing time and energy deliberating over possibilities, the long-term and large-scale consequences of which are usually negligible for their own lives, but which latently serve to rejuvenate the circulation of capital.

Because consumers are regularly presented with multiple options that force them to refine their wants more precisely than they might otherwise, they are unlikely, in the normal run of things, to discover just how overdetermined their world really is. Thus their subjective sense of freedom lacks an objective basis. Joined in their belief in the cunning of reason in history, Dawkins and Marx see this point very vividly in a way that Rose does not.

Consider what Rose rejects under the rubric of "reductionism." There is more at stake than simply a denial of the gene's-eye view of the world. Also at issue is the very idea of a coherent systemic perspective from which the biological world can be regarded. To be sure, reductionism is not the only such perspective, but Rose appears to throw the baby out with the bath water in his postmodern acceptance of the relative autonomy of the different levels of biological organization. Nevertheless, from the standpoint of theodicy, a systemic perspective is necessary to what followers of Hegel would consider a "gold standard" of objective freedom, whereby an agent inhabiting a world can be said literally "to know what it is doing."

For the gold standard to be met in a given population, the diversity of its members' actions must be matched by an equal or greater diversity of outcomes. In addition, these outcomes must generally correspond to what the members wanted, ideally in the terms they expected. If both conditions are satisfied, then there are good grounds for concluding that the population is objectively free. From a systemic perspective, such a population exerts significant control over its collective future.

Although this gold standard of objective freedom is impossibly high, it does enable us to distinguish between types of intervention one might make to improve the human condition. Specifically, the most convenient level of intervention is not necessarily the most efficacious, if it turns out that once a cause is removed, its deleterious effects are largely reproduced by another factor either present or latent in the environment. The freedom exemplified by the intervention, then, would be merely subjective. Rose potentially falls foul of this critique in his discussion of lung-cancer treatment (Rose 1997: 305).

Tobacco companies are currently major funders of research into the molecular biology of the lungs and the localization of "predisposing" genes for cancer. Rose regards this research as a strategic misdirection that capitalizes on the persuasiveness of reductionist rhetoric. A more direct route to cutting lung cancer, according to Rose, is simply to restrict the sale of tobacco-based products, the use of which is known to be highly correlated with the incidence of lung cancer.

Before judging the adequacy of Rose's proposed intervention, we would need to know its ultimate aim. What is the curtailment of tobacco sales meant to eliminate: lung cancer *per se*, premature death, excessive healthcare costs, a certain kind of lifestyle, or the unpleasantness of a smoke-filled environment? In some of these cases, the intervention would have the efficacious results Rose seeks. But in others, tobacco may simply be replaced by another set of products that engender largely the same or even worse effects.

Which is which depends equally on a clarification of ends, the state of scientific knowledge and the activation of political will. From the standpoint of theodicy, these three conditions must be integrated in a world view that defines the conditions under which we can act so as to bring about the world we want, or at least so as to recognize that such a world has not been brought about. Because Rose fails to provide such a systematic perspective, his conception of freedom does not have the objective character promised by his reliance on the Marxist motto.

Before concluding this section, let me offer some general remarks about the interaction effects between the present and future that need to be incorporated in any adequate theory of objective freedom, especially in the context of claims that actions taken now may limit our descendants' possibilities for action. This may enable interested readers to bring Rose's admirable initiative to fruition. Here I draw upon the implications of time-discounting introduced in the previous section.

Suppose we consider a perspective sufficiently long that the people affected by our actions are spatiotemporally detached from us: that is, we do not know their identities and they barely know ours. These descendants of ours are likely to have benefited from whatever we happen to have done, at least in the weak formal sense of our having provided the conditions of their possibilities for action. Even if we had imagined alternative futures for them, the actions we actually took will have rendered most of those possibilities implausible for our descendants to pursue in their day.

The only context in which it would make sense to talk about our having harmed our descendants is if they are close enough to us causally that we managed to change the living conditions of, say, the immediately following generation, since these people would have known a time when things were better. In that case, their harm would be motivated by a feeling of "relative deprivation." Similarly, any strong sense that we substantially benefited them would also presuppose adequate publicity of ideas of an improved existence, only this time in relation to the deprived conditions of recent memory.

Conclusions: meeting Weber's challenge and transcending the science wars

Max Weber claimed that only those who surrender their scientific scruples to religious impulses could believe that the distribution of good and bad in the world can be systematically explained. Such people have, in Weber's terms, an "enchanted" view of reality. According to Weber, a properly "disenchanted" view sees the world as intractably complex and open-ended. Thus, outside the self-consciously artificial strictures of the law, it is impossible to isolate clear causal paths that would enable the agent and recipient of morally significant action to recognize each other as such. This failure of mutual recognition—or "accountability," to use the current term of art—effectively short-circuits the value nexus.

Nevertheless, what the disenchanted world view loses in terms of providing meaning in life, it gains by providing what Weber regarded as a "value-neutral" basis for scientific inquiry. Weber's perspective, in turn, has legitimized what I have characterized here as the "neo-puritanical" attitude of the natural scientists who have been most vocal in their opposition to the "Academic Left" in the science wars.

In conclusion I want to drive home a point that I have made throughout this chapter, namely that the disenchanted view seriously misrepresents the spirit that has motivated the conduct of scientific inquiry, which is epitomized by "scientism," a recurrent yet repressed theme in the history of science. It is here that the interests of science and religion merge, especially in the arena of theodicy.

A full return to an enchanted science would target the scientific method itself, especially what Stephen Toulmin (1953) has called the "ideal of natural order" that a scientific theory presumes. This consists of the theory's simplest concepts or models, out of which explanations of complex concrete phenomena are constructed. Three familiar examples include: (1) according to Newtonian mechanics, the "natural state" of objects is to be at rest or moving in a straight line, subject to the state of other objects and gravity's universal pull; (2) in most renderings of natural history, each species is given an archetypal morphology, in relation to which pathologies and other deviant formations can be identified; (3) in neoclassical economics, people are ideally regarded as making the most of the conditions under which they are forced to pursue their individual interests, which include other similarly positioned agents.

Most philosophies of science regard such ideals of natural order as matters of convention designed to ease a theory's extension and application. In this respect, the ideals function as default positions, the value of which is to be judged almost entirely in terms of the research developments they enable. However, in nearly every case, these conceptual starting points were originally chosen because they captured a normative ideal upheld by proponents of the theory, be it the Greek one of simplicity as the mark of purity (an ideal that pervades the entire history of physics) or some rather specific notions about what counts as a "healthy" organism or a "rational" person.

This point is often overlooked in discussions of the scientific method because we have come to hive off the original, value-laden sense of "norm" from its use in summarizing empirical phenomena. Thus, often in the spirit of "political correctness," we treat the common appeal to "norms" in statistics and sociology as a mere play on words, as if there were no reason to think that a statistical "norm" would correspond to a "norm" possessing deeper social significance. Yet this was precisely what Karl Pearson thought, when he introduced "norm" into the social science lexicon at the dawn of the twentieth century.

Perhaps not surprisingly, Pearson held a chair in "social genetics," and many keen on reenchanting science in our own time have believed that intelligence has a strong racial component, based on apparently robust correlations between racial identity and IQ scores. Of course, there are many ways to demystify this particular form of scientific enchantment, especially such pedestrian ones as diagnosing errors in statistical reasoning. But from the perspective pursued in this chapter, those moves may be a bit too convenient.

In particular, most of the normative ideals that have been advanced on behalf of all of humanity are based on norms that were originally thought to hold for only a small subset. Sometimes these norms roughly captured patterns of behavior and other social traits that empirically distinguished the elite from the rest. But often they were invoked to reinforce such distinctions, especially when the interaction of people of different "types" threatened to blur them. Consequently, behind every seemingly benevolent initiative to extend education, representation, and welfare provision to the populace has been a prehistory in which they were justifiably perceived as vehicles of domination and segregation.

As heirs to the Enlightenment, we would like to say that all this shows is that the human spirit progresses gradually, diffusing from its origins in a vanguard of the species. However, the history is actually more sobering, yet familiar from our earlier discussion of theodicy. It may be that without a strong discrimination of "better" and "worse" people, backed by political force, there would never have been the impetus to produce the concrete models and corresponding forms of research and applications that have ultimately enabled an overall improvement of the human condition. In other words, some very bad politics may be needed to supply raw material for the kind of utopian vision that has informed our most widely shared normative ideals.

This point has been recently driven home with a vengeance by the historian Robert Proctor, who suggests that the Nazis pioneered what we now take to be enlightened views concerning the promotion of organic foods, vegetarianism, smoke-free environments, and related forms of "healthy living," because of their belief that a superior race needs to have a superior lifestyle (Proctor 1999). While such ideas had been previously floated by various eugenics and public hygiene groups in North America and Scandinavia, it took a state as committed to the cultivation of a "master race" as Nazi Germany to follow through on the implications of "healthy living" in ways that have become second nature for many (though not all) of us.

In the end, perhaps the most constructive way to understand the position of the Academic Left is as challenging the institutional preconditions of Weberian disenchantment. From that standpoint, what I call "social epistemology" (Fuller 1988), Weber reified as a particular development in the history of the university, whereby bureaucratic differentiation has (mis)begotten ontological depth (Fuller 1999a: Chapter 3). The Weberian motto of "science for its own sake" makes sense only if research programs have been made the preserve of fellow specialists and insulated from the demands of state, industry, taxpayers, and especially students.

To be sure, this flies in the face of the "unity of research and teaching" that marked the modern rebirth of the university in the hands of Wilhelm von Humboldt. Here the emphasis was placed on academics striving to synthesize disparate modes of inquiry into a comprehensive world view. While it is natural to deem the liberal arts orientation "interdisciplinary," it is worth recalling that it was pursued long before academia consisted of specialized disciplines.

The fact that now (though not in the past) most of those who would reenchant the natural sciences are humanists and social scientists speaks to the resurgence of the liberal arts orientation to academia, largely in reaction to the climate of disciplinary specialization that Weber's disenchanted view of inquiry has promoted. In this respect, the much-vaunted postmodern aversion to "master narratives" is a misdirection, and perhaps a dangerous one at that.

For we have reached not the end, but only the beginning, of the story of the reenchantment of science in our time. Academic puritans pose a much smaller obstacle to the reenchantment of science than patrons outside academia who would mold the products of specialized inquiry to their own rather specific ends, often in a proprietary spirit that would inhibit its use for more collective ends (Fuller 2000a: Chapter 8). Not surprisingly, but no less disturbingly, theodicy's two leading modern descendants—the invisible hand and natural selection—have been invoked to legitimize just such tendencies. It is time for us—both scientists and humanists—to come up with alternatives.

Acknowledgments

I wish to thank Adrian Melott and Phil Baringer for having invited me to debate Alan Sokal at the University of Kansas in February 1997, and to thank Phil and Keith Ashman for their helpful and probing comments on this chapter.

Bibliography

Ainslie, George (1992) *Picoeconomics*, Cambridge, UK: Cambridge University Press.
Berger, Peter (1967) *The Sacred Canopy*, New York: Free Press.
Bricmont, Jean and Sokal, Alan (1997) *Impostures intellectuelles*, Paris: Odile Jacob.
Cassirer, Ernst (1950) *The Problem of Knowledge: Philosophy, Science, and History since Hegel*, New Haven: Yale University Press.
Collins, Harry and Pinch, Trevor (1993) *The Golem: What Everyone Needs to Know about Science*, Cambridge, UK: Cambridge University Press.
Dawkins, Richard (1982) *The Extended Phenotype*, Oxford: Freeman.
Dusek, Val (1999) *The Holistic Inspirations of Physics*, New Brunswick, NJ: Rutgers University Press.
Elster, Jon (1980) *The Logic of Society*, Chichester, UK: John Wiley and Sons.

Elster, Jon (1984) *Sour Grapes*, Cambridge, UK: Cambridge University Press.

Feyerabend, Paul (1979) *Science in a Free Society*, London: Verso.

Fuller, Steve (1985) "Bounded rationality in law and science," University of Pittsburgh: Ph.D. in History and Philosophy of Science.

Fuller, Steve (1988) *Social Epistemology*, Bloomington: Indiana University Press.

Fuller, Steve (1992) "Knowledge as product and property," in Stehr, N. and Ericson, R. (eds) *The Cultures of Power and Knowledge*, Berlin: Walter de Gruyter.

Fuller, Steve (1993) *Philosophy, Rhetoric, and the End of Knowledge: The Coming of Science and Technology Studies*, Madison: University of Wisconsin Press.

Fuller, Steve (1997) *Science*, Milton Keynes and Minneapolis: Open University Press and University of Minnesota Press.

Fuller, Steve (1999a) *The Governance of Science: Ideology and the Future of the Open Society*, Milton Keynes: Open University Press.

Fuller, Steve (1999b) "What does the Sokal hoax say about the prospect for positivism?" in Despy-Meyer, A. and Devriese, D. (eds) *Positivismes*, Brussels: Brepols.

Fuller, Steve (2000a) *Thomas Kuhn: A Philosophical History for Our Times*, Chicago: University of Chicago Press.

Fuller, Steve (2000b) "Social epistemology as a critical philosophy of multiculturalism," in McCarthy, C. and Mahalingam, R. (eds) *Multicultural Curriculum: New Directions for Social Theory, Practice and Policy*, London: Routledge.

Gross, Paul R. and Levitt, Norman (1994) *Higher Superstition: The Academic Left and Its Quarrels with Science*, Baltimore: Johns Hopkins University Press.

Gross, Paul, Levitt, Norman and Lewis, Martin (eds) (1996) *The Flight from Science and Reason*, Baltimore: Johns Hopkins University Press.

Hakfoort, Caspar (1995) "The historiography of scientism: a critical review," *History of Science* 33: 375–395.

Harrington, Ann (1996) *The Reenchantment of Science: Holism in Germany from Wilhelm II to Hitler*, Princeton: Princeton University Press.

Hayek, Friedrich von (1978) *New Studies in Philosophy, Politics, Economics and the History of Ideas*, London: Routledge and Kegan Paul.

Hayles, N. Katherine (1998) *How We Became Posthuman*, Chicago: University of Chicago Press.

Kelsen, Hans (1943) *Society and Nature: A Sociological Inquiry*, Chicago: University of Chicago Press.

Knight, David (1986) *The Age of Science*, Oxford: Blackwell.

Koyre, Alexandre (1957) *From the Closed World to the Infinite Universe*, Baltimore: Johns Hopkins University Press.

Kuhn, Thomas, Heilbron, John, Forman, Paul and Allen, Lini (1967) *Sources for the History of Quantum Physics*, Philadelphia: American Philosophical Society.

Latour, Bruno (1988) *The Pasteurization of France*, Cambridge, MA: Harvard University Press.

Mendelsohn, Everett (1964) "Explanation in nineteenth century biology," in Cohen, R. S. and Wartofsky, M. (eds) *Boston Studies in the Philosophy of Science*, Vol. 2, Dordrecht: Reidel.

Pettit, Philip (1993) *The Common Mind*, Oxford: Oxford University Press.

Price, Colin (1993) *Time, Discounting and Value*, Oxford: Blackwell.

Proctor, Robert (1991) *Value-Free Science?*, Cambridge, MA: Harvard University Press.

Proctor, Robert (1999) *The Nazi War on Cancer*, Princeton: Princeton University Press.

Rabinbach, Anson (1990) *The Human Motor: Energy, Fatigue, and the Origins of Modernity*, New York: Basic Books.

Rose, Steven (1997) *Lifelines: Biology, Freedom, Determinism*, Harmondsworth: Penguin.

Shapin, Steven and Schaffer, Simon (1985) *Leviathan and the Air Pump*, Princeton: Princeton University Press.

Simon, Herbert (1977) *The Sciences of the Artificial*, 2nd edn, Cambridge, MA: MIT Press.

Sokal, Alan (1996) "Transgressing the boundaries: toward a transformative hermeneutics of quantum gravity," *Social Text* 46–47: 217–252.

Sorell, Tom (1991) *Scientism*, London: Routledge.

Sowell, Thomas (1972) *Say's Law*, Princeton: Princeton University Press.

Suppe, Fred (ed.) (1977) *The Structure of Scientific Theories*, 2nd edn, Urbana: University of Illinois Press.

Toulmin, Stephen (1953) *Philosophy of Science: An Introduction*, London: Hutchinson.

Toulmin, Stephen (1999) "The rediscovery of reasonableness," Unpublished manuscript.

Weber, Max (1965) *The Sociology of Religion*, Boston: Beacon Press.

Weinberg, Steve (1996) "Sokal's hoax," *New York Review of Books* 43(13) (8 August): 11–15.

Williams, Bernard (1981) *Moral Luck*, Cambridge, UK: Cambridge University Press.

Wolpert, Lewis (1992) *The Unnatural Nature of Science*, London: Faber and Faber.

12 Anticipations

A science-fiction author dramatizes the issues

James Gunn

Preface

When the subject for this symposium was announced, I realized that I had been thinking about this matter for much of my adult life: the two poles of human existence, the emotional and the rational, and how they can reinforce each other but often come into conflict. So when Adrian Melott suggested that I might want to read something from my science-fiction writing, I thought of two pieces that framed much of my writing career: "Witches Must Burn," which I wrote back in the early 1950s, used the McCarthy attacks upon academia as the point of departure for a story about the way in which science has replaced witchcraft without providing the same kind of tribal security, and about the basic anti-intellectualism of American culture. The story begins with the burning of the (unnamed) University of Kansas. Eventually I continued the story with "Trial by Fire" and "Witch Hunt," and brought them together in the novel *The Burning*.

"The Day the Magic Came Back" was written in the mid-1990s and published shortly after my retirement from the University I burned in "Witches Must Burn." By this time my thoughts had focused on the healing process and our desire for magical cures that lead people these days to seek out all kinds of alternative treatments, some of them apparently successful, some of them delusions or outright frauds. But do we really want "faith healers"? Maybe we do, particularly when we or those we love are ill and modern medicine cannot come up with a cure. But what are we willing to give up? It seems to me there is a hidden price.

Witches must burn

The nightmare began when he was still five miles from the campus. For as long as he lived it would be *the nightmare* to him, never far from his unguarded moments. But then his life expectancy, at that moment, was not long.

The burning of the law building started it. The building was old and dry; it burned briskly, the flames leaping and dancing on the hill like malicious demons, spearing upward into the night, painting the other buildings with scarlet fingers.

There's been an accident, he thought, and poured kerosene to the old turbine under the hood. It responded nobly; the '79 Ford lunged forward.

An instant later he realized that the other buildings were burning, too; the scarlet fingers were their own.

When he reached the edge of town, the hill was a vast bonfire. The town sprawled under it, bathed in a sullen glare, dark-shadowed and lurid like a village in hell.

As he got closer to the campus, the streets became jammed with cars. He drove as far as he could, and then he got out and ran. Before he reached the top of the hill, some instinct of self-preservation made him strip off his tie and turn up his coat collar.

There were no fire trucks, no police cars. There was only the silent crowd, its dark face reddened occasionally by a leaping flame, its ranks impenetrable, its hydra-heads impassive. Only its eyes, holding within them their own small flames, seemed alive.

The law building was a crumbled ruin of stone and glowing coals. Beyond it was a tossing sea of fire, melting islands within it—the political science building, the library, the behavioral science building, the Union, the journalism school, the humanities tower, the auditorium . . . For a moment he thought the administration building was untouched. But that was the illusion; it was a shell—blank windows reddened by a dying glow.

It was summer, and the night was hot. The fiery death of what had been one of the Midwest's loveliest and finest universities made it hotter. But he was cold inside as he watched the labor and devotion of a hundred years burning, burning . . .

A man ran toward the waiting crowd, a torch flaring in his hand, his face dark and unreadable, yelling, "Come on! They're running the eggheads now!"

For a moment longer the crowd waited and then, silently, it surged forward. For a few hundred yards he was carried with it, unable to fight free. At the brink of the hill, it dropped him. He stood there, unmoving, jostled by people who pushed past, not feeling them.

Beyond the hill were the physical science building, the experimental biology building, the building for business and economics. They were more isolated, more secure than those on top of the hill. Or so it may have seemed.

Now they, too, were burning. They were fire resistant and they burned less readily, but they burned. The flames roared in the night, and between the flames the forked, black figures ran back and forth. At every exit, the silent crowd waited for them with clubs and pitchforks and axes. Some of the black figures turned back into the flames.

The flames behind him and the flames in front, he watched, and all he could think about was that his papers were gone, charred and irretrievable, and the intolerable waste of five long years of labor and research. Even the Tool was gone.

Then like a wave of nausea, the truth hit him. The black figures down there were people, people he knew and liked and respected, professors and their wives and their children. He turned aside and was sick.

As he straightened, he fought the impulse to run down the hill, to scream at the mob: "Stop it, you blind, killing fools! These are people like you, living, working, loving, obeying the laws! You're killing yourself, the finest thing in you, and you're killing your country! Stop before it's too late!"

But it was already too late. Logic said it was futile. He would only die himself. He was important, not for himself but what he knew and the promise that knowledge held.

Too many good men had died there already.

He closed his eyes and thought of Sylvia Robbins, who was intelligent, beautiful, as good a friend as any man ever had and might have been more if he had given it a chance, and who now lay dying down there. He thought of Dr. William Nugent, that tall, lean, iron-gray man of quick intuitions and relentless determination in his search for the truth. He thought of Dr. Aaron Friedman and Professor Samuel Black and a dozen others . . .

And he thought: *If you are down there in that hell, my friends, forgive me. Forgive me, all of you, for being logical while you are dying . . .*

And forgive them the logicless, murderous mob.

He knew the people that formed this mob, their fears, their passions. He knew the savagery that moved them, the frustrations that demanded a scape-goat, the consciousness of guilt, of wrongdoing, of failure that cried out for an external soul to punish, that created one on demand.

They were unable to face the realization of "I was wrong—I made a mis-take—Let's try a new line" that every scientist, every creative thinker must face daily. They needed the age-old, pain-killing drug of "He did it, the Other Guy—He's Evil—He made me Fail!"

And yet, knowing them so well, he did not know enough to stop them. He was five years, perhaps ten years away from the knowledge that he could take down the hill with him into their midst and find the right words and the right actions to make them stop—to turn them back into sane human beings.

The intuitive psychologists like the Senator were more capable than the scientists. But it is always easier to drive men insane than to lead them into sanity.

"Witches Must Burn" originally published in *Astounding Science Fiction*, August, 1956, © 1956 by James E. Gunn; reprinted in *The Burning*, © 1972 by James E. Gunn.

The day the magic came back

Dr. Knowland looked around the isolation room at the masked faces of the nurse and of Susan Grinnell, his resident physician in internal medicine, and then back to the face of the child on the hospital bed. Her name was Linda

Constant. She was seven years old. With her red cheeks and her long, golden hair spread out upon the pillow, she looked like an angel, but the color in her cheeks came from fever, not good health. Her eyes were closed. Knowland thought they might never reopen. If she were awake to see the three of them standing over her he wondered if she might think they were apparitions from the past, witch doctors come to drive the demons from the body they had possessed.

But the powers of medicine were more limited. Knowland's gaze went to the two bottles of antibiotics hanging inverted from their stands, one on each side of the bed, each with a tube leading to a pump on the IV pole and from there to a needle inserted into a vein at the inner elbow of each small arm. All their medical knowledge, all their armamentarium, were failing before the onslaught of this child's illness, and he was dreading the moment when he would have to face her parents and tell them that science had been defeated by a simple bacterium, *mycobacterium tuberculosis*.

Knowland turned and walked from the room. He was a man of medium height and graying hair and a slight paunch. He walked on his heels with his feet turned out, like a duck, as he made his way down the hall. No one smiled. He was a man of great dignity, and his patients, and many of his fellow workers, thought he was the next thing to God.

He went to the nearest lavatory, washed his hands, and removed his mask. When he emerged Susan was waiting for him.

"Isn't there something else we can try?" she asked. Ordinarily she was a plain woman, but when her concern transformed her face, Knowland thought she was beautiful and that her frequently neglected husband was luckier than he knew.

Knowland shook his head. "The strain is antibiotic resistant. We've tried the whole spectrum."

She looked at him as if willing him to work a miracle. Knowland shook his head again, this time as if trying to rid himself of a heavy burden. "I'm going to have to tell them."

"The Constants? Do you want me to do it?"

"You'd be better at it," Knowland said. "But they need to hear it from me."

"They've asked me if they could bring in someone to see Linda."

"What kind of someone?"

"Someone to pray for her, or something like that."

Knowland folded his arms across his chest. "They've lost faith in me. I can understand that. But they might have asked me."

"They belong to a sect that believes in healers. They feel that they sinned by bringing Linda to a hospital. They were afraid to go with their own beliefs. Now they're afraid again. Afraid to ask you."

"If they can bring in a healer?"

She nodded.

"Why not?" Knowland said.

"You're going to let them?"

"We've failed. Why shouldn't they try what they believe in? I've never understood why medicine should deny people the comfort of alternatives."

"You think there's a chance –?"

Knowland looked at her like a teacher disappointed in a promising student. "Faith healers and snake oils don't work. Medicine does not oppose them because of that, but because they keep the ill from seeking effective treatment. Well, the Constants have done that and we've failed. Now they can make their peace with their daughter's dying in their own way."

Over the next few days Knowland got accustomed to seeing the tall thin man sitting next to the bed of the tubercular child. He was of that indeterminate age reached by some men between the middle years and the old. He had dark eyes and a beak of a nose like an owl. His hair, though thin, was still black and his skin was unlined, but his face reflected the serenity obtained through long years of experience with the world's tragedies. He said nothing. When he was offered a mask, he shook his head. He held the child's hand and stared at her as if the power of his will was enough to force open her eyes, to turn on her smile, to make her well again.

Linda's parents, one at a time or both, often were present as well, but they stood on the other side of the bed, smoothing their daughter's hair or cooling her fever with a wet cloth. They asked Susan and then Knowland to stop the antibiotics. They pointed at the places on the child's arms and hands where the needles had left ugly hematomas on their daughter's delicate skin and agonized over the nurses' struggles to find new places to insert their heparin locks.

"I can't," Knowland said. "If you want the treatment to stop, you'll have to remove her from my care."

"You said you can't help her," the mother said. She was a sturdy woman with freckles and a sunburned nose. Her hair had once been yellow, like her daughter's, but now was an indeterminate brown.

"I know," Knowland conceded, "but I can't stop trying." They were standing outside the isolation room. He nodded toward the door where their healer sat with the sick child. "Just as you can't."

The Constants gave up their efforts to stop the medical treatment. They feared removing her from the antisepsis and the round-the-clock attentions of the hospital, and their healer seemed not to care. He did not care, either, about the activities of the hospital staff around him. He kept his vigil and ignored everything else, leaving only, Knowland presumed, to take care of his physical needs. It was only a presumption: He was always there when Knowland opened the door on his rounds.

On the fourth day, the healer was gone and Linda looked better. Her temperature had dropped, and the false flush of fever in her cheeks had faded. She had not opened her eyes, but she had summoned the strength to cough again.

On the fifth day she was awake and recognizing her parents. On the sixth day she was sitting up and talking to everyone, her parents, the nurses, Susan, even Knowland. She had been everyone's favorite patient in the hospital and they all celebrated the normality of her temperature and pulse. Her cough had disappeared, and her chest sounded better. A few rails and cracks, but even they seemed to be diminishing. The sputum samples came back negative.

"When are you going to release her?" Susan asked.

"Tomorrow."

"Shouldn't we continue the antibiotics for a few more days?"

Knowland did not like questions about his judgment, and sometimes he snapped at students. But this time he seemed distracted. "Look at the record," he said mildly. He had admitted to himself, although he had not yet come to the point of admitting it to his resident, that the antibiotics had done nothing.

"If it wasn't the antibiotics," Susan said, "then what was it?"

Knowland shook his head. Next day, as the Constants checked their daughter out of the hospital, Knowland asked them the name of their healer.

"Mr. Alma," Constant said. He was a sturdy man, a farmer, with weathered hands, a pale forehead, and a brown face from the cheeks down.

"That's his real name?"

"That's his name," Constant said.

"Why didn't you call him in sooner?"

"He was on another mission," Mrs. Constant said. And then she added, as if admitting a lapse of faith. "We were afraid."

"And where can I find Mr. Alma?"

"Why'd you want to?" Constant asked.

Knowland shrugged. "I don't know. We might have something to talk about." He didn't know what it might be, yet.

A week later he had figured it out. The address the Constants had given him turned out to be a storefront in a part of the city that had made a good part of the cycle from decent housing to slum to restoration. The storefront, however, was still in the slum stage. It had once been a hardware store, but the glass had been broken out of the front windows and replaced by plywood. The plywood had been painted green at one time, scrawled with graffiti, and then painted pink, graffitied, painted blue and later other colors so that words, drawings, and colors came through indistinctly like palimpsests from the beginning of the world. Where a sign had once said "Hardware," other words had been neatly lettered: "All Souls Chapel."

The first time Knowland knocked at the battered wooden door he got no answer. The second time, a service of some kind was in progress—he could hear someone speaking and the mumble of an audience—and Knowland couldn't wait. The third time, late in the afternoon, he heard a voice asking him to enter. The interior of the room was gloomy after the sunshine outside, and a few moments elapsed while his vision was adjusting. The room was neat and clean but shabby. Folding chairs were arranged carefully across the floor, eight across and eight deep. Beyond them was an old wooden desk. Behind the desk was the dark-haired man the Constants had called Alma.

"I'm Dr. Knowland," he said.

"I know you." The man's voice was thin and reedy, and Knowland realized it was the first time he had heard it.

"I wanted to ask you about Linda Constant."

Alma nodded.

Knowland approached the desk that perhaps also served as a rostrum or pulpit or maybe even an altar. "How is she?"

"She's well," Alma said, "but you don't need me to tell you that."

"No," Knowland said. He sat down in one of the folding chairs, suddenly feeling as if his knees were unable to support him. He looked down at his soft, white hands and then up at Alma waiting patiently behind the desk. "How did you do it?"

"It weren't you and your medicines?"

"You know it wasn't."

"Most doctors take credit for what happens in their hospitals," Alma said.

"I'd failed. I know that. I want to know why you succeeded. Was it faith? Some kind of supernatural intervention? God?"

The tall, thin man stood up, towering now above the seated physician. "None of them. You may use it agin me, but I'll give you truth—"

Knowland waved his hand impatiently. "I just want to know one thing. All my life have I been wrong about the world and the way it works?"

"Once upon a time people would have called me shaman and give me honor," Alma said. "Later folks'd call me a witch and burn me at the stake. Today I'm called a faith healer and scorned." His soft voice was without passion. "All I do is put sick people right with the way things is, underneath, where the real stuff is."

Knowland's hands tightened and he was sorry he had come, but he could think of no easy way to leave and as he listened to Alma's soft voice he began to realize that what the man was talking about in his inadequate vocabulary was physics and biology.

Later, he was seated in his office when Susan arrived for their daily conference. His desk was broad and polished, and he had an oriental rug on the floor, a broad window behind him opening on trees and a carefully tended green lawn dotted with flower beds, and bookcases filled with medical texts on either side. For several minutes he stared without speaking at a medical file in front of him. Finally Susan asked if something was bothering him.

"The healer's name is Alma," Knowland said without looking up. "That isn't his real name, of course, but he wouldn't tell me that. He told me other things. It is easier to be considered a preacher than a healer, he said. Preachers are unregulated; anybody else can be prosecuted for practicing medicine without a license."

Susan looked at him with concern. "Why did you go to see him?"

"Something happened in that hospital room with Linda Constant, and I wanted to know what it was. No, that's wrong—I had to know what it was."

"The antibiotics finally took effect," Susan said.

"You know that isn't true," he said. "It was something else, something frightening."

People have always understood, Knowland said, that the mind could influence the body. Even medical science conceded the reality of psychosomatic illnesses and sometimes the fact that recovery was aided by a positive attitude. It could be called psychosomatic healing. But medical science had no mechanism for the operation of psyche on the soma, and it denied the ability of someone else's mind to heal another person's sickness.

Alma had come up with a mechanism, and as Knowland had listened to Alma's thin voice only able to hint at the abstractions the healer was attempting to describe, Knowland had come to understand it, too. The underlying reality of the universe, Alma had said, lies far beneath the perceptions of the creatures that live within it. "In the beginning was the word," said an astronomer named Harlow Shapley, Knowland thought, "and the word was hydrogen."

Humanity cannot see or hear or touch or smell or taste the basic reality, because it is atomic and molecular and cellular. The only thing humanity has that can compare with that intangible micro-stuff from which all the macro-stuff is built is the mind. Thought, like atoms and molecules and cells, exists without being tangible, and thought not only can encompass the basic reality, it can influence it. Alma could persuade the body's cells and the bacteria and the viruses to work together rather than like selfish individuals.

That is what Alma had told the physician. In spite of the evidence provided by Linda's recovery, Knowland could not accept such far-fetched claims, but he also could not deny the bare possibility that Alma might not be a charlatan.

Once, Alma said, magic had worked because people believed in it. It wasn't a case of ignorant people trying to explain a world filled with uncontrollable forces and inexplicable events by peopling it with spirits and demons and gods. A few of them, the shamans, perceived a deeper truth than the deceptive world of everyday reality. And their perceptions enabled some of them to shape that deeper truth to the needs of the people around them. It was easy to make a mistake, of course, or as such positions paid off with honor and privilege, to pretend to a power that one didn't possess. Sometimes the truths also became confused, became visions that were interpreted differently by prophets and messiahs, became religions and superstitions, but all were reflections of the underlying reality that is and always has been unified and available. It was nature, not the supernatural. And then science came along, with its objective reality and demonstrable power over nature, faith weakened, and shamans forgot and were forgotten. The magic was lost.

"And you believed this?" Susan asked.

Knowland could tell she was concerned about his mental stability. Had the experience with Linda unhinged his mind? "What's remarkable about it is that this man of almost no education has come up with a theory about the nature of the universe that is not much different from that of our most learned physicists."

Susan frowned. "That sort of thing is out there in the popular press, on science programs. If it worked, that would be remarkable."

"Yes," Knowland said. "It seemed to work in the case of Linda Constant."

"Medical literature is filled with spontaneous cures."

"Do you know how weak that sounds? What we cannot explain, we call spontaneous, as if that explains anything."

"What are you going to do?"

"I've asked Alma to let me go along on a few of his healing sessions. You may have to cover for me."

"Of course. But aren't you concerned about being too—?"

"Gullible?" He knew his expression reflected an inner turmoil, and he knew Susan was watching him for signs of a mental breakdown. But he could not conceal the doubts that were eating away at a lifetime of belief. "Of course I am. My reputation would be ruined if anyone found out I was taking Alma seriously. But I'm also concerned, as a man of science, about denying the existence of phenomena that I can see in front of me."

They formed an odd team, the thin, dark haired healer and the shorter, plumper physician. Their visits never took them to hospitals. Instead, they met in bedrooms of decaying houses and apartments. Sometimes the bedroom was the only room or the only one presentable enough for visitors, and the ailing person had been moved into it. Many were neat, but whether the rooms were clean or filthy, Alma went about his business without a glance or a word.

He allowed Knowland to check the ailing person's pulse, temperature, and blood pressure, and to make a routine physical examination, listening to the heart and the lungs, feeling the lymph glands, taking a blood sample, coming to a tentative diagnosis that he later checked, as best he could, in the laboratory. Then the vigil began. Knowland could not take the time from his normal practice and teaching to monitor the entire process of healing, but he checked on each person at the beginning of the vigil, in the middle, and at the end. Over a period of four weeks, Alma had recorded a remarkable string of successes.

As nearly as Knowland could tell without full clinical examinations, one elderly woman had a blood infection, an old man had kidney failure, a middle-aged woman had pancreatic cancer, a middle-aged man had pneumonia, and a ten-year-old boy had leukemia. All were poor and some were virtually without means. Two lived in the country on small plots; one was a squatter, and the other had been reduced from more extensive farmland. Three lived in the inner city. The rural residents, at least, had gardens and neighbors. Those in the inner city subsisted on welfare and food stamps and junk food.

Knowland resisted the urge to get them into a hospital where their conditions could be treated. He tried to tell himself that this was a scientific experiment, but he could not shake the feeling that he had violated his Hippocratic Oath and, more important, his personal principles. He thought about the studies in syphilis allowed to continue in Alabama and the experiments conducted in Nazi Germany under the guise of science. He felt that way, that is, until the ailing individuals began to show improvement. All but the old man with the renal condition were out of their beds and back to normal activities after a week. They seemed, as far as Knowland could discern, to be cured, although if his original diagnoses had been correct, the pancreatic cancer at least was terminal. The leukemia might have gone into remission, but the rapidity and the extent of recovery were uncharacteristic. Without proper diagnoses and data, the cases were without scientific standing and would be worthless as anything but anecdote, but Knowland knew that with the best of luck he might have been successful with only two of the illnesses.

At the end of the month, Knowland congratulated Alma on his healings. They were standing outside one of the tenements surrounded by litter and uncollected garbage. The odor was strong, but Knowland did not notice. "If anybody had told me about these cases, I wouldn't have believed him."

"They'll not believe you, either," Alma said.

"What about the man with the renal condition?"

"The what?"

"The old man with the kidney problem. The one who died."

"He'd much to overcome," Alma said. "And I couldn't reach his—I know not what to call it."

"How many do you lose?"

"A few. Here and there. Sometimes I can't touch their will to live. Sometimes my power fails. Sometimes they fight me."

"Skepticism?"

"I give it no name," Alma said. "Some cling too strong to the world of the senses; some won't hold with the unseen."

"Have you ever tried to teach someone else to do what you do?" Knowland asked.

"People can be showed how to heal if they can see the hidden truth and if they has the power. I was taught as a boy and have taught some others the same; many cannot learn. But those that can, they spread far and wide. Beyond the seas, there may be many, I sense. Maybe some places never lost the truth."

Knowland thought for a moment and then asked, "If I could set up some controlled experiments, would you participate? While we worked, could we check your pulse, your blood pressure, your brain waves?"

"No," Alma said.

"No?" Knowland said. "And yet you allowed me—"

"You cared about Linda. You let me help her. But this other would not work. Even with evidence, people would doubt, and I would be shamed. My people would wonder. Maybe question my power." Alma looked at Knowland. "This troubles you."

When Knowland spoke, his voice was uneven. "How can we control this power, turn it into a science, if we cannot study it?"

"Some things science ain't never going to control," Alma said.

Susan found Knowland in the doctor's lounge, a clean, sterile room with shiny chromium furniture, a coffee maker, a small refrigerator with soft drinks, and no humanizing touches, not even curtains at the windows. "Look who I've got?" Susan said, too brightly. She was holding Linda Constant's hand, and the seven-year-old was hanging back, the other hand to her mouth, looking overwhelmed by the building and its official-looking occupants. "Her mother brought her to say hello."

"Hello, Linda," Knowland said gently, holding out his hand.

The child hesitated for a moment and then reached for his hand with the hand that had been at her mouth and put it trustingly in his. It felt wet, but Knowland shook it and said, "How are you feeling, Linda?"

"I'm fine," Linda said. "You don't have a mask."

"No, it isn't necessary now, is it?" The little girl shook her head. "I feel all well," she said.

"That's good," Knowland said. "Stay that way."

"I will," she said with conviction, and turned toward the door. She looked back. "My mother said to tell you 'thanks,'" she said.

"You're welcome," Knowland said.

When Susan returned, Knowland was looking at his stethoscope, turning it over and over in his hands as if he had never seen one before and was trying to figure out what it was good for. He looked up. "De nada," he said.

"She's well again," Susan said. "That's what counts."

"Is it?" Knowland looked toward the window where the afternoon sunshine was struggling through the leaves of the giant pin oak that shielded this side of the hospital.

"You can't blame yourself for someone else's success. If that is what it was."

"That would be mean-spirited, wouldn't it," Knowland said. "Alma's method works. He heals people."

"Even if that's true," Susan said, "there has always been room in the world for the people of faith and the people of science. You'll have plenty of work to do."

Knowland turned on the bench seat of the couch. "You think I'm concerned because Alma and his kind will put me and you out of business?"

Susan looked surprised at Knowland's question.

Knowland looked back toward the window. "I suppose there's some of that. Some jealousy is hard to avoid. But more than that is at stake here."

"What is at stake?" she asked.

"It's not just the healing. It's science itself. The ability to manipulate the basic reality of the universe may start with restoring people to health, but what is to stop it from working miracles of other kinds?"

"Like what?" Susan asked.

Knowland shrugged. "Creating food. Loaves and fishes, say. Or gold. Or death for our enemies and good fortune for our friends. Energy for free if our supplications are proper; atomic explosions if they are not. Once magic is let loose upon the world again, there is no place it cannot touch."

"I didn't have your experience with Alma. But even if magic worked," Susan said, catching her breath in the middle, "surely there would be rules and controls."

"The very essence of magic is that there are no controls," Knowland said. "Only other magic."

Susan raised her chin stubbornly. "Then you'll just have to learn how to do it yourself."

"That's just it," Knowland said. "I can't. I'm too tied to the sensory world I perceive around me, that I have lived with all my life. I'm too committed to science, to ways of understanding that have nothing in common with faith. I'm bound by the physical laws I learned long ago."

"Is that why you're upset?"

"No," Knowland said. "That isn't it. The important thing is not who does it but that it can be done only by those chosen by some unseen power to possess this unique ability. Like the princess and the pea or King Arthur and the sword in the stone. Not earned but given. The image of the future is the Middle Ages. That's Camelot under another name. The divine right of kings and the magical rites of the Elect."

"Even so," Susan said, "isn't it worth a great deal to have something to fall back on. Something that can help when medical science can't?"

"To everybody seeking mercy, the appeal of magic is irresistible," Knowland said. "But it means that medicine and science are finished. All science can offer is justice. Science has much to answer for, including its neglect of mercy, but it transformed the world into something egalitarian instead of hierarchical. Science created democracy and affluence and individual choice. Now the magic has come back and the world is going to be changed beyond recognition, and it is not going to be in the hands of those who work hard and study and understand but of the Elect. They may do good, they may do evil, but science is ended, and with it any possibility of getting ahead, and of pulling the rest of humanity along, by anything but good fortune or the blessings of the Chosen."

"I don't think I ever told you," Susan said, "that my brother is HIV-positive."

Something snapped. As Susan watched, Knowland walked to the wastebasket beside the coffee machine and dropped into it his broken stethoscope.

"The Day the Magic Came Back" originally published in *Science Fiction Age*, January 1996, © 1996 by James E. Gunn.

Index